Digital Media and the Preservation of Indigenous Languages in Africa

COMMUNICATION, GLOBALIZATION, AND CULTURAL IDENTITY

Series Editor: Jan Servaes

The *Communication, Globalization, and Cultural Identity* series explores and complicates the interlinked notions of "local" and "global" by integrating global dependency thinking; world-system theory; local, grassroots, interpretative, and participatory theory; and research on social change.

In the current world state, globalization and localization are seen as interlinked processes, and this marks a radical change in thinking about change and development. It also marks the arising of a new range of problems. One of the central problems is that the link between the global and the local is not always made clear.

The debates in the field of international and intercultural communication have shifted and broadened. They have shifted in the sense that they are now focusing on issues related to "global culture," "local culture," "(post)modernity," and "multiculturalism," instead of their previous concern with "modernization," "synchronization," and "cultural imperialism." With these new discussions, the debates have also shifted from an emphasis on homogeneity toward an emphasis on differences. With this shift toward differences and localities, there is also an increased interest in the link between the global and the local and in how the global is perceived in the local.

Recent titles in the series:

Digital Media and the Preservation of Indigenous Languages in Africa: Toward a Digitalized and Sustainable Society, edited by Fulufhelo Oscar Makananise and Shumani Eric Madima

Indigenous Language for Social Change Communication in the Global South, edited by Abiodun Salawu, Tshepang Bright Molale, Enrique Uribe-Jongbloed, and Mohammad Sahid Ullah

Communication Theory and Application in Post-Socialist Contexts, edited by Maureen C. Minielli, Marta N. Lukacovic, Sergei A. Samoilenko, Michael R. Finch, with Deb Uecker

Transcultural Images in Hollywood Cinema: Debates on Migration, Identity, and Finance, edited by Uğur Baloğlu and Yıldız Derya Birincioğlu

Media and Public Relations Research in Post-Socialist Societies, edited by Maureen Minielli, Marta Lukacovic, Sergei Samoilenko, and Michael Finch with Deb Uecker

Rethinking Post-Communist Rhetoric: Perspectives on Rhetoric, Writing, and Professional Communication in Post-Soviet Spaces, edited by Pavel Zemliansky and Kirk St.Amant

Representations of Islam in the News: A Cross-Cultural Analysis, edited by Stefan Mertens and Hedwig de Smaele

The Praxis of Social Inequality in Media: A Global Perspective, edited by Jan Servaes and Toks Oyedemi

Digital Media and the Preservation of Indigenous Languages in Africa

Toward a Digitalized and Sustainable Society

Edited by

Fulufhelo Oscar Makananise
Shumani Eric Madima

LEXINGTON BOOKS
Lanham • Boulder • New York • London

Published by Lexington Books
An imprint of The Rowman & Littlefield Publishing Group, Inc.
4501 Forbes Boulevard, Suite 200, Lanham, Maryland 20706
www.rowman.com

86-90 Paul Street, London EC2A 4NE, United Kingdom

Copyright © 2024 by The Rowman & Littlefield Publishing Group, Inc.

All rights reserved. No part of this book may be reproduced in any form or by any electronic or mechanical means, including information storage and retrieval systems, without written permission from the publisher, except by a reviewer who may quote passages in a review.

British Library Cataloguing in Publication Information Available

Library of Congress Cataloging-in-Publication Data

Names: Makananise, Fulufhelo Oscar, 1986- editor. | Madima, Shumani Eric, editor.
Title: Digital media and the preservation of indigenous languages in Africa: toward a digitalized and sustainable society / edited by Fulufhelo Oscar Makananise, Shumani Eric Madima.
Description: Lanham : Lexington Books, 2024. | Series: Communication, globalization, and cultural identity | Includes bibliographical references and index. | Summary: "This edited volume argues that digital media technologies and platforms are essential for the preservation of Indigenous languages and African epistemologies in modern-day African societies. Contributors also provide a methodology for African researchers, practitioners, and marginalized communities to integrate digital technology into their lives"—Provided by publisher.
Identifiers: LCCN 2024006289 (print) | LCCN 2024006290 (ebook) | ISBN 9781666957525 (cloth) | ISBN 9781666957532 (epub)
Subjects: LCSH: Language maintenance—Africa. | Language revival—Africa. | Indigenous peoples—Africa—Languages. | Digital media—Africa. | Mass media and language—Africa. | Language and culture—Africa.
Classification: LCC P40.5.L322 A3535 2024 (print) | LCC P40.5.L322 (ebook) | DDC 306.44096—dc23/eng/20240325
LC record available at https://lccn.loc.gov/2024006289
LC ebook record available at https://lccn.loc.gov/2024006290

♾️™ The paper used in this publication meets the minimum requirements of American National Standard for Information Sciences—Permanence of Paper for Printed Library Materials, ANSI/NISO Z39.48-1992.

Contents

Acknowledgments ix

Introduction: Theorizing Digital Media and Epistemic Indigenous Languages Preservation for Sustainable Development in the Fourth Industrial Revolution 1
Fulufhelo Oscar Makananise and Shumani Eric Madima

PART I: DIGITAL PRESERVATION, EPISTEMIC AFRICAN KNOWLEDGES, AND THE FOURTH INDUSTRIAL REVOLUTION 19

Chapter 1: Digital Preservation of Indigenous Languages and Participatory Epistemic Knowledge Systems of the Global South: Insights from South African Experiences 21
Fulufhelo Oscar Makananise

Chapter 2: Indigenous Language Preservation and Promotion through Digital Media Technology in the Fourth Industrial Revolution 49
Yusuf Ayodeji Ajani, Adeyinka Tella, and Nhlavu Petros Dlamini

Chapter 3: Positioning South African Indigenous Languages on Social Media Communication in the Fourth Industrial Revolution 77
Shumani Eric Madima

Chapter 4: Computational Linguistics and Indigenous Languages: WhatsApp Emoji Use and the Reclamation of Shona and Ndebele Language and Culture 95
Jennings Joy Chibike

Contents

PART II: DIGITAL MEDIA STRATEGIES AND INDIGENOUS LANGUAGE PRESERVATION IN THE FOURTH INDUSTRIAL REVOLUTION   111

Chapter 5: Global Initiatives for Digital Preservation of Indigenous Languages in the Fourth Industrial Revolution   113
Adeyinka Tella and Joseph Ngoaketsi

Chapter 6: Indigenous Language Development and Preservation in the Age of the Fourth Industrial Revolution   135
Remah Joyce Lubambo

Chapter 7: Kivunjo Names and Naming as an Indigenous Language Preservation and Digitization Strategy   153
Zelda Elisifa

PART III: ENDANGERED LANGUAGE REVITALIZATION, SOCIAL MEDIA LANGUAGE PROSPECTS, AND MEDIA TRAINING   173

Chapter 8: Using Social Media to Promote Indigenous Languages: Reality or Delusion: A Critical Review of Shona Facebook Television   175
Memory Mabika

Chapter 9: Exploring the Role of Indigenous Languages in Journalism and Media Training in the Fourth Industrial Revolution Era   203
Toyosi Olugbenga Samson Owolabi

Chapter 10: Indigenous Language Preservation, Challenges, and Opportunities in the Social Media Age   223
Mawethu Glemar Mapulane, Amukelani Collen Mangaka, Edgar Julius Malatji, Nhlayisi Cedrick Baloyi, and Rudzanimbilu Muthambi

PART IV: ORALITY ON SOCIAL MEDIA, INDIGENOUS EPISTEMIC CULTURES, AND MINORITY LANGUAGES IN DIGITAL MEDIA   239

Chapter 11: Promotion of Indigenous Languages and Culture through Social Media   241
Kganathi Shaku

Contents vii

Chapter 12: Orality On Social Media Language: Linguistic Texts
and Images Portraying Elements of Isizulu Folklore 263
Beryl Babsy Boniwe MaMchunu Xaba

Index 285

About the Editors and Contributors 287

Acknowledgments

This volume is one of the two books that emerged from the theme "Indigenous Language Preservation and Promotion through Digital Media Technology in the Fourth Industrial Revolution." The call attracted many articles from local, continental, and global scholars, and the editorial team decided to publish two books with different titles. The editorial team would like to extend their deepest gratitude to the authors and contributors whose expertise, dedication, and insights have made this book possible. We want to further express our honest appreciation to all the blind reviewers who provided valuable feedback and guidance throughout the development of chapters for this book.

Our deepest gratitude goes to the indigenous communities in Africa whose knowledge, language preservation efforts, and wisdom have inspired this valuable work. As such, this book is a testament to the collaborative effort of many individuals and organizations who share a commitment to the preservation of indigenous languages across Africa. Their contributions have been invaluable in advancing the cause of a digitalized and sustainable society.

Furthermore, we would like to extend our heartfelt gratitude to Lexington Books for their unwavering support and commitment to bringing this book to life. Their expertise, guidance, and professionalism throughout the production process have been invaluable. Our sincere gratitude to the cover designer for creating a captivating and thought-provoking cover that perfectly encapsulates the essence of this book.

Finally, we want to express our deepest gratitude to our families and friends for their understanding, and steady support during the journey of editing this book. Had it not been for your support, this book project would have not been a success. In a nutshell, we are humbled by the contributions of everyone involved and deeply grateful for their dedication.

Introduction

Theorizing Digital Media and Epistemic Indigenous Languages Preservation for Sustainable Development in the Fourth Industrial Revolution

Fulufhelo Oscar Makananise and Shumani Eric Madima

Indigenous languages, alternative knowledge epistemologies, and the experiences of people of African origin are integral parts of the cultural heritage and legacies of many indigent African societies. These societies are former colonies of the European and Western colonial systems, which in all domains undermined and excluded the existence of the African way of knowing, cultural celebrations, and multiple epistemic participatory knowledge traditions. Ndlovu-Gatsheni (2018) postulated that colonialism and imperialism were systems of domination by power and force that were carefully orchestrated to spread, establish, and celebrate scientific Westernized epistemologies, hegemonic knowledges, and dominant colonial languages. Ndlovu-Gatsheni (2018) further argued that the colonialism regimes did not only dehumanize and demoralize the colonized peoples from Africa but also excluded and marginalized their indigenous languages and epistemic knowledge systems that are based on lived experiences and social interactions. In addition, it can be argued that the impact of the colonial systems and hegemonic colonial languages such as Afrikaans, English, French, Portuguese, and Spanish are still apparent as official languages in many African countries today. However, Makalela (2019), Makalela (2022), and Nkadimeng and Makalela (2023) asserted that these Eurocentric colonial systems and hegemonic languages that continue to undermine, discriminate against, exclude, and marginalize indigenous languages and the epistemic participatory legacies of the Africans, need to be equally challenged and dismantled in global discourses. As argued in this book, one area that deserves distinct attention is preserving and revitalizing indigenous languages and alternative knowledges in the African context. This book contends that African societies should acknowledge and embrace digital media platforms as "epistemic colonial sites" for preserving indigenous languages and revitalizing their celebrated cultures in the digital age.

Furthermore, UNESCO (2020) indicated that as the world becomes increasingly interconnected and globalized, the risk of indigenous languages fading into obscurity is a pressing concern in many developing countries. Drawing on an extensive variety of current case studies, practical discourses, and empirical research from the African continent, the volume is a timely response to the United Nations General Assembly's declaration that 2022–2032 was dedicated to the development, safeguarding, preserving, and revitalizing indigenous languages with the expectation of shaping a global digital linguistic society that offers enduring development support to all marginalized languages and knowledges. As indicated above, the book resonates well with the current scenario of ensuring the development, revitalization, and preservation of the African knowledge economy and cultural sustenance without discrimination against any epistemic knowledge, cultural legacies, or linguistic systems. As such, other scholars like Gwagwa, Kraemer-Mbula, Rizk, Rutenberg, and De Beer (2020) argued that with the rise of technological algorithms, artificial intelligence, globalization, and urbanization in the Fourth Industrial Revolution, these indigenous languages and epistemological practices are at risk of extinction in global discourses. Research conducted by Lor (2012), supported by Lucibella (2023), demonstrated that half of the 7,000 documented languages spoken worldwide are at high risk of being lost or disappearing in the coming decades or centuries. As such, this makes this volume essential to advocating that these African languages and local knowledges, which were subjected to unjust colonial laws of being marginalized and excluded in popular debates and discourses in the past, adapt to a rapidly changing technological age.

Purvis, Mao, and Robinson (2019) articulated that indigenous languages are spoken by local or native peoples in their respective societies, while Makananise, Malatji, and Madima (2023) and Nkadimeng and Makalela (2023) underscored that these are languages that have not been globally recognized and accepted as languages of politics, education, economy, business, or trade for centuries because they are not known for activities that could sustain a society's way of knowing and its environment on a global scale. Madingiza (2020) said that the non-recognition, unappreciation, and ingratitude of these previously marginalized languages have led some indigenous speakers to consider their languages primitive and inferior to the dominant languages of the colonial masters, settlers, and colonizers. As such, these are ideologies and practices that the discourses in this volume seek to address so that indigenous peoples should not only support the development and promotion of their local languages but also their revitalization and preservation to advance their indigenous epistemologies of knowing and being.

In addition to this epistemic discourse, Mekonmen, Bires, and Berhanu (2022) underscored that the advent of digital preservation offers new opportunities to safeguard and revitalize these cultural practices and language legacies to ensure a sustainable development of African society that embraces its rich linguistic diversity and subjective alternative epistemologies. However, Cakata (2015) and Kapatika (2022) once asserted that the importance of these epistemic cultural practices and indigenous languages cannot be overstated as they serve as essential repositories of traditional knowledge, cultural heritage, and a unique way Africans could understand the world's experiences and knowledges. In addition, Nhung (2016) argued that these languages offer insights into ancient practices, historical events, and cultural values that are often distinct from mainstream narratives. It is argued in this volume that, besides neocolonialism and coloniality, various factors contribute to the decline and marginalization of indigenous languages in many African societies, including but not limited to societal changes, migration, urbanization, and the dominance of global languages in local contexts. As such, the concept of digital preservation, as deliberated in this volume, emerges as a powerful solution to counteract the continual decline and exclusion of indigenous languages in global economic and sustainability discourses (Dutta, 2019; Masenya & Ngulube, 2021).

Most essentially, the digital revolution has democratized access to the technology of things, local communications, and epistemic knowledges that should empower African peoples to document, revitalize, and preserve their heritage and native identities (Nilson & Thorell, 2018). It can further be argued that, through harnessing technological advancements, African societies have the potential to create sustainable initiatives that safeguard indigenous languages for future generations. In this context, the need for the digital preservation of indigenous languages and revitalization of African cultural legacies and epistemologies through "epistemic colonial sites" is particularly urgent in Africa. This is because Africa is home to unparalleled linguistic diversity, with over 2,000 distinct indigenous languages spoken across the continent (Tshabangu & Salawu, 2021). However, most of these African languages and indigenous epistemologies are endangered, necessitating immediate action to prevent their extinction. As such, digital preservation offers a viable pathway to address these important issues that could contribute to people connecting with their roots and fostering a sense of cultural identity.

Furthermore, Lucibella (2023) argued that between 1950 and 2021, approximately 230 languages worldwide disappeared from human memory because they were not developed, safeguarded, and preserved using colonial technological systems. However, most African countries and societies are home to various understated and endangered indigenous languages (Salawu, 2019), and the struggle for their survival and recognition in political and economic global discourses requires resources and a rigorous obligation from their users to develop, document, and preserve these languages (Tshabangu & Salawu, 2021; Malatji, Makananise, & Madima, 2022). This volume demonstrates that African peoples on the continent and in the diaspora should entirely embrace digital media technology and technological algorithms to preserve their epistemic knowledges and language legacies from possible disappearance. As Wetzel (2018) argued, a language is only in danger of vanishing if its speakers do not make any efforts to revitalize and preserve it or use it in fewer areas of communication, and it can no longer be passed on from one generation to another.

In this instance, it is argued in this book that in this era of decolonization, technological innovations, transformation, and digital media platforms such as the internet, AI technologies, Web3, and other new technologies are perfect tools that Africans should take advantage of as "epistemic sites of knowledge production" (Ndlovu-Gatsheni, 2018). As Schoon, Mabweazara, Bosch, and Dugmore (2020) indicated that, this is done to digitally revitalize, preserve, and document their indigenous languages and cultural legacies (Mpungose, 2020). In addition, Makananise and Sundani (2023) underscored that since the rise of the internet, new media technology, and digital media, there has been a pioneering transformation and modification of how African leaders and societies communicate and interact with each other in their countries and the diaspora. However, the main argument is that even though these languages and native epistemologies in Africa had suffered from unreasonable colonial laws in the past, they now must adapt to a rapidly changing technological age, threats, and opportunities in the age of the Fourth Industrial Revolution (see Makananise, 2022). It is most important that these technological systems be adopted not only as sites of resistance to the scientific Westernized epistemologies and dominant colonial languages but also as epistemic sites for the development, revitalization, and preservation of indigenous African languages, the voice epistemologies of the South, and the creation of a peaceful and sustainable African digital society.

In their description of sustainability development, Purvis, Mao, and Robinson (2019) considered human, social, economic, and environmental as the most important pillars of sustainable development in any society.

Introduction 5

Schwartz (2021) highlighted that in the Fourth Industrial Revolution, the use of precision application equipment and advanced technologies like robots, artificial intelligence, the Internet of Things, and drones in various sectors such as agriculture, building, infrastructure, and transportation types of digital media play a vital role in societies' sustainable development. Makananise (2023a) argued that the Fourth Industrial Revolution, which is characterized by the rapid advancement of digital technologies, has brought about significant changes in various aspects of African society. Furthermore, in the Fourth Industrial Revolution (4IR) era and artificial intelligence (AI), the digital preservation of indigenous languages and revitalization of diverse cultural epistemologies have become crucial issues for ensuring their survival, promoting cultural diversity, and contributing to a digitalized sustainable African society in the future (Galla, 2016).

It has been further argued by Makananise (2023b) that in this contemporary period of the Fourth Industrial Revolution, digital technological innovations, and social media such as Facebook and X (formerly known as Twitter) have exponentially increased, and their use in localized contexts has been globalized over the past decades. However, in their description of the impact of the Fourth Industrial Revolution on diplomatic practices, Makananise and Sundani (2023) asserted that the global South leaders, including the Africans, use these new technological algorithms to address various critical issues such as poverty eradication, socioeconomics, education, peace, and political stability that affect their respective countries. In addition, Makananise (2023b) indicated that language is central to the distribution of essential information and the promotion of awareness on issues of national and international importance in most democratic and developing states in Africa. Makananise, Malatji, and Madima (2023) and Nkadimeng and Makalela (2023) underscored that the use of indigenous African languages in digital media platforms is essential to solving epistemic African problems such as poverty, education, agriculture, and health that distress local peoples. This demonstrates the need to develop, revitalize, and preserve indigenous languages and use them in global discourses to address genuine glitches that are affecting African societies.

Therefore, the central argument on aligning African experiences, preserving indigenous legacies, and recognizing African ways of being, knowing, and participatory knowledge epistemologies on the African continent is hinged on digital media as an epistemic sphere to engage in global scholarship on language development and knowledge revitalization processes through local languages. In this instance, African intelligentsias should engage using colonial media systems, in this case, digital media platforms, to prevent indigenous language loss, also known as "linguicide," that is not only felt locally but globally due to the presence of technological algorithms, globalized systems, the internet of things, and artificial intelligence (Schoon et al., 2020). The presence of these technologies in the African context has led to unrest and the need to revitalize and preserve these languages through digital media formats, especially in the 4IR era. As a result, scholarly debates and discourses have erupted among academics and researchers from various disciplines such as media, communication, journalism, and languages to discuss the current status quo of indigenous languages in the era of the Fourth Industrial Revolution and the artificial intelligence–saturated world (Schoon et al., 2020; Tshabangu & Salawu, 2021; Meighan, 2021; Salawu et al., 2022; Makananise et al., 2023; Salawu et al., 2023; Hukmi & Khasri, 2023).

This should help to address the best ways and practices Africans can use their local languages and epistemic knowledges for economic and educational purposes, "demonstrate self-improvement, motivation, and a sense of community" (Schoon et al., 2020: 4). For sustainable development, individuals can digitally document and preserve their indigenous languages. But the main questions dealt with in this volume are: How can these efforts to use digital media as epistemic centers to revitalize local languages and preserve epistemic cultural legacies contribute to social and economic development, empowerment, and cultural valorization in Africa? What are the implications for education, research, and linguistic revitalization systems? How far have African societies, researchers, and scholars gone to digitally document and preserve their indigenous languages to thwart linguicide in the Fourth Industrial Revolution?

A critical discourse on the role of digital technologies as epistemic sites in local language revitalization and cultural epistemology preservation and the potential of 4IR and AI technologies to support this effort are central issues of concern with everyday struggles in African societies (Oliver, 2022; Oke & Fernandes, 2022). These various challenges facing indigenous languages and different strategies of knowledge production that could be utilized to revitalize the endangered languages for sustainable development and social change are at the epicenter of any epistemic African discourse. From the African perspective, it can be contended that there is an urgent need for technology development and digital algorithm growth that should be culturally appropriate and sensitive to the needs and hurdles of indigenous knowledge epistemological communities; as Schoon et al. (2020) asserted, this would assist these African cultural legacies and their great successes to continue to be celebrated and flourish notwithstanding the perpetuation of colonialism and neocolonialism systems in the continent.

As such, Outakoski, Cocq, and Steggo (2018) and Masenya and Ngulube (2020) underscored that this would assist in societal development and emphasize the potential of indigenous language digital preservation to contribute to a sustainable African digital society. This has been underscored by Makananise and Madima (2020) and Ligidima and Makananise (2020) that technological algorithms offer Africans an opportunity to voice their imbalances in society, exchange knowledges, and access vital information, and social media could equally advocate for equality in societies. This is because the epistemic African discourse of preserving and revitalizing these indigenous cultural legacies and their way of knowing is not only a matter of cultural heritage but also issues of epistemologies of justice, social justice, linguistic justice, and human rights (Msuya, 2019). When Africans start to embrace digitalization as a sphere for indigenous language preservation and revitalization, we will equally promote linguistic diversity, cultural pluralism, and social inclusion and eventually contribute to the sustainable development of the continent through digital media (Shrinkhal, 2021; Russ, 2023).

Russ (2023) further highlighted that the universal and uninterrupted connectivity to the Internet has reached humanity's appreciation with the mass take-up of smartphones and the consequent access to information, social networks, audio-visual entertainment, artificial intelligence, the Internet of Things, language development, and epistemic preservation in the Fourth Industrial Revolution. In addition, Păvăloaia and Necula (2023) asserted that the acceleration of technical progress in the digital realm has made the use of technological devices and applications such as cloud computing, big data analysis, blockchains, and artificial intelligence a daily practice for digital preservation and revitalization of indigenous languages. So, if these smart technologies and their algorithms are utilized well, they could contribute to a sustainable digital society in the future by preserving cultural diversity and indigenous languages. Hoosain, Paul, and Ramakrishma (2020) underscored that the technological revolution has been combined with a change in the strategies of the companies at the forefront of digital technology use to greatly increase the role of global media platforms in the development and preservation of indigenous languages and cultures. Redvers, Menzel, Ricker, Lopez-Carmen, and Blondin (2023) concluded that for decades, most world organizations, such as the United Nations Educational, Scientific, and Cultural Organization (UNESCO) and the International Decade, have recognized and supported the need for indigenous peoples to preserve and revitalize their indigenous languages and to incorporate aspects of linguistic diversity and multilingualism into sustainable development and social change efforts. Most essentially, this volume demonstrates that every revolution has its own various technological opportunities, challenges, and threats in different aspects of life, including media, society, education, health, business, and the preservation of indigenous languages in African communities, which are discussed in detail within the subsequent chapters.

Against this backdrop, *Digital Media and the Preservation of Indigenous Languages in Africa: Toward a Digitalized and Sustainable Society* is a collection of various African voices, debates, case studies, and research findings on how digital media technology and social media platforms affected the development and usage of indigenous languages for communication and how these technological innovations should be applied to advance the protection and preservation of these previously marginalized languages across various cultures and backgrounds. In addition, the book advocates that for indigenous languages to not only survive but also thrive in this ever-changing technological period, global societies should efficiently practice various strategies and innovative techniques to develop, safeguard, and preserve their languages and cultures. Digital media technology, social media platforms, and AI technologies are cutting-edge and avant-garde approaches to ensuring longevity, sustainable development, and the preservation of these previously marginalized indigenous languages in the 4IR.

The chapters in this volume address critical issues about how Africans use digital media platforms and AI technologies to participate in global economic discourses, political debates, gender equality, and digitalized narratives for sustainable development in Africa. In addition, this book provides cutting-edge discourses on digital, indigenous languages, and epistemic knowledge experiences and legacies that contribute to the best digital practices, techniques, innovative strategies, theoretical and conceptual frameworks, and empirical research findings; that are critical to the 4IR's digital media documentation, revitalization, and preservation of these popular African cultural artifacts. This book underscores the need for African practices for the digital preservation of indigenous languages; positioning South African indigenous languages on social media communication in the Fourth Industrial Revolution; social media, artificial intelligence, and indigenous culture; and the relationship between indigenous language development and preservation in the Fourth Industrial Revolution. As such, the preservation and promotion of indigenous languages are not only about linguistic diversity but also about cultural identity and human rights. These languages embody the unique knowledge, worldview, and history of indigenous communities. Through concerted efforts, including documentation, education, and embracing digital tools, indigenous languages can continue to thrive and enrich the cultural tapestry of our world.

DIGITAL PRESERVATION, EPISTEMIC AFRICAN KNOWLEDGES, AND THE FOURTH INDUSTRIAL REVOLUTION

This book is divided into four sections based on theoretical perspectives that connect the chapters on related topics. Part I, "Digital Preservation, Epistemic

Introduction 9

African Knowledges, and the Fourth Industrial Revolution," contains the first collection of chapters. This section begins with Makananise's (chapter 1) argument that in recent years, the United Nations Sustainable Development Goals have been viewed as substantially incorporating some of the vivacious features, principles, and values of indigenous language and knowledge systems. The chapter also indicates that indigenous languages and knowledge systems have acquired traction as a strategic resource for socioeconomic growth and social transformation; thus, proper management, promotion, and persistence through digitized platforms are critical. Makananise goes on to argue that participative epistemic knowledge and indigenous languages of the South, including African communities, are equally important as scientific knowledge and hegemonic colonial languages of Western and European provenance. He asserts that indigenous African institutions of knowledge production, conservation, and sharing, such as initiation schools, indigenous games, agricultural systems, dances and songs, storytelling, and proverbs, as well as digital media platforms, continue to be pillars of indigenous African ways of knowing. It is also urged that, as long as a wealth of knowledge and information exists among African elders and other knowledge holders, digital media should be used to quickly document, disseminate, and conserve indigenous knowledge for global access and usage. Finally, the chapter recommends how these formerly excluded folks might use digital media to conserve and safeguard their indigenous language for social change and development communication in the Fourth Industrial Revolution.

Ajani, Tella, and Dlamini (chapter 2) argue in their contribution to this book that, amid globalization, technological advancement, artificial intelligence, and the Fourth Industrial Revolution, indigenous language preservation and promotion have become critical. The authors argue that these languages have rich cultural, historical, and ecological value, as well as distinct knowledge systems and identities. Nonetheless, problems arising from historical, social, resource, and institutional limits impede preservation; however, digital media technology emerges as a critical tool in this attempt. Furthermore, Ajani, Tella, and Dlamini contend that in light of globalization and the 4IR, the maintenance and advancement of indigenous languages have assumed ever-more-important significance. Indigenous languages are distinctive knowledge systems and identities that have great cultural, historical, and ecological significance. They think that language documentation, preservation, learning, and revitalization become more approachable and interesting with the use of digital tools and applications. The writers of this chapter contend that successful language preservation programs require cooperative methods involving indigenous populations, linguists, and technology specialists. The chapter's conclusion made clear that, for the most part, governments are essential in fostering and advancing indigenous languages by putting supportive policies, sufficient money, and pertinent legislation into place.

Madima's (chapter 3) contribution to this book highlights that, in this age of technological algorithms and AI, the survival of indigenous languages is dependent on their use and promotion via social media communication platforms such as WhatsApp, Facebook, YouTube, X, Instagram, and Snapchat, to name a few. Madima believes that language is and has always been a tool from which indigenous people have obtained their identities, values, and indigenous knowledge systems to relate to their territories in a dignified and values-based manner. Madima argues in this chapter on what should be done to position the usage and promotion of indigenous languages in the Fourth Industrial Revolution using various social media platforms. Moreover, Chibike's (chapter 4) contribution elaborates on the widespread usage of online platforms for communication in the digital age. The focus of the chapter is on how WhatsApp group members and message recipients react to visuals on the app in their native tongues. Furthermore, Chibike provides an example of how the emoji answers help users imagine their unique African identities, cultures, and backgrounds. As a result, he contends that this aids in illuminating for common people the advantages of the Fourth Industrial Revolution in terms of identity formation and communication. In the context of marriage, Chibike shows how the use, interpretation, and reactions to emojis in an epistemic unlearning trajectory were essential in cascading, conserving, and reviving pristine local languages and cultures that are currently in danger of going extinct. In his findings, Chibike indicates that Shona and Ndebele are just as significant to the creation and dissemination of information as English, especially when it comes to marriage. He goes on to say that emojis, a type of computational linguistics, provide clues about the gender, ethnicity, work status, skin tone, and behavior of people who are talking about marriage. This demonstrates how the use of indigenous language and meaning to comprehend emojis exposes the challenges posed by Western colonial linguistics and creates a relationship between language, identity, and culture.

DIGITAL MEDIA STRATEGIES AND INDIGENOUS LANGUAGE PRESERVATION IN THE FOURTH INDUSTRIAL REVOLUTION

Part II of the book titled "Digital Media Strategies and Indigenous Language Preservation in the Fourth Industrial Revolution" brings together topics dealing with digital media strategies that could be used to preserve indigenous languages in the 4IR. Indigenous languages are often at risk of extinction due to various factors, including the dominance of major world languages, urbanization, and cultural assimilation. Digital media offers innovative tools and platforms for indigenous communities to document, promote, and pass on their languages to future generations. In their chapter, Tella and Ngoaketsi (chapter 5) commence by raising the concern that many indigenous, minority, and low-resourced languages are excluded from the advantages and opportunities presented by the 4IR. They further assert that global initiatives for the digital preservation of indigenous languages in the 4IR represent crucial efforts to preserve the linguistic diversity and cultural heritage of indigenous people. Their discussion in this chapter is centered on conceptual and theoretical frameworks related to linguistic diversity, cultural heritage, and digital technologies, digital initiatives to preserve indigenous languages worldwide, 4IR technologies for preserving indigenous languages, digital preservation of indigenous languages, approaches, and strategies for digital preservation of indigenous languages, and opportunities and challenges associated with using digital technology. Their analysis focused on the various global initiatives across the world concerning the digital preservation of indigenous languages in the 4IR, featuring the 4IR technologies relevant to preserving indigenous languages. Tella and Ngoaketsi conclude that efforts to conserve the linguistic diversity and cultural history of indigenous peoples worldwide are vital for the digital preservation of indigenous languages in the 4IR. Therefore, these projects would ensure that indigenous languages continue to flourish and contribute to the global cultural landscape by utilizing the potential of digital technologies.

In addition, Lubambo (chapter 6) highlights that an indigenous language is referred to as a language spoken by indigenous peoples in a specific region, in this case, Africa. These are languages that belong to the native people from which they originated, and thus they are central to indigenous peoples' identities, even though new cycles of innovation evoke and expand beyond those attributed to previous waves of innovation. She further argues that though English is the global language of communication, it does not mean that native speakers can sit back and watch their languages perish. The author indicates that the neglect of these languages has created some difficulties for native speakers in sociocultural and socio-political contexts, particularly in education and economic participation potential. In this chapter, Lubambo further suggests that the challenges faced by indigenous languages can be overcome by adopting digital methods such as social media platforms, television, mobile devices, and digitization of language resources for future generations. In a nutshell, Lubambo validates that the study of this nature may necessitate the rebirth of native languages and encourage optimal conceptualization of ideas, allowing for language development and preservation. Lastly, Elisifa (chapter 7) demonstrates that the Kivunjo speech community, which is indigenous, has rich and diverse means of naming places. The author further argues that these names have their origins in pre-colonial Tanzania and reflect the socio-economic and religio-cultural aspects of that time. In other words, what the place names suggest is that the Kivunjo speech community were crop cultivators, iron smelters, and traders, had chiefdoms and had strong beliefs and taboos. Elisifa, however, indicates that what is unknown is that Tanzania's indigenous language had a chance of having its place names documented in a digital online repository. The author further argues that even when the names are now homes to modern institutions and religious houses, they still bear witness to relics of the non-perishability of cultures (spiritual and material) of Kivunjo's past. Elisifa concluded that the digitalization of indigenous language names via online retrieval means a contribution to the African rich cultural past, made known by Kivunjo toponymy.

ENDANGERED LANGUAGE REVITALISATION, SOCIAL MEDIA LANGUAGE PROSPECTS, AND MEDIA TRAINING

Part III of the book is titled "Endangered Language Revitalization, Social Media Language Prospects, and the Fourth Industrial Revolution," which focuses on the revitalization of the languages that are at risk of being endangered due to a combination of various factors. These are languages that are typically spoken by small, marginalized communities and face a number of challenges that threaten their survival. As an opening chapter, Mabika (chapter 8) makes a case for how Facebook television could be used to promote the Shona language in Zimbabwe. She establishes that the language in which one communicates a certain message reflects certain social realities. The author mentions that the role of digital technologies in undermining minority cultures and indigenous languages globally is a topical issue for researchers and academics. In this chapter, Mabika argues whether there is hope for the Shona language to be preserved due to the exponential growth of the use of television and Facebook, or if it is just another delusion. Owolabi (chapter 9) begins by underscoring that existing research has shown that African languages are not inferior to their European counterparts (English and French) and could function alike. He further asserts that, despite that certainty, it is ironic to note that some African languages have gone into extinction while many others are on the same path. In this chapter, Owolabi further deals with the impact of state politics and power play on indigenous language development, especially in a multi-ethnic society like Nigeria. He argues that indigenous languages should be engaged beyond the level of information sharing and cultural exchange and be employed in digital transformation, digital skills, and digital literacy, as well as systematic integration into the journalism and media training curricula of universities to guarantee their continuity.

Mapulane, Mangaka, Malatji, Baloyi, and Muthambi (chapter 10) present both challenges and opportunities for the preservation of indigenous languages through social media platforms. They demonstrate that in recent years, the relationship between technology and language endangerment has experienced a shift in attitude, more especially toward the development, promotion, and preservation of indigenous languages. They argue that in the recent past, technology was perceived as a threat to the advancement of endangered and minority languages. However, with the development of technological algorithms, digital media, and social networks, these technologies are now viewed as vital tools in language preservation and revitalization endeavors. In this chapter, Mapulane et al. make several discoveries. First, the use of social media to preserve indigenous languages is a welcome move toward preserving African culture. Second, the native speakers of the indigenous languages are the mainstay of their preservation. Third, linguistical aspects such as code-switching, translanguaging, and multilingualism are presenting new opportunities and challenges. As such, code-switching can adversely affect the use of indigenous languages since English is mostly used in this exercise. They further argue that, unfortunately, code-switching among indigenous languages is rare, which is detrimental to these languages. Translanguaging has some elements of eroding the key attributes of these indigenous languages. The authors conclude that multilingualism presents an alternative way of promoting indigenous languages. This is because most languages are given fair opportunities through multilingualism. Also, it does not stifle minorities or previously marginalized languages.

ORALITY ON SOCIAL MEDIA, INDIGENOUS EPISTEMIC CULTURES, AND MINORITY LANGUAGES IN DIGITAL MEDIA

Part IV is the last section, titled "Orality on Social Media, Indigenous Epistemic Cultures, and Minority Languages in Digital Media," which focuses on the preservation and promotion of minority languages, oral communication, and indigenous epistemic cultures in digital media. Many indigenous and minority language communities have strong oral traditions and folklore. Digital media and social platforms can be used to document and share oral traditions, such as storytelling, songs, and oral histories. Platforms like YouTube, podcasts, and social media networks allow for the dissemination of oral narratives in their original languages. Similarly, the use of indigenous and minority languages in digital media may transmit and preserve cultural knowledge. In addition, YouTube videos, blogs, and websites in indigenous and minority languages can serve as repositories for traditional knowledge, rituals, and practices, helping to maintain the cultural fabric of these communities. As such, Shaku (chapter 11) uses Facebook, X, and TikTok to advocate that Internet linguistics concerns itself with how language is used on digital platforms. He argues that the use of language on digital platforms has recently gained scholarly attention; as a result, the sociolinguistics of the e-community has become a case of analysis in the field of linguistics. In this chapter, Shaku argues the role of social media platforms such as Facebook, X, and TikTok in the promotion of the Sepedi language and culture. As part of his analysis, Shaku demonstrated different initiatives taken by the Bapedi speech community on Facebook, X, and TikTok regarding the promotion of their language and culture. He argues that through social media, Bapedi social media users are given the chance to understand and know their surroundings. He concluded that social media must be appreciated for playing an important role in enabling the promotion of language and culture.

Lastly, Xaba (chapter 12) begins by implying that the oral tradition, which was transmitted orally from one generation to the next through word of mouth, changed with the advent of literacy and the creation of folklore literature. Due to the continual introduction of new applications for computers and smartphones that enhance communication, social media has recently taken over. This chapter has, however, used discourse and textual analysis to demonstrate how indigenous proverbs, idioms, and folktales are spread and promoted through the Facebook platform. In this context, Xaba reveals that the folklore components under investigation were presented on social media platforms as condensed proverbs, photographs, and visuals that convey both educational and indigenous knowledge systems perspectives. She further argues that technology, including social media platforms such as Facebook, is currently used and has the potential to educate about languages, disseminate knowledge, and preserve cultural heritage. Xaba asserts that old linguistic information is presented in new ways (social media platforms) for preservation and accessibility to generations of the Fourth Industrial Revolution and beyond. Xaba concludes her argument with a suggestion that to enhance the preservation and archiving of this traditional knowledge that language users and non-language speakers around the world share, oral tradition apps and compilations of social media sites should be established.

FINAL REMARKS ON THE BOOK

This book provides cutting-edge epistemological debates, academic insights, and linguistic discourses from renowned African scholars on the continent

Introduction 15

and abroad regarding the utilization of digital media technologies, and artificial intelligence (AI) toward feasible growth, revitalization, and preservation of the previously marginalized indigenous languages and epistemic African oral knowledges for socio-economic and sustainable African development in the Fourth Industrial Revolution. The volume argues the ways African researchers and ordinary citizens in the periphery could adopt and integrate digital technologies such as fifth-generation mobile networks (5G), the Internet of Things, cloud computing, artificial intelligence, big data analytics, Web3, and other technologies to advance the documentation and preservation of previously marginalized languages and African emerging epistemologies. It investigated the practical aspects of implementing digital preservation initiatives while also examining the sociocultural and ethical dimensions associated with language preservation. This is achieved by shedding light on successful case studies, innovative technologies, and community-driven efforts to provide a comprehensive framework for building sustainable strategies for the preservation of indigenous languages.

In addition, through a multidisciplinary approach, this book examines the intersections of language, technology, and societal well-being, with the overarching goal of fostering a sustainable African society that values and preserves its indigenous languages. The volume argues that the Fourth Industrial Revolution presents both challenges and opportunities for the preservation of indigenous languages in Africa. As such, the book provides that digital preservation can act as a catalyst for maintaining linguistic diversity, empowering communities, and revitalizing cultural heritage. This research book contributes to the ongoing discourse on language preservation and provides practical insights for policymakers, researchers, language activists, and technology developers. As such, by working together, African societies can ensure a future where indigenous languages flourish, enriching African societies and promoting a more inclusive and sustainable world.

REFERENCES

Cakata, Z. 2015. In search of the absent voice: The status of indigenous languages in post-apartheid South Africa. Doctor of Philosophy in Psychology diss., University of South Africa.

Dutta, U. 2019. Digital preservation of indigenous culture and narratives from the global south: In search of an approach, *Humanities* 8, 68; doi:10.3390/h8020068.

Galla, C. K. 2016. Indigenous language revitalization, promotion, and education: Function of digital technology. *Computer Assisted Language Learning,* 29(7), 1137–1151.

Gwagwa, A., Kraemer-Mbula, E., Rizk, N., Rutenberg, I., & De Beer, J. 2020. Artificial intelligence (AI) deployments in Africa: Benefits, challenges, and policy dimensions. *The African Journal of Information and Communication (AJIC),* 26, 1–28. https://doi.org/10.23962/10539/30361.

Hoosain, M. S., Paul, B. S., & Ramakrishna, S. 2020. The impact of 4IR digital technologies and circular thinking on the United Nations sustainable development goals. *Sustainability,* 12(23), 10143. MDPI AG. Retrieved from http://dx.doi.org /10.3390/su122310143.

Hukmi, R. & Khasri, M. R. K. 2023. The epistemic status of indigenous knowledge: A socio-epistemological approach, *Digital Press Social Sciences and Humanities,* 1–7.

Kapatika, H. W. 2022. Epistemicide: A conceptual analysis in African epistemology. Master of Philosophy diss., University of the Western Cape, South Africa.

Ligidima, M. & Makananise, F. O. 2020. Social media as a communicative platform to promote indigenous African languages by youth students at a rural-based university, South Africa. *Gender and Behaviour,* 18(2), 15824–15832.

Lor, P. 2012. Preserving, developing, and promoting indigenous languages: Things South African librarians can do. *Journal of Appropriate Librarianship and Information Work in Southern Africa,* 45(1), 28–50.

Lucibella, M. 2023. Preserving endangered languages as 3D shapes. (Date accessed, January 27, 2023). https://phys.org/news/2023-01-endangered-languages-3d.html

Madingiza, T.S. (2020). Indigenous languages must be celebrated. This is why. (Date accessed, January 26, 2023). https://www.news24.com/citypress/voices/ indigenouslanguages-must-be-celebrated-this-is-why-20200220

Makalela, L. 2019. Uncovering the universals of Ubuntu translanguaging in classroom discourses. *Classroom Discourse,* 10(3–4): 237–251.

Makalela, L. 2022. Not eleven languages: Translanguaging and South African multilingualism in concert. Boston, MA: Walter de Gruyter Inc.

Makananise, F. O. & Madima S. E. 2020. The use of digital media technology to promote female youth voices and socio-economic empowerment in rural areas of Thohoyandou-South Africa. *Gender and Behaviour,* 18(2):15851–15861.

Makananise, F. O. & Sundani, N. D. 2023. Digital media and their implications on diplomatic practices in the Fourth Industrial Revolution: A global South perspective. In F. Endong (ed.), *The COVID-19 Pandemic and the Digitalization of Diplomacy* (pp. 1–26). Hershey, PA: IGI Global Publisher.

Makananise, F. O. 2022. Youth experiences with news media consumption: The pursuit for newsworthy information in the digital age. *Journal of African Films & Diaspora Studies,* 5(2), 29–50

Makananise, F. O. 2023a. Digital media endorsement on COVID-19 vaccination hesitancy among women in the Vhembe District, Limpopo Province of South Africa, *African Journal of Gender, Society, and Development.* 12(1), 133–155.

Makananise, F. O. 2023b. Reimagining South African political campaigns through indigenous language posters in the 4IR: A political communication perspective, communicare: *Journal for Communication Studies in Africa, 42(1),52–63.*

Makananise, F. O., Malatji, E. J., & Madima, S. E. 2023. Indigenous languages, digital media, and COVID-19 pandemic in the Global South: A South African Discourse. In A. Salawu, A. Molale, E. Uribe-Jongbloed and M. S. Ullah (eds.), *Indigenous Language for Social Change in the Global South* (PP. 76–92), London: Lexington Books.

Malatji, E. J., Makananise, F. O., & Madima, S. E. 2022. Critical language matters: The fate of indigenous languages amid Covid-19 pandemic in South Africa. In A. Salawu, A. Molale, E. Uribe-Jongbloed and M. S. Ullah (eds.), *Indigenous Language for Development Communication in the Global South* (pp. 269–286), London: Lexington Books.

Masenya, T. M. & Ngulube, P., 2020. Factors that influence digital preservation sustainability in academic libraries in South Africa. *South African Journal of Libraries & Information Science,* 86(1), 52–63.

Masenya, T. M. & Ngulube, P., 2021, Digital preservation systems and technologies in South African academic libraries, *South African Journal of Information Management,* 23(1),12–49.

Meighan, P. J. 2021. Decolonizing the digital landscape: The role of technology in indigenous language revitalization. *AlterNative: An International Journal of Indigenous Peoples*, 17(3), 397–405.

Mekonnen, H., Bires, Z. & Berhanu, K. 2022. Practices and challenges of cultural heritage conservation in historical and religious heritage sites: Evidence from North Shoa Zone, Amhara Region, Ethiopia. *Heritage Science* 10, 172. https://doi .org/10.1186/s40494-022-00802-6.

Msuya, N. H. 2019. Concept of culture relativism and women's rights in Sub-Saharan Africa. *Journal of Asian and African Studies,* 54(8), 1145–1158. https://doi.org/10 .1177/0021909619863085

Ndlovu-Gatsheni, S. J. 2018. Epistemic freedom in Africa: Deprovincialization and decolonization. New York: Routledge.

Nhung, M.T. 2016. Why Language and Culture are inseparable. (Date accessed, July 21, 2023). https://matteotalotta.medium.com/ language-and-culture-areinseparable-707cc51c136b

Nilson, T. & Thorell, K. 2018. Cultural heritage preservation: The past, the present and the future. (Date accessed, June 13, 2023). https://www.semanticscholar.org/ paper/Cultural-Heritage-Preservation-%3A-The-Past%2C-the-and-Nilson-Thorell/ 7a8b11e0db13502298851cf27f50cc14a48aa909

Nkadimeng, S. & Makalela, L. 2023. The (re)making of an African language: Revisiting epistemologies for quality assessment practices, *Southern African Linguistics and Applied Language Studies*, 41:1, 5–15, DOI: 10.2989/16073614.2023.2185973.

Oke, A. & Fernandes, F. A. P. 2022. Innovations in teaching and learning: Exploring the perceptions of the education sector on the 4th industrial revolution (4IR). *Journal of Open Innovation: Technology, Market, and Complexity*, 6, 31; doi:10.3390/joitmc6020031.

Oliver, E. 2023. Global initiatives and higher education in the fourth industrial revolution. Johannesburg: University of Johannesburg Press.

Outakoski, H., Cocq, C., & Steggo, P. 2018. Strengthening indigenous languages in the digital age: Social media–supported learning in Sápmi. *Media International Australia*, 169(1), 21–31.

Păvăloaia, V. D. & Necula, S. C. 2023. Artificial intelligence as a disruptive technology—A systematic literature review. *Electronics*, 12(5), 1102. MDPI AG. Retrieved from http://dx.doi.org/10.3390/electronics12051102.

Purvis, B., Mao, Y., & Robinson, D. 2019. Three pillars of sustainability: In search of conceptual origins. *Sustainability Science*, 14:681–695 https://doi.org/10.1007/s11625-018-0627-5.

Redvers, N., Menzel, K., Ricker, A., Lopez-Carmen, V. A., & Blondin, B. 2023. Expanding the scope of planetary health education: The international decade of indigenous languages. *Crossmark,* 17, 4–5.

Russ, A. 2023. Preserving indigenous languages and promoting multilingualism, international mother language day. (Date Accessed, July 14, 2023). https://phys.org/news/2023-01-endangered-languages-3d.html

Salawu, A. 2019. African language digital media and communication, New York: Routledge.

Salawu, A., Molale, T. B., Uribe-Jongbloed, E. & Ullah, M. S. (eds.) 2023. Indigenous language for social change communication in the global south. London: Lexington Books.

Schoon, A., Mabweazara, H. M., Bosch, & Harry Dugmore, H. 2020. Decolonising digital media research methods: Positioning African digital experiences as epistemic sites of knowledge production, *African Journalism Studies,* 41:4, 1–15, DOI :10.1080/23743670.2020.1865645.

Schwartz, M. 2021. How technology can provide a more sustainable future for the industrial sector. Forbes Technology Council. (Date accessed, July 14, 2023). https://www.forbes.com/sites/forbestechcouncil/2021/08/31/how-technology-can-provide-amore-sustainable-future-for-the-industrial-sector/?sh=af5492a50c19

Shrinkhal, R. 2021. Indigenous sovereignty and right to self-determination in international law: A critical appraisal. *AlterNative: An International Journal of Indigenous Peoples*, 17(1), 71–82. https://doi.org/10.1177/1177180121994681.

Tshabangu, T. & Salawu, A. 2021. Indigenous-language media research in Africa: Gains, losses, towards a new research agenda, *African Journalism Studies,* 43:1, 1–16, DOI: 10.1080/23743670.2021.1998787.

UNESCO, 2020. Unesco celebrates the international decade of indigenous languages. (Date Accessed, July 22, 2023). https://www.unesco.org/en/articles/unesco-celebratesinternational-decade-indigenous-languages

Wetzel, A. 2018. Preserving linguistic diversity in the digital world. *Multilingual,* 1–6.

PART I

Digital Preservation, Epistemic African Knowledges, and the Fourth Industrial Revolution

Chapter 1

Digital Preservation of Indigenous Languages and Participatory Epistemic Knowledge Systems of the Global South

Insights from South African Experiences

Fulufhelo Oscar Makananise

Toward the imagined termination of colonization, imperialism, and capitalism systems that subjected the global South, including African countries such as South Africa, to a state of inferiority complex and marginalization, there has been an urgency in academic and political discourses to recognize and position indigenous languages and participatory epistemic knowledge systems as equal contributors in the global debates and discourses. The process to advocate the priority and inclusion of participatory epistemic knowledge systems and indigenous languages in the global discourses has for decades been undertaken through the formation and manifestation of several movements from African scholars, such as postcolonialism, decolonization, and Africanization systems. These movements were established as systems the colonies used to counter-discourse or challenge the dominant colonial systems and struggles that undermined and discriminated against the local knowledges, and indigenous languages of the peoples in the South. Furthermore, Santos and Meneses (2020:19) argued that these epistemologies of the South sought to challenge and "transform the Eurocentric canon and to change Southern struggles and experiences into sources of capable generating theory and insight into the diversity that exists in our world." In addition, Reyes (2019) asserted that these movements began to oppose the unequal relations of power of the colonization and colonialism system which for decades marginalized and undermined the indigenous peoples' ways of knowing, being, minds, culture, and their languages. As such, Santos and Meneses (2020) maintained that even though colonization and the colonialism systems that undermined and marginalized the African way of knowing, knowledge production, being, and language usage are believed to have ended, the repercussions are still felt and continue to reproduce its economic, political, and ontological domination over the global South societies such as South Africa. Santos and Meneses (2020:20) indicated that for most of "the epistemologies of the South, the independence of the colonies did not mean the end of colonialism, but it only meant that it underwent a mutation." This is through neocolonialism and the dominant coloniality of power systems of Eurocentric canon and nature.

Furthermore, Khupe (2017) once asserted that African participatory knowledges and indigenous languages have for years been undermined and marginalized as equal epistemic systems of communication, interaction, media, knowledge production, economics, and education. Nkadimeng and Makalela (2023:2) argued that "despite the plethora of knowledge systems available in linguistics and educational research worldwide, African languages of Bantu origin have been residually neglected and versioned from Germanic languages" for education and sustainable development. In addition, Meighan (2021) maintained that digital media and technological algorithms are one of the colonial ways and processes that the global North continues to perpetuate its colonial dominance of knowledge production and colonial languages. As such, the chapter argues that digitalization or digital technology is equally one of the contemporary technological and ideological systems that African scholars in the continent and the diaspora should use as sites of the contest to reproduce and preserve their participatory epistemic knowledges as well as indigenous languages of the South. Hence, the main thesis of this epistemic discourse in the African context is to argue that as much as the participatory African epistemologies and indigenous languages are valid and thus, should be celebrated, reproduced, promoted, and preserved through digital media platforms and technological algorithms. As such, the process to digitize indigenous languages and knowledges of the global South would contribute and open avenues toward their equal promotion, use, and preservation in the global discourses for economic and educational purposes.

It is against the popular narrative that one could contend that participatory epistemic knowledges and indigenous languages of the South including African societies are as imperative as scientific knowledges and dominant colonial languages of Western and European origin. In support of this assertion, Hukmi and Khasri (2023) observed that what makes participatory knowledge and their indigenous languages imperative is that they are rooted in the ideological system, which advocates that knowledge in African epistemologies is produced, constructed, and negotiated through social inter-action, collective participation, and life experiences of individuals in society. In this instance, it can be argued that the epistemic African ways of being and knowing are not based on the use of scientific, colonial, and Western perspectives of individualism which is perpetuated through the Anglophone and Francophone languages (Demeter, 2020) but is an ongoing process of negotiation and co-creation of that, which involves multiple indigenous languages, perspectives, and accumulated experiences (Ndlovu-Gatsheni, 2015). It is further maintained that in this era of technological algorithms and the Fourth Industrial Revolution, the Internet of Things, and Artificial Intelligence (Makananise, 2023), the most appropriate platform that African societies could use to negotiate, recognize, and co-create an accurate picture of African cultures, values, and epistemic knowledges to the entire world is through digital media platforms (Hukmi & Khasri, 2023). Hence, it is sig-nificant in this current discourse to interrogate and theorize how the use of digital media platforms preserves the African knowledge systems, identity, languages, culture, and values which are the individual's best pride. As Santos and Meneses (2020:19) argued that "all knowledges of the world are incomplete," and as such digital media are the most relevant platforms to reproduce the African participatory epistemic knowledge systems, preserve indigenous languages, and recapture the inexhaustible experience and diver-sity of the global South World.

PROBLEMATIZATION OF THE AFRICAN EPISTEMIC KNOWLEDGES AND INDIGENOUS LANGUAGES

Furthermore, this chapter's major argument is that in the face of globaliza-tion, technological advancement, and cultural modernization, there is an urgent need to preserve and revitalize indigenous languages and epistemic knowledge systems of the global South, with a particular emphasis on the South African context. As such, digital media technology and social media platforms such as artificial intelligence, the internet, Facebook, X (formerly known as Twitter), Instagram, YouTube, and TikTok provide a once-in-a-lifetime chance to capture, safeguard, and transmit this invaluable history, promoting cultural diversity, sustainable development, and social fairness. In addition, this chapter aims to explore and assess various chal-lenges, opportunities, and implications in the process of digital preservation for indigenous languages and participatory epistemic knowledge systems, with a focus on their critical role in shaping the cultural and intellectual landscape of the global South. However, grounded on the Afrocentric and decolonial expressions, the central objectives addressed in this chapter are to explore how the African societies in the global South could best reproduce and preserve indigenous knowledge epistemologies and languages through digitized and technologically advanced platforms in the Fourth Industrial Revolution; to outline strategies that could be used to preserve and promote the African knowledges, indigenous languages, oral traditions in the global South; to identify challenges that affect the documentation and preservation of the African epistemic knowledges and indigenous languages using digital media platforms; to determine the impact and possible implications of policies and protocols in the protection and promotion of the African participatory epistemic knowledges and indigenous languages; and finally, to suggest the possible solutions and opportunities that could best accelerate the promotion and preservation of the African epistemic knowledges and indigenous languages using digital media platforms.

To address these objectives, the following questions were critically addressed in the chapter: What are the possible digital ways that could be used to best document the African epistemic participatory knowledges and indigenous languages for access and use by the global community? Which strategies can the African people in the South use to preserve oral traditions, participatory epistemology, and indigenous languages through available technological platforms? What are the challenges that affect the documentation and preservation of indigenous languages and participatory knowledge systems using digital media platforms? Therefore, the need for its effective management and preservation through digitized platforms is essential. In addition, the current discourse focuses on how digital media platforms can be used not only to preserve African knowledges and languages but also for African societies to participate in the creation of global, economic, and social sustainability knowledges. In light of the intensifying neoliberal discourses and decoloniality practices in the global South, this chapter further interrogates the critical digital ideologies that underpin indigenous language activism and theorizes how they contribute toward the creation of indigenous identities and epistemologies. In a nutshell, Santos and Meneses (2020) indicated that these participatory knowledges, alternative thinking, and indigenous languages are the most significant resources of the South that should be reproduced and preserved through these contemporary digital platforms to challenge and decolonize any dominant knowledge and colonial languages that are imposed as the only core epistemic knowledge and language in the political, economic, and educational global discourses.

CONTEXTUALIZATION: SILENCED PARTICIPATORY EPISTEMOLOGIES AND INDIGENOUS LANGUAGES

During the colonial systems and colonization, African epistemic knowledge systems and indigenous languages were treated as silenced epistemologies that were excluded from dominant debates and discourses in the global context. Demeter (2020) stated that in any given context, whether in the global North or South, epistemic knowledges and languages are the epicenter in the production and dissemination of significant knowledges, epistemic ideologies, and ontological philosophies, hence they should be digitally preserved and reproduced. It is further indicated by Whiten, Biro, Bredeche, Garland, and Kirby (2022) that, unlike the European and Western countries in the global North, African societies in the South have their unique process of ontological and epistemological restitution that could reproduce and transfer epistemic knowledges from one individual to another. This process mostly relies on memory, taboos, collective wisdom, and lived collective experiences. As Santos and Meneses (2020) argued, most epistemologies and ontological processes of the South aim to create a humanistic knowledge outside of the historical colonial trail, aspirating to a plural, simplified history of humanity that considers both the accomplishments and the atrocities committed in the name of mankind. Rousseau and Dargent (2019) asserted that though the global society plays a pivotal role in the process of generating space for indigenous languages and participatory epistemologies in the digital public sphere; however, African societies and language users in the global South continue to face, cultural subjugation, epistemic knowledge marginalization, silencing, and linguistic discrimination. Nevertheless, Phyak and De Costa (2021) highlighted that such forms of unfairness generally stem from government policies and laws that still embrace and magnify colonial languages, nationalist materials, neoliberal ideologies, and coloniality of power in public sphere discourses. Additionally, these participatory epistemologies and indigenous languages of the South must be promoted and afforded an equal opportunity in the global spheres and discourses as languages of technology, the internet, development, and science. The whole process would recompense and reposition these African epistemic knowledge systems, ontological ideologies, and indigenous languages from the South to become equal role players and contributors in the global economic spheres, politics, education, and sustainable development discourses in the digital age.

African participatory epistemic knowledge systems and ontological ideologies are the localized knowledges based on praxis, and experiences of the previously silenced, marginalized, and underrepresented societies of the South. For decades, these silenced knowledges and languages were undocumented and could only be sustained through accumulated experiences as alternative thinking for intercultural and knowledge production (Santos & Meneses, 2020). As presented in this discourse, participatory epistemologies were previously silenced and excluded knowledges that are transferred from one person to another through word-of-mouth, folklore, and storytelling, which are also known as verbal communication (Akinwale, 2012). In the same vein, word-of-mouth and oral communication have been some of the ancient strategies and practices or oral traditions used to disseminate and transfer indigenous knowledge, culture, traditions, beliefs, values, and other cultural practices (Raphalalani, 2017) from one generation to another in most global South countries in Africa, including South Africa. In addition, identical to any other kinfolk in the African continent, the silenced participatory epistemologies and indigenous languages have for years been acknowledged through traditional media platforms, house painting, noisy singing, oral communication, and tribal or traditional dancing practices (Kugara & Mokgoatšana, 2022). It is argued that just like other traditional communities in the African continent and the diaspora, the African societies used to preserve, manage, and promote their cultural traditions, norms, values and beliefs, and other cultural practices through word of mouth and oral communication. In the same vein, it is maintained in this discourse that the process to recapture, manage, reproduce, and preserve these knowledges and languages through digitalized resources would require skilled personnel and capital. Ritchie (2014) postulated that digital technology and social media platforms should be approached with vigilance concerning the reproduction of participatory epistemology knowledges, indigenous languages and oral traditions of the South.

Hukmi and Khasri (2023) highlighted that African societies like those in the global South have an affluence of indigenous cultures, values, languages, oral traditions, and participatory knowledge epistemologies that need to be reproduced and preserved through digital media platforms. However, the silenced participatory epistemic knowledges are based on accumulated subsisted experiences and observations of the collective. Nxumalo and Mncube (2018) once indicated that through oral history, tradition, and languages, societies continue to learn about the most significant features of their communities and traditions. As Kugara and Mokgoatšana (2022) indicated this would in return support them in the perpetuation of societal structures, traditional laws, indigenous languages, and values inherited from the ancient generations. Lazar (2020) maintained that for indigenous languages and silenced African participatory epistemic knowledge systems to be recognized as role players in knowledge production, political, and economic changes, Makananise (2023) asserted that this must be a collaborative effort by scholars from the South and North to engage within knowledge ecologies as self-reflexive and intellectually humble collaborators in identifying critical epistemological projects that have not been done and which remain to be done. It has been argued that most of these indigenous languages and silenced epistemic knowledge systems were hitherto neither documented nor written compared to the scientific knowledges and colonial languages but were only based on lived participatory experiences and preserved through memories of the adults. Hence, it is sustained in this chapter the need for these indigenous epistemic knowledges and languages to be managed, reproduced, promoted, and preserved through contemporary media platforms such as digital media.

Furthermore, digital preservation and digital production of cultural products for heritage and historical practices are the best processes the global South could adopt to reproduce, promote, and preserve the previously silenced African epistemologies, ideological ontologies, and indigenous languages. This is because traditional methods of relying on memories, community participation, adults' storytelling, and observations are weakening and could contribute to the demise of these precious commodities and resources. As such, Ligidima and Makananise (2020) asserted that digitalization is the central technique these previously marginalized, and inferior communities in the South could use to promote, preserve, and reflect the diversity of the world's experiences and reproduce their silenced and excluded epistemic participatory knowledges and oral traditions for future generations to access and use. In addition, Akinwale (2012:5) once argued that "indigenous knowledge management is a process in which communities recapture, reproduce, control and share their knowledges through indigenous languages to meet specific local needs." Kugara and Mokgoatšana (2022: 4) further asserted that the process of promoting African epistemic knowledge and digitizing indigenous languages "opens up various opportunities for long-term preservation and wider dissemination of oral history." As Anshari, Syafrudin, and Fitriyani (2022) and Makananise and Malatji (2021) argued that the emergence of the Fourth Industrial Revolution presented what is now known as "humanities digitalization" which could be helpful in the process of digital preservation of indigenous knowledge systems and native languages. Therefore, scholars need to engage in these discourses in global South societies like Africa to determine how these preciously silenced African knowledges, native languages, and oral traditions like dominant colonial languages and knowledges could best be recaptured, reproduced, and preserved through digitized media platforms in the Fourth Industrial Revolution.

It is imperative to designate those African participatory epistemic knowledges and indigenous languages that play a fundamental role in the sustainable development and growth of every society, either in the global North or South. These previously excluded knowledges and oral traditions are embedded with momentous messages and information that not only regale but also enlighten, educate, and change society about their substantial traditional customs, cultures, values, and behaviors. For instance, to highlight the significance and hegemonic thinking of African participatory knowledges, Sillitoe, Dixon, and Barr (2005) designated that in their respective corners, most African societies used and relied on participatory epistemologies as imperative strategies to maintain peace, calmness, synchronization, and order in society. In addition, Kugara and Mokgoatšana (2022) noted that most of the world's heritage resources have been lost, and some cannot be recovered due to neglect and improper documentation, and preservation of their epistemic indigenous resources. Most absolutely, the use of digital media platforms would allow South Africans to practice indigenous knowledge preservation and redocumentation in ways other mediums may fall short of. At the same time, Biyela, Oyelude, and Haumba (2016) postulated that digitization could be viewed as a technique that could provide long-term preservation and global access to local indigenous knowledges and languages. It is against this contextual locus that this chapter advocates for the digitalization, management, preservation, and promotion of the African epistemic participatory knowledge and indigenous languages for access and use in the global economic, political, and sustainable development discourses. Henceforth, the chapter encourages and promotes a holistic approach to embrace multiple platforms to overcome the challenges faced in the digitization of indigenous knowledge and oral traditions in the global South.

THEORETICAL PERSPECTIVE: MODERNIZATION THEORY

This chapter is reinforced by the modernization theory of contemporary studies and knowledge production processes in the globalized world. Thus, there is a need to provide a historical overview and a basic description of the theory as well as explain the selected principles that are pertinent to the chapter.

Modernization Theory

According to Janos (2000), modernization theory was one of the central models in the disciplines of the contemporary social sciences between the 1950s and 1960s, before going into a cavernous occultation and it reemerged after 1991 through the Fourth Industrial Revolution period. The theory is grounded on the popular expression that for African societies to increasingly transit from a premodern to modern epistemic and ontological ideological thinking, the global South must recognize and accept the utilization of new technological innovations, digital algorithm systems, the internet, and digital media platforms to reproduce the previously excluded diversified epistemologies of the world's experiences in the contemporary age. This process could assist in building a better epistemic future and a modern society that is highly complex and sophisticated with its knowledge that hinges on digital technology. The model further proposes that the previously disadvantaged or marginalized societies would develop and progress well as they adopt the new modernized and contemporary practices, norms, and behaviors. It is further argued in this discourse that the only way African societies could transform, and grow is through the recognition and acceptance of the modernized practices and processes of knowledge gain, indigenous language preservation, and information dissemination in the digital age. Within the context of this chapter, modernization theory confirms that various transformations and growths such as information community technology, new media, digital media, the internet, social media, and the need to update traditional techniques like communication, socialization, and protection processes make rejuvenation and modernization more necessary than ever in this era.

Furthermore, Mdhluli et al. (2021) designated that the technique and popular practice that indigenous peoples use to preserve, manage, and share participatory epistemic knowledges and native languages is reasoned to have contributed to their knowledge being threatened with extinction. It is further illustrated that modernization theory not only stresses the process of knowledge transformation and the alternatives to modern hegemonic thinking but also *how* the change should occur and the responses to that transformation. As Janos (2000) asserted, the model theorizes the internal dynamics while referring to social and digital cultural structures and the variation of digital media technology for social change and economic development. Whereas Mdhluli et al. (2021: 34) indicated that "the speedy use of digital media in the modern, dynamic world gives valuable opportunities to facilitate the process of preserving, managing, and sharing participatory epistemic knowledge and indigenous linguistic features that are unique to the African societies." More so, it is maintained in this chapter that the process of digitalization and modernization should be fully introduced and locally embraced by the African scholars in the South to safeguard and preserve indigenous knowledge, information, and languages against "intellectual theft." It also allows knowledge holders from previously marginalized and excluded alternative hegemonic thinking societies of the South to benefit from such initiatives and struggles against epistemic oppression.

The model has been applied in this chapter to theorize how the traditional societies in the global South could adopt the contemporary practices of using digital resources and media platforms to promote, reproduce, and preserve their participatory epistemic knowledges and indigenous languages to be recognized as core players and producers of fundamental knowledges in the economic and sustainable development discourses. This is because participatory epistemologies and indigenous languages of the South are essential actors in the production of acceptable knowledges and information that could foster economic stability, sustainable development, and peace worldwide. The theory would emphasize the promotion and preservation of African indigenous knowledges and language discourses among the previously disadvantaged, undermined, and marginalized communities in the global South.

METHODOLOGICAL PERSPECTIVE: AFROCENTRICITY APPROACH

This chapter draws from the Afrocentricity approach and decolonial expressions (Asante, 2003) to center African experiences, languages, and knowledge systems. It aligns with Afrocentric principles of valuing indigenous languages and embracing participatory knowledge systems while countering Western-centric narratives, and fostering cultural and intellectual sovereignty. Through this approach, this chapter underscores the significance of digital media as a means of preserving and celebrating the unique cultural heritage and knowledge systems of the Global South, particularly from a South African standpoint. In addition, this chapter employed a systematic review research design using secondary sources and research materials to explore the current trends and debates on the digital preservation of oral traditions and indigenous knowledge systems from the South African perspective. These secondary sources and materials used were accessed from various and relevant research repositories such as Google Scholar, ResearchGate, ScienceDirect, Scopus, Embase, and PubMed. This chapter included scholarships that reported discussions and conclusions related to the digital emancipation of epistemic participatory knowledges and languages; digital management and preservation of participatory knowledges and indigenous languages; participatory epistemologies for sustainable economic development and social change; challenges of promoting and preserving indigenous knowledge and oral traditions, new ways to promote access to oral traditions and indigenous knowledge and excluded any research studies that focus on hegemonic knowledges and languages. This chapter further followed the preferred reporting items for systematic reviews and meta-analysis model in screening different publications, using appropriate keywords relevant to the topic. The Newcastle Ottawa scale was used to assess the quality of all cross-sectional studies included in this review. Furthermore, the thematic analysis was carefully used to synchronize how the indigenous knowledge systems and information could be promoted and preserved through the new media technologies.

DIGITAL EMANCIPATION OF EPISTEMIC PARTICIPATORY KNOWLEDGES AND LANGUAGES

The United National Human Rights Office of the High Commissioner (OHCHR, 2020) indicated that participatory marginalized knowledges and indigenous languages are in various continents such as the Arctic, Asia, Australia, Africa, and the Americas. However, regardless of their distinct differences and geographical distances, these previously silenced epistemologies and marginalized languages face similar challenges in the global spaces. They are not officially recognized and offered equal opportunities as knowledges and languages of science, technology, and education. In addition, as a response to these colonial projects that marginalize indigenous resources, the indigenous African peoples would fight using decolonial practices and processes to have their epistemic participatory knowledges, indigenous languages, identities, and their way of life emancipated, recognized, and offered equal opportunities as colonial hegemonic thinking in the global context (O'Brien, Pan, Sheikh, & Prideaux, 2023). As such, in recent years, the global South has experienced popular discourses and decolonial movements on the epistemic emancipation of participatory epistemologies and indigenous languages to reflect on the diversity of experiences and practices of knowledge production.

Ndlovu-Gatsheni (2018) indicated that participatory epistemologies are the decolonial studies of the politics of knowledge production and indigenous language promotion of African struggles for epistemic emancipation. Ritchie (2014) argued that over the years, traditional media such as print and broadcast have emerged as the most conventional media that are used for ontological and epistemological restitution and promotion of African epistemic participatory knowledges, ontological ideological thinking, and indigenous languages of the South. In addition, Constant and Tshisikhawe (2018) indicated that the advent of digital media platforms and the epistemic decolonial thinking of digitalization processes and information systems have expedited various institutions to prioritize the reproduction of diversified participatory knowledges and preservation of indigenous languages through technological systems in the South.

Furthermore, Ndlovu-Gatsheni (2018:1) indicated that "as a result of the long-term consequences of modernity, enslavement, and colonialism, African people have been reproduced as agents in a Eurocentric history." As such, Green (2007) once indicated that the process to emancipate participatory knowledges and indigenous languages through digital media platforms is a complex one as these ontological knowledges and diversified technologies are developed and utilized around specific conditions of indigenous populations and communities in a particular geographic area and their interfaces with others. The participatory epistemic knowledge and indigenous languages are diverse, as Ndlovu (2015) designated those African knowledges and languages are also known as "living heritage" or "living culture" that depend on memory and word of mouth for continuity. As such, Kugara and Mokgoatšana (2022) indicated that from time immemorial, the custodians of participatory cultural practices, silenced knowledges, and vulnerable languages have been the elders of the society.

Unfortunately, O'Brien et al. (2023:173) asserted that throughout human history, epistemic participatory knowledges or alternative hegemonic thinking and their languages "have been violated, making them one of the most disadvantaged and vulnerable groups globally." As Madima, Makananise, and Malatji (2022) argued, for decades indigenous languages and participatory knowledges have been predominantly perceived as undocumented cultural, local, traditional, and community knowledge produced and owned by local people in their specific communities. As such, their use and promotion on digital media platforms would assist with their preservation and emancipation process from the colonial thinking and systems of being marginalized and undermined as valuable resources of technology, science, economics, and education.

Most significantly, van den Berg (2018) highlighted that in this era of using the internet and digitalized platforms, the traditional roles of cultural heritage institutions as platforms to emancipate epistemic participatory knowledges and indigenous languages have been confronted and challenged in terms of the relevancy of their content in line with the needs of the diverse users they serve. Whereas Akinwale (2012:5) underscored digitalization as an essential process and practice African societies in the South could employ to advocate for the emancipation of the participatory epistemologies and indigenous knowledges to be recognized as equal contributors in the different spheres of life. Concurrently, it can be argued that digitization has become a burning topic because it has been viewed as a process that can be best used to emancipate, reproduce indigenous knowledges, preserve indigenous African languages for future generations, and increase their visibility. As Smith (2002) once highlighted that the process to emancipate participatory epistemologies and indigenous languages through digital media platforms could assist the global South from the African societies to bridge the knowledge and digital divide and thus, curb the scores of poverties and other socioeconomic challenges.

In contrast, Kugara and Mokgoatšana (2022), concluded that South Africa is currently behind the rest of the global South World in terms of emancipation and digitization of participatory epistemologies and indigenous languages for global access and participation in the knowledge production and economic discourses. Moreover, it is argued in this chapter for the global South societies to use balanced practices and methods such as traditional and technological innovations to emancipate and preserve the epistemic participatory knowledges and indigenous languages for easy access and use by the global society.

Digital Management and Preservation of Participatory Knowledges and Indigenous Languages

Over the years, the global South scholars in the African context followed the postcoloniality and decoloniality practices and processes to challenge the colonial status quo that marginalized and silenced the African participatory epistemologies and indigenous languages in cultural and structural ways within health, economic, science, technology, and sustainable development (Malatji, Makananise & Madima, 2022). In addition, Reyes (2019) advocated that in different ways this coloniality of dominance and power has been normalized, naturalized, and rationalized in many colonies in the global South World. In addition, dismantling these Eurocentric and Westernized dominant ideologies would assist African societies to navigate processes that could be used to construct and reconstruct their epistemic epistemologies, indigenous languages, and cultural heritage sites. This would ensure that these knowledges and languages that have been previously undermined, excluded, and silenced are reproduced and recognized as equal participants in global discourses and debates. In the South African context, the Protection, Promotion, Development, and Management of Indigenous Knowledge Act of 2019 outlines the best practices and processes that the previously marginalized societies could manage, preserve, promote, and protect their African participatory knowledges, oral traditions, and indigenous languages from unauthorized use, misappropriation, and misuse. As O'Brien, Pan, Sheikh, and Prideaux (2023) theorized, the international community is gradually acknowledging that special measures are necessary to protect Indigenous rights and maintain their distinct cultures and ways of life.

Furthermore, the emancipation and digital management of the participatory epistemologies, African ontological ideologies, and indigenous languages are essential struggles to validate, evaluate, and recognize these African knowledges and languages of the previously marginalized societies of the South. Similarly, these measures were strictly introduced to digitally protect and manage these participatory epistemologies and oral traditions, which were previously disseminated through word of mouth, and collective memory for continuity and preservation. In addition, these traditional cultural preservation techniques have been utilized for centuries by most marginalized African societies as the only way to reproduce, manage, and preserve their oral traditions and cultural discourses until the start of writing, printing, broadcasting, technology, and digitization practices.

As such Biyela, Oyelude, and Haumba (2016) asserted that the marginalization and exclusion of African participatory knowledges and indigenous languages in the public discourses had had a massive negative impact on Africa's economic development and knowledge growth. However, many indigenous knowledge scholars are "still lamenting those heritage resources especially digitally born will become inaccessible in the future unless they are digitised" (Breytenbach, Lourens & Marsh, 2013:1). Smith (2002:231) once asserted that "the lack of relevance is perpetuated by the continued social, economic, and technological ties between African countries and their former colonising powers." Hence, digitization of African epistemic knowledges and indigenous languages seems to be the only technique local African peoples could use to manage, preserve, and digitalize their cultural ideologies and oral traditions. These struggles against the coloniality of knowledge and dominance of languages still have an enormous impact on how the global South would do agricultural farming that contributes to socioeconomic development and social change.

Participatory Epistemologies for Sustainable Economic Development and Social Change

Epistemic African participatory knowledges and indigenous languages discourse need our concern because they play an essential part in cultural, sustainable economic development, and social change in the global South World (Makananise, Malatji, & Madima, 2023). Over the past recent years, these knowledges and languages across the global South have been viewed as fundamentally integrating some of the vivacious traits, principles, and values of the sustainable development goals (Ndlovu, 2015). It is in this context that African participatory knowledges are equally considered to play a vibrant role in ensuring the socioeconomic development and social change that would benefit the global South World. Scholars in the global South such as Rasmussen and Nolan (2011), Ndlovu, (2015), Hukmi and Khasri (2023), and Makananise, Malatji, and Madima (2023) have all argued that participatory epistemologies of the South and indigenous languages that have been marginalized and undermined for decades have a significant contribution to the socioeconomic development and bringing to realization the sustainable development goals such as peace, justice, climate action, sustainable cities and communities, reduced inequalities, gender equality, quality education, good health, and well-being.

Furthermore, Mutula (2008), Ocholla (2009), and Chisita (2011) established that there is substantial theoretical and empirical evidence that the marginalization of indigenous knowledges and native languages have had some adversative effects on Africa's socioeconomic development, and social change. In addition, Kaya and Seleti (2013:32) indicated that this is "perpetuated by the continued social, economic, and technological ties between the African countries and their former colonial powers." However, it was during the postcolonial, decolonial, and digital eras that these so-called backward and marginalized indigenous knowledges and their traditional roles have been advocated to be more relevant and to be afforded an equal space in the global discourses. To substantiate these claims, WHO (2016) indicated that in Africa, up to 80 percent of the population uses traditional medicine to help meet their healthcare needs, and the most important issues affecting the practice of traditional medicine fall into national policy, and regulatory framework, safety, efficacy and quality, access, and rational use. Scholars in the global South are of the view that most digitalized materials published on and about indigenous medicines and their effective use in Africa are slowly growing (Lor, 2005; Ocholla & Onyacha, 2005); others such as Akinwale (2012) and Ngulube (2002) are of the view that majority of African countries are currently behind the rest of the world in terms of the digitization of their participatory epistemologies and indigenous languages to dismantle the ongoing exploration of African knowledges.

Constant and Tshisikhawe (2018) highlighted that the available empirical evidence and literature show that the marginalization and degrading of local knowledges and indigenous languages have adversely affected Africa's economic growth and social change for the better. As Santos and Meneses (2020) argued that currently the global North is getting smaller in economic as well as political and cultural terms, and it cannot make sense of the world at large other than through general theories and universal ideas. Medie and Kang (2018) the global South refers to African, Asian, Latin American, and Middle Eastern countries that are also members of the Group of 77. Heine (2023) asserted that the global South are various countries around the world that are described as developing, less developed, and underdeveloped. In this context, the global South refers to the countries in the African context and societies. This is evident as the BRICS summit held in South Africa in August 2023 sought a wide range of alternatives to decrease their dependence on the United States dollar.

As Heine (2023) highlighted, by 2030 it is projected that three of the four largest economies will be from the global South with the order being China, India, and Indonesia. Already the GDP in terms of purchasing power of the global South-dominated BRICS nations such as Brazil, Russia, India, China, and South Africa. This was previously indicated by Santos (2016) that the global North seems to have very little experiences to teach and offer the whole world, hence it is essential for the global South and their participatory knowledges and languages to emerge as the major contributors in the economic development discourses. These arguments demonstrate that the proper management, preservation, and promotion of African epistemic knowledges, cultural discourses, and indigenous languages through digital platforms might significantly contribute to the socioeconomic development, and social transformation of the global South community, livelihood, and their small-scale economy.

Epistemic Strategies to Preserve African Knowledges and Indigenous Languages

African scholars, philosophers, and theorists from the hitherto marginalized and underrepresented communities in the global South should formulate numerous strategies and techniques that could hasten the preservation of their participatory epistemologies, oral traditions, and indigenous languages. As such, Hunter (2005) specified that there is no doubt that technological algorithms, communication technologies, new media, the internet, and digital media platforms hold significant potential for supporting the recording, management, dissemination, and long-term preservation of indigenous knowledge and oral traditions. In addition, Kugara and Mokgoatšana (2022) underscored that it would be through digital media platforms such as scanners, computers, the internet, social media, and external storage drives that the indigenous peoples can learn how to digitize, manage, preserve, and exchange indigenous knowledge and oral history in South Africa. The aforementioned authors further revealed that this is because the country faces the danger of losing out on the benefits of African oral history, indigenous languages, and participatory knowledges. This epistemic discourse encourages and promotes a holistic approach embracing multiple stakeholders to overcome the challenges faced in digitizing participatory knowledges, oral tradition, and indigenous languages.

The study conducted by Hunter (2005) revealed that the equipment used for digitizing participatory knowledges, native languages, and data includes large high-production scanners, computers, and a special kind of software. In addition, copyright issues as one of the strategies should also be well-taken cognisance of and access is provided to all who request materials with the proper permissions adhered to. During this process, the content of the participatory knowledge would be protected and preserved through a license called Creative Commons license. This type of license helps creators or licensors to retain copyright while also allowing others (licensees) to copy, distribute, and make some use of their work at least for non-commercial purposes. Access to the portal is password protected. Small digitization projects take place according to the demand at the time. In addition, maps, books, pamphlets,

Digital Preservation of Indigenous Languages

rare books, letters, albums, photos, and negatives are all digitized depending on the demand at the time. In this regard, computers, cell phones, laptops, tablets, and large-format scanners are used. Moreover, it is essential to note that these strategies would assist the previously disadvantaged communities to manage, preserve, and promote their indigenous knowledge for the global community to access and use.

According to Lor (2005:67), most "repository libraries wishing to play the role in the preservation of digital indigenous knowledge resources need to consider factors such as technical; organisational; economic; political; legal and ethical." In addition, Hoppers (2002) explained that the developing world should create an indigenous knowledge digital library. Ngulube (2002) avowed that information professionals should ensure the longevity of the documented indigenous knowledge by devising preservation strategies. Also, Hunter (2005) strongly believes that significant time, patience, funding, resources, support, training, and a collaborative effort by indigenous communities, multidisciplinary researchers, staff from cultural institutions and software engineers and designers could help to accelerate the preservation and protection of indigenous knowledge. Biyela et al. (2016) concluded that there is a need for training in the digital preservation of African epistemic participatory knowledge systems and indigenous languages so that people can be able to cascade the skill to colleagues and community members as the need arises. As such, it can be argued that African scholars and those previously marginalized should embrace the use of new technology, digital libraries, and digitalized media platforms as techniques or strategies to quicken the preservation and promotion of their indigenous knowledge and data for access and use by the global community.

Challenges with Preserving African Epistemic Knowledges through Digital Media

The global South World which refers to African societies faces challenges when rethinking, reimagining, recreating, reproducing, and preserving African epistemic knowledges and indigenous languages through digital media platforms. As Van den Berg (2018) and Makananise and Sundani (2023) asserted that like other ethnic groups and societies, African peoples are also faced with challenges and threats from the modern industrial world, artificial intelligence, and the Internet of Things which could erode the African history, cultural ideologies, and epistemic participatory knowledges of the South. Accordingly, the comparative study conducted by Biyela et al. (2016) on the digital preservation of participatory epistemologies of the South revealed that the digitization of African cultural ideologies, indigenous language discourses, and behaviors is so slow as to be almost nonexistent.

In addition to this, Kugara and Mokgoatšana (2022) revealed that it is well known that the digitization of participatory knowledge systems and indigenous languages specifically, the oral tradition carries both the good and the bad about society. As Masoga (2005) once designated that the challenge that still faces most African societies is the perpetuation and continuation of colonization through the coloniality of power and dominant colonial languages which happen alongside decolonization and Africanization processes. African societies in the global South are still indirectly affected by the colonization systems that have displaced their identities, native languages, epistemic knowledges, and cultural ideologies. Reyes (2019) argued that the coloniality process or neocolonialism system manifests how the colonial system that underwent a mutation controls power, knowledge, identity, and human languages. As such, the colonization system and the technological algorithms have been major challenges toward the growth, reproduction, and digitalization of African epistemic participatory knowledge systems and indigenous languages.

Furthermore, Kugara and Mokgoatšana (2022) explained that despite the attacks and challenges on African indigenous thought (predominantly their knowledge and culture), the indigenous societies in South Africa did not controvert their participatory knowledge systems and indigenous languages. These African scholars further argue that digitization problems should not hinder the work of native oral historians, but their work should be tailored and designed to make the enterprise flourish. Whereas Mdhluli et al. (2021) asserted that during colonialism and coloniality systems, the African community structures were disturbed to an extent that indigenous ways of preserving, managing, and sharing knowledge on digital platforms were abandoned and had little or no room. For instance, Ngulube (2002:31) indicated that the "archival fraternity was not fully conversant with the opportunities and challenges of preserving digital records." As such, Mdhluli et al. (2021) revealed that the digitalizing participatory epistemologies and indigenous languages were a Western-driven project that wishes to use African knowledge holders as tools to benefit financially from their indigenous knowledge, without sharing any benefits with the African knowledge holders.

Of utmost importance, Mdhluli et al. (2021) highlighted that these unique knowledges and languages are in danger of disappearing and becoming extinct if proper intergenerational measures are not taken to preserve, manage, and share them in digital media platforms. Whereas Biyela, Oyelude, and Haumba (2016) once argued that one of the challenges with the process of documenting, reproducing, and preserving indigenous knowledge is that digitization standards are not fully implemented due to a lack of satisfactory funding. In addition, regarding copyright compliance, a requestor must provide written approval from the copyright holder permitting the digitization

(Mdhluli et al., 2021). As such, challenges of documenting and preserving the indigenous languages and African participatory epistemic knowledge systems through digital media platforms include but are not limited to the lack of funding, scarcity of high-quality equipment, and lack of information technology support.

Regulatory Policies and Protocols for Epistemic Knowledges and Indigenous Languages

Regulatory policies and protocols are essential for the management and digitalization of epistemic African participatory knowledge systems and indigenous languages for sociocultural and economic development. As such, the global South societies should develop and implement policies and protocols that recognize and support various organizations and African societies to manage, monitor, evaluate, and regulate the development and Digitalization of these essential participatory knowledges and native languages. In addition, it is argued that, if participatory knowledges and language elevation policies and protocols are well developed, managed, and implemented, first, they could help strengthen ways indigent societies could protect and preserve their indigenous knowledge and oral traditions from unauthorized use, misappropriation, and misuse. Second, they could assist to affirm African indigenous values, norms, and practices in the face of globalization, digitalization, and the Fourth Industrial Revolution process.

Third, they may assist with how to develop and advance the services offered by various indigenous knowledge holders and practitioners, especially in the global south. Fourth, these policies and procedures could assist how in creatively advancing the course of indigenous knowledge within the context of complex economic, social, and cultural rights. Lastly, these policies might also assist in how the marginalized communities including African societies may best promote and endorse their various indigenous knowledge better on the digitalized media platforms available. As Kalusopa and Zulu (2009:98) explain, "digital preservation and policy implications as the way of preserving information materials such as digital surrogates created because of converting analogue materials to digital format and those which are born digital and were not in the analogue format before." This means that indigenous knowledge policies and procedures could place a great emphasis on the promotion of international linkages in indigenous knowledge systems from the perspective of sharing best practices and commitment to common objectives in developing countries.

Furthermore, these regulatory policies protocols and procedures are significant for the safeguarding and fortification of these epistemic African knowledge systems and indigenous languages that have been in existence for centuries. Whereas Dewah and Feni-Fete (2014:77) are of the view that "digital preservation differs from digital archiving in that the former refers to a series of adopted management activities that are undertaken to ensure continued access to digitised materials for as long as the agreement prevails while the latter refers to the process of creating backup as opposed to strategies for long-term digital preservation." However, as a way to protect and preserve indigenous knowledge (Lusenet, 2007:164; South African Department of Arts & Culture, 2010) indicated that in October 2003 during the thirty-second session of the general conference, the United Nations Educational, Scientific and Cultural Organization (UNESCO) adopted a charter on the preservation of the digital heritage with the principal aim to strengthen ventures for the preservation and protection of documented heritage resources and sites.

In addition, UNESCO Memory of the World Programme (2015:21) indicated that "in 2015 the International Federation of Libraries Association (IFLA) stressed its support for the UNESCO Vancouver Declaration of the libraries' role of providing access and safeguarding of heritage resources." Moreover, Battiste (2002) asserted that African intellectuals should help Africa close the gap created by over four hundred years of domination and marginalization of African people's knowledge systems, by rejecting the utilization of the dominant Western worldview of knowing and knowledge production as the only way of knowing.

Through the Protection, Promotion, Development, and Management of Indigenous Knowledge Act of 2019, Chapter 2; Section (3), the South African government endorsed its support to manage and protect the indigenous knowledge of indigenous communities from unauthorized use, misappropriation, and misuse; second, to promote public awareness and understanding of indigenous knowledge for the wider application and development thereof; third, to develop and enhance the potential of indigenous communities to protect their indigenous knowledge; and last, to provide for registration, cataloguing, documentation, and recording of indigenous knowledge held by indigenous communities (The Republic of South Africa, 2019:10).

Moreover, Ngcobo (2010:1) noted that the establishment of the National Ingenuous Knowledge Systems Office (NIKSO) by the Department of Science and Technology (DST) was one of the ways to nurture national indigenous knowledge system priorities through proactive engagement in the field of science and technology, to protect and recognize indigenous knowledge as property owned by indigenous communities, to facilitate and coordinate the development of indigenous knowledge, and to empower the indigenous communities through academic discourse and awareness campaigns that would enable them to recognize and utilize indigenous knowledge for cultural and economic benefit. In a nutshell, this shows that the idea and project of preserving and promoting the participatory epistemologies in Africa and indigenous languages through digital media platforms in the developing world is endorsed and supported by various stakeholders both international bodies such as UNESCO and national ones such as the South African Government through DST, and NIKSO and the National Research Foundation (NRF).

DISCUSSION: THE AMALGAMATION OF SIGNIFICANT DISCOURSES AND CONSIDERATIONS

It is argued in this chapter that indigenous languages and participatory epistemic knowledge systems are the most imperious legacies of African societies and if they are preserved could continue to shape their African identity, knowledge production, and distinctiveness on a global scale. Most critical to this, participatory epistemologies and indigenous languages need to be safeguarded and promoted using technological innovations and digital media platforms. In addition to the indigenous knowledge discourses, studies in various parts of the African continent demonstrate that most people including those living in South African regions; still deeply depend on African indigenous knowledge for existence and livelihood (Biyela, Oyelude & Haumba, 2016). Take for instance, an elderly woman who cooks pumpkin and vegetables and dries them to be eaten after the summer season has indigenous knowledge and information on how to preserve food or practice food security without using a refrigerator or modernized technology. This would be known as dried vegetables also known as *Mukusule* that could after months be cooked with tomatoes and enjoyed with porridge. Such knowledge needs to be promoted among the younger generations to see how best they can preserve their food or contribute to food security without using modernized techniques and methods.

Furthermore, the chapter accentuated that the African participatory knowledges, oral traditions, and indigenous languages have for years gained serious popularity and momentum as strategic resources for socioeconomic development and an agent of social transformation (Biyela, Oyelude & Haumba, 2016). The strong cultural focus would help future generations to learn and be informed about their cultural norms, behaviors, and oral traditions concerning food security, farming, health, and education just to mention but a few. Furthermore, it is argued that the process of knowledge sharing on a global scale could assist African countries including South Africa to bridge the knowledge and digital divide that could further assist to control food scarcity and other socioeconomic challenges faced by the global South (Akinwale, 2012; Enhuber, 2015). For instance, from the African perspective, a traditional healer who can cure a particular disease using a specific herb has the knowledge and theory of the plant species and their characteristics and in return could contribute to the socioeconomic development of the community (Kaya & Seleti, 2013). This demonstrates that the process of promoting indigenous knowledge systems and languages through digital media platforms does not only contribute to the preservation of such knowledge but also to the socioeconomic development and social transformation of the community.

A study conducted by Kugara and Mokgoatšana (2022) further established that the African epistemic participatory knowledges, oral traditions, and languages had faced severe challenges following the thorny issues of dominant colonial languages, sponsorship, and politics of preference. For centuries, the marginalized local communities have relied on their indigenous knowledge systems, native languages, and accumulated expertise to cope with the challenges posed by severe environmental and climate change such as droughts, epidemic pests, and infertile soils to mention but a few (Kaya & Seleti, 2013). Research shows that over time, many marginalized local communities, and people managed to develop their coping strategies to get the most out of their natural environment by using indigenous knowledge. whereas some African scholars and philosophers argue that in their endeavor to digitize indigenous knowledge, cultural heritage institutions are dissatisfied by many challenges such as lack of or insufficient funding; digital rights management; the complexity of ownership protocols; loss or misappropriation of digitized indigenous knowledge; lack or limited skills; inadequate infrastructure; lack of resources; and unreliability of the preservation media (Dewah & Feni-Fete, 2014; Sithole, 2007). Whereas Akinwale (2012:1) reports that "albeit indigenous knowledge of Africans remains a gold mine, the challenge was that Africans are currently behind the rest of the world in terms of indigenous knowledge digitisation for global access." In addition, in most cases, the success of digitization projects in the African continent is determined by the sustenance of the intercontinental subsidy (Kugara & Mokgoatšana, 2022). As such, to meet these challenges, there is a need to create a more intensive environment for the development, management, and protection of indigenous knowledge through digital media platforms.

Akinwale (2012) asserted that indigenous knowledge management implicates the use of both traditional and modern methods. These traditional methods include but are not limited to word of mouth, storytelling, folklore, and communities of practice. For years, most African communities in the global South depended more on storytelling, folklore, and interpersonal communication through which information and knowledge were narrated by the elderly people to the younger generations. In those instances, the elders in the community were considered the sole custodians, managers, and protectors of this imperious information and knowledge that is essential to the community concerned. It is recently argued that these conventional methods are not accurately reliable, and societies cannot continue to use them because information, ideas, and crucial concepts get lost in the process. This is simply because the information is not written, stored, or preserved through modernized technological techniques and platforms. Henceforward, African scholars should advocate for the best techniques that could be used to protect and preserve their oral traditions and indigenous knowledge through digitalized platforms which for years have been undermined and relied on word of mouth.

CONCLUSION AND RECOMMENDATIONS

This chapter explored the current debates and trends on how best to promote and preserve the African participatory epistemic knowledge systems, indigenous languages, and oral traditions through digital media platforms. As such, the chapter argued that digitalization or digital technology is equally one of the contemporary technological and ideological systems that African scholars in the continent and the diaspora should use as sites of the contest to reproduce and preserve their participatory epistemic knowledges as well as indigenous languages of the South. Hence, it has been highlighted that these participatory African epistemologies and indigenous languages are valid and thus, should be celebrated, reproduced, promoted, and preserved through digital media platforms and technological algorithms. As such, the process to digitize indigenous languages and knowledges of the South should contribute and open avenues toward their equal promotion, use, and preservation in the global discourses for economic and educational purposes. It has been distinguished that indigenous languages, African participatory epistemic knowledge systems, and oral tradition have for years gained serious popularity and momentum as strategic resources for socioeconomic development and an agent of social transformation. Hence, it must be widely promoted and preserved through digitalized systems or platforms for global access and use.

It has been highlighted in this chapter that indigenous knowledge is Africa's identity, and it needs to be always managed and safeguarded using a holistic approach to knowledge preservation. The chapter further contended that participatory epistemic knowledges and indigenous languages of the South including African societies are as imperative as scientific knowledges and dominant colonial languages of Western and European origin. In addition, it has been indicated in this chapter that African indigenous institutions of knowledge production, conservation, and sharing such as initiation schools, indigenous games, agricultural systems, dances and songs, storytelling, and proverbs, remain pillars of indigenous African ways of knowing. In addition, the chapter advocates that if the wealth of knowledge and information still exists among the elders and other knowledge holders in African local communities, digital media should be used to document, promote, and preserve indigenous knowledge for global access and use. In a nutshell, the chapter strongly recommends the need for intensifying digitization projects of participatory epistemologies, indigenous languages, and oral traditions found in rural communities, a collaborative approach, increased funding, and capacitating information professionals in digitizing heritage resources. Last, the global South governments in the African context should also be at the forefront to implement policies that promote the preservation and digitalization of African participatory epistemic knowledge systems, indigenous languages, and oral traditions through digital media platforms.

REFERENCES

Akinwale, A. A. 2012. Digitisation of indigenous knowledge for natural resources management in Africa. Proceedings of the AERN Summit. Paper presented at the 20th Anniversary Summit of the African Educational Research Network at North Carolina State University, Raleigh, USA, 19 May, pp. 1–18.

Anshari, M., Syafrudin, M., & Fitriyani, N. L. 2022. Fourth Industrial Revolution between Knowledge Management and Digital Humanities. *Information,* 13(6), 292. MDPI AG.

Asante, M. K. 2003. *Afrocentricity: The theory of social change.* New York: African American Images.

Battiste, M. 2002. Protecting Indigenous Knowledge and Heritage. Saskatoon, SK: Purich Publisher.

Biyela, N., Oyelude, A. & Haumba, E. 2016. Digital preservation of indigenous knowledge (IK) by cultural heritage institutions: A comparative study of Nigeria, South Africa, and Uganda. (Accessed June 14, 2023). http://hdl.handle.net/20.500.11910/10196

Breytenbach, A., Lourens, A. & Marsh, S. 2013. The role of the Jotello F. Soga Library in the digital preservation of South African veterinary history. *Journal of the South African Veterinary Association,* 84 (1), 1–7.

Chisita, C. T. 2011. Role of libraries in promoting the dissemination and documentation of indigenous agricultural information: A case study of Zimbabwe. Paper presented at the 77th IFLA Conference on Information Systems for indigenous knowledge in Agriculture, August 13–18, San Juan, Puerto Rico.

Constant, N. L. & Tshisikhawe, M. P. 2018. Hierarchies of knowledge: Ethnobotanical knowledge, practices, and beliefs of the Vhavenḓa in South Africa for biodiversity conservation. *Journal of Ethnobiology and Ethnomedicine,* 14(56), 1–28.

Demeter, M. 2020. Academic Knowledge Production and the Global South: Questioning Inequality and Under-representation. Switzerland: Springer Nature.

Department of Arts & Culture, 2010. South African National Policy on Digitization of Heritage Resources. Final Draft for Public Review. http://www.dac.org.za (Accessed June 10, 2023).

Dewah, P. & Feni-Fete, V. 2014. Issues and prospects of digitising liberation movements' archives held at the University of Fort Hare, South Africa. *Journal of the South African Society of Archivists,* 4(7), 77–88.

Enhuber, M. 2015. Art, space, and technology: How the digitalisation and digitalisation of art space affect the consumption of art—A critical approach. *Digital Creativity,* 26 (2): 121–137.

Green, L. 2007. The Indigenous Knowledge Systems Policy of 2004: Challenges for South African Universities. *Social Dynamics,* 33(1), 130–154.

Heine, J. 2023. The Global South is on the rise—but what exactly is the Global South? https://theconversation.com/the-global-south-is-on-the-rise-but-what-exactly-is-the-global-south-207959 (Accessed July 04, 2023).

Hoppers, C. A. 2002. *Indigenous knowledge and the integration of knowledge systems: Towards a philosophy of articulation.* Claremont: New Africa Books (Pty) Ltd.

Hukimi, R. & Khasri, R. K. 2023. The Epistemic Status of Indigenous Knowledge: A Socio-epistemological Approach, *Digital Press Social Sciences and Humanities,* 9(1), 1–8.

Hunter, J. 2005. The role of information technologies in indigenous knowledge management. *Australian Academic & Research Libraries,* 36(2), 109–124.

Jonas. K. 2000. *Modernization as ideology: American social science and "Nation Building" in the Kennedy era.* New York: Johns Hopkins University Press.

Kalusopa, T. & Zulu, S. 2009. Digital heritage material preservation in Botswana: Problems and prospects. Collection Building 28 (3) pp. 98–107. www.emeraldinsight.com/0160-4953.htm (Accessed May 28, 2023).

Kaya, H. O. & Seleti, Y. N. 2013. African indigenous knowledge systems and Relevance of higher education in South Africa. *The International Education Journal: Comparative Perspectives,* 12(1), 30–44.

Khupe, C. 2017. Language, Participation, and Indigenous Knowledge Systems Research in Mqatsheni, South Africa. P. Ngulube (ed.), Handbook of Research on Theoretical Perspectives on Indigenous Knowledge Systems in Developing Countries (pp. 100–126). Pennsylvania: IGI Global Publisher.

Kugara, S. L. & Mokgoatšana, S. 2022. Challenges presented by digitisation of Vhavenḓa oral tradition: An African indigenous knowledge systems perspective. *HTS Teologiese Studies/Theological Studies,* 78(3), 1–8.

Lazar, M. M. 2020. Politics of the 'South': Discourses and praxis. *Discourse & Society,* 31(1) 5–18.

Ligidima, M. & Makananise, F. O. 2020. Social Media as a Communicative Platform to Promote Indigenous African Languages by Youth Students at a Rural Based University, South Africa. *Gender and Behaviour,* 18(2), 15824–15832.

Lor, P. J. 2005. Preserving African digital resources: Is there a role for repository libraries? *Library Management,* 26(1), 63–72.

Lusenet, D. Y. 2007. Tending the garden or harvesting the fields: Digital preservation and the UNESCO Charter on the preservation of the digital heritage. *Library Trends,* 56 (1), 164–182.

Madima, S. E., Makananise, F. O., & Malatji, E. J. 2022. The Role of Indigenous African Language Newspapers in Deepening South African Democracy. In A. Salawu, A. Molale, E. Uribe-Jongbloed and M. S. Ullah (eds.), Indigenous Language for development communication in the global South (pp. 191–201). London: Lexington Books.

Makananise, F. O. & Malatji, E. J. 2021. The use of Twitter by South African television news channels to engage the rural-based youth about the coronavirus Pandemic. *Journal of African Films & Diaspora Studies,* 4(3), 85–105.

Makananise, F. O. & Sundani, N. D. 2023. Digital Media and Their Implications on Diplomatic Practices in the Fourth Industrial Revolution: A Global South Perspective. In F. Endong (ed.), The COVID-19 Pandemic and the Digitalization of Diplomacy (pp. 1–26). Hershey, PA: IGI Global Publisher.

Makananise, F. O. 2023. Reimagining South African Political Campaigns through Indigenous Language Posters in the 4IR: A Political Communication Perspective, *Communicare: Journal for Communication Studies in Africa,* 42(1), 52–63.

Makananise, F. O., Malatji, E. J., & Madima, S. E., 2023. Indigenous Languages, Digital Media, and COVID-19 Pandemic in the Global South: A South African Discourse. In A. Salawu, A. Molale, E. Uribe-Jongbloed, and M. S. Ullah (eds.), Indigenous Language for Social Change in the Global South (pp. 76–92). London: Lexington Books.

Malatji, E. J., Makananise, F. O, & Madima, S. E. 2022. Critical Language Matters: The Fate of Indigenous Languages amid Covid-19 Pandemic in South Africa. In A. Salawu, A. Molale, E. Uribe-Jongbloed & M. S. Ullah (eds.), Indigenous Language for development communication in the global South (pp. 269–286). London: Lexington Books.

Masoga, M. 2005. South African research in indigenous knowledge systems and challenges of change. *African Journal of Indigenous Knowledge Systems,* 4(1), 15–30.

Mdhluli, T. D., Mokgoatšana, S., Kugara, S. L., & Vuma, L. 2021. Knowledge management: Preserving, managing, and sharing indigenous knowledge through a digital library. *HTS Teologiese Studies/ Theological Studies,* 77(2), 1–7.

Medie, P. A. & Kang, A. J. 2018. Global South Scholars are missing from European and US Journals. What can be done about it? https://theconversation.com/global -south-scholars-are-missing-from-european-and-us-journals-what-can-be-done -about-it-99570. (Date accessed: July 04, 2023).

Meighan, P. J. 2021. Decolonizing the digital landscape: The role of technology in Indigenous language revitalization. *AlterNative: An International Journal of Indigenous Peoples,* 17(3), 397–405.

Mutula, S. (2008). Local content development projects in Africa. *South African Journal of Libraries and Information Science,* 74(2), 105–115.

Ndlovu, N. 2015. Living heritage vs. heritage legislation: Exploring the preservation of living heritage in the post-apartheid South Africa. Paper presented at the Human Sciences Research Council Seminar, 21 September, Pretoria, South Africa.

Ndlovu-Gatsheni, S. 2015. Genealogies of coloniality and implications for Africa's development. *Africa Development,* 7(3), 13–40.

Ndlovu-Gatsheni, S. J. 2018. Epistemic Freedom in Africa: Deprovincialization and Decolonization. New York: Routledge.

Ngcobo, N. 2010. Indigenous knowledge systems: Impact of policies of Department of Science & Technology. https://pmg.org.za/committee-meeting/12337 (Accessed June 2, 2023).

Ngulube, P. 2002. Managing and preserving indigenous knowledge in the knowledge management era: Challenges and opportunities for information professionals. *Information Development*, 18(2), 95–101.

Nkadimeng, S. & Makalela, L. 2023. The (re)making of an African language: Revisiting epistemologies for quality assessment practices, *Southern African Linguistics and Applied Language Studies*, 41:1, 5–15, DOI: 10.2989/16073614.2023.2185973.

Nxumalo, S. A. & Mncube, D. W. 2018. Using indigenous games and knowledge to decolonise the school curriculum: Ubuntu perspectives. *Perspectives in Education,* 36(2), 103–118.

O'Brien, G., Pan, P. C., Sheikh, M., & Prideaux, S. 2023. Indigenous emancipation: The fight against marginalisation, criminalisation, and oppression. *Social Inclusion*, 11(2),173–176.

Ocholla, D. N. & Onyacha, O. B. 2005. The marginalized knowledge: An informetric analysis of indigenous knowledge publications (1990–2004). *South African Journal of Libraries and Information Science*, 71(3), 247–258.

Ocholla, D. N. 2009. Are African libraries active participants in today's knowledge and information society? *South African Journal of Libraries and Information Science*, 75(1), 20–27.

Phyak, P, & De Costa, P.I. 2021. Decolonial struggles in Indigenous language education in neoliberal times: Identities, ideologies, and activism. *Journal of Language, Identity & Education*, 20:5, 291–295.

Raphalalani, T. D. 2017. The significance and appropriateness of Tshivenḓa proverbs in new South Africa. *Journal of Sociology and Social Anthropology*, 8(3), 98–105.

Rasmussen, T. & Nolan, J. S. 2011. Reclaiming Sámi languages: Indigenous language emancipation from East to West. *Int'l. J. Soc. Lang.* 29(), 35–55.

The Republic of South Africa. 2019. Protection, Promotion, Development, and Management of Indigenous Knowledge Act No. 6 of 2019. *Government Gazette.* No 42647 of 19 August 2019: Cape Town.

Reyes, G. T. 2019. Pedagogy of and towards Decoloniality. M. A. Peters (ed.), Encyclopaedia of Teacher Education, (pp, 1–7). Singapore: Springer Nature.

Ritchie, D. A. 2014. *Doing Oral History,* Oxford University, New York.

Rousseau, S., & Dargent, E. 2019. The construction of Indigenous language rights in Peru: A language regime approach. *Journal of Politics in Latin America*, 11(2), 161–180.

Santos, B. S. & Meneses, M. P. 2020. Knowledge Born in the Struggle: Constructing the Epistemologies of the Global South, New York: Routledge.

Santos, B. S. 2016. Epistemologies of the South: Justice against Epistemicide. New York: Routledge.

Sillitoe, P., Dixon, P., & Barr, J. 2005. *Indigenous knowledge inquires A methodologies manual for development,* The University Press.

Sithole, J. 2007. The challenges faced by African libraries and information centres in documenting and preserving indigenous knowledge. *IFLA Journal*, 33(2), 117–122. http://www.ifla.sagepub.com/content/33/2/117 (Accessed October 27, 2022).

Smith, A. 2002. Power and hierarchy of knowledge. *Geoforum*, 40(1), 230–248.

South African Department of Arts and Culture. 2010. Department of Arts and Culture Annual Report 2010/2011. https://www.gov.za/documents/annual-reports/department-arts-and-culture-annual-report-20102011-25-oct-2011 (Accessed May 20, 2024).

UNESCO. 2015. Memory of the world programme. https://www.nationalarchives.gov.za/node/821#:~:text=The%20vision%20of%20the%20Memory,accessible%20to%20all%20without%20hindrance (Accessed May 20, 2024).

The United Nations Human Rights Office of the High Commissioner. 2020. OHCHR Surge Initiative Seeding-Change Projects (distinct projects managed by the OHCHR Surge Initiative). https://sdgs.un.org/un-systemsdg-implementation/office-united-nations-high-commissioner-human-rightsohchr-44205 (Accessed July 1, 2023).

van den Berg, J. 2018. Intergenerational knowledge transfer in the Vhavenda communities in South Africa. MSc Dissertation. Amsterdam: University of Amsterdam. [Online] Available: https://inclusivevcc.files.wordpress.com/2018/09/thesis-final-jvdb.pdf (November 30, 2022).

Whiten, A., Biro, D., Bredeche, N., Garland E. C. & Kirby, S. 2022. The emergence of collective knowledge and cumulative culture in animals, humans, and machines. Phil. Trans. R. Soc. B3772020030620200306.

WHO, 2016. Indigenous knowledge systems for appropriate technology and development. (Accessed April 10, 2023).

Chapter 2

Indigenous Language Preservation and Promotion through Digital Media Technology in the Fourth Industrial Revolution

Yusuf Ayodeji Ajani, Adeyinka Tella, and Nhlavu Petros Dlamini

The Fourth Industrial Revolution (4IR) marks a significant shift where technology doesn't just affect society, the economy, and culture but also extends its influence into the human mind and body. Industry 4.0 leads this transformation, driven by cyber-physical systems, signifying a substantial technological advancement. In this new era, the internet, along with complementary technologies and embedded systems, serves as the foundation for seamlessly integrating physical objects, human agents, intelligent machines, production lines, and processes, crossing organizational boundaries. This integration gives rise to a novel and interconnected value chain known as the smart factory. Essentially, 4IR encompasses both an economic aspect, triggering a broader restructuring of the modern economy and society, and a technological aspect rooted in computer science and information science. During the 2016 World Economic Forum, Mr. Klaus Schwab, the executive chairman, introduced the concept of the Fourth Industrial Revolution (4IR). This concept embodies the impact of digitization and its progress on the global economy.

What sets 4IR apart from previous industrial revolutions is the convergence and interplay of these technologies across physical, biological, and digital domains. This convergence leads to significant disruptions in traditional strategies and methods. Moreover, 4IR technologies are driving transformative changes across various industries and institutions, reshaping how individuals and organizations interact and collaborate. These technologies are bringing about a revolution in our society by enabling the preservation and promotion of indigenous knowledge through tangible objects created with innovative materials. As 4IR represents a major era characterized by profound technological advancements reshaping global societies and industries, it is vital to acknowledge its influence (Oosthuizen et al., 2023). It is defined by the seamless integration of digital technologies, automation, artificial intelligence, and the Internet of Things, resulting in transformative changes in how we live, work, and communicate. Amid this sweeping technological revolution, the preservation and revitalization of indigenous languages via digital media technologies emerge as a vital and pressing concern. Indigenous languages serve as crucial repositories of cultural heritage, embodying unique systems of communication, knowledge, and identity for diverse communities (Gwerevende & Mthombeni, 2023).

However, the relentless forces of globalization and sociocultural dynamics expose these languages to a genuine risk of extinction. In response, digital media technology assumes a central role, providing a dynamic and innovative tool kit to address the formidable challenges faced by indigenous languages. Digital media technology enables meticulous documentation, comprehensive archiving, and seamless digitization of indigenous languages, extending their accessibility to a broader and more diverse audience (Hinton, 2019). It also serves as a canvas for the creation of interactive and immersive language learning applications, online resources, and social media platforms designed to engage and empower indigenous communities. The true significance of digital media technology emerges as it bridges gaps between disparate communities, fostering cultural and linguistic diversity. By harnessing digital tools and platforms, speakers and advocates of indigenous languages can foster collaborations, share valuable resources, and revitalize their languages in unprecedented ways (Gwerevende & Mthombeni, 2023). Amid the ongoing 4IR, it is imperative to recognize the pressing issue of indigenous language preservation (Bagea, 2023).

As globalization and digital transformation reshape our world, understanding the profound cultural, historical, and ecological significance of indigenous languages becomes paramount. These languages are not merely repositories of linguistic diversity but also storehouses of unique knowledge systems and cultural identities. Consequently, comprehending the importance of preserving indigenous languages is the linchpin for effective conservation efforts. In conjunction with acknowledging the value of indigenous language preservation, it is equally crucial to identify and address the multifaceted challenges they face (Montero, 2022). These challenges, stemming from historical factors, social dynamics, limited resources, and inadequate institutional support, present complex obstacles. Understanding these hurdles is fundamental for developing robust preservation strategies and ensuring the holistic safeguarding of these linguistic treasures. Another challenge arises from the need to explore the evolving role of digital media technology in indigenous language preservation (Onyenankeya, 2022). In an era where digital technologies and communication platforms have become ubiquitous, assessing how they can be leveraged to protect and revitalize indigenous languages becomes a pressing issue.

This exploration encompasses the innovative use of digital tools and applications, enabling the documentation, archiving, and digitization of indigenous languages. It also entails the creation of interactive and engaging language learning applications and online resources, which are crucial elements in the preservation tool kit. In light of these complexities, effectively addressing these issues demands a thorough evaluation of the various digital tools and applications available for language preservation. The goal is to discern which tools are most effective in meeting the unique requirements of indigenous language preservation. This task is of particular significance as it guides the selection of tools that align best with the specific needs and challenges faced in this context. The sustainability of indigenous languages is intrinsically linked to the promotion of collaborative approaches that engage indigenous communities, linguists, and technology experts (Meighan, 2023).

Determining the most effective collaborative strategies is essential for the success of preservation initiatives. This collaborative effort must also consider and address ethical considerations, such as intellectual property rights and informed consent, ensuring that resource utilization is responsible and respectful. In the forthcoming discussions, we will embark on a comprehensive exploration of the multifaceted challenges and opportunities that underpin the preservation and promotion of indigenous languages through digital media technology in the context of the Fourth Industrial Revolution. Our journey will also encompass a detailed examination of specific applications, the pivotal role of collaborative approaches, ethical dimensions, the vital role of government support, and the intriguing prospects that shape this critical endeavor.

PURPOSE OF THE STUDY

The purpose of this study is to investigate indigenous language preservation and promotion through digital media technology in the Fourth Industrial Revolution. To further the investigation, the following research objectives were considered, namely: examine the importance of indigenous language preservation; determine challenges faced in language preservation; explore the role of digital media technology in preserving indigenous language; compare digital tools and applications for language preservation; and determine collaborative approaches toward the sustainability of indigenous language.

METHODOLOGY

The research methodology for this study involves a comprehensive exploration of the various aspects related to the preservation of indigenous languages, the challenges encountered in this preservation effort, and the role played by digital media technology. It is a systematic approach that comprises the following steps:

In-Depth Literature Review

Scope and Source Selection: Initially, we define the scope of our literature review, specifying the relevant themes, indigenous languages, and geographic regions under consideration. We select sources from scholarly articles published in reputable journals, detailed case studies, and insights from subject-matter experts. This approach ensures a diverse and comprehensive representation of knowledge.

Search Strategy: We employ a structured search strategy, utilizing databases like JSTOR and Google Scholar. A combination of keywords and controlled vocabulary terms is used to conduct a thorough and exhaustive search.

Inclusion and Exclusion Criteria: To maintain the quality and relevance of the sources, we establish clear inclusion and exclusion criteria. This ensures that the selected literature is directly related to indigenous language preservation, digital media technology, and collaborative efforts.

Data Collection: We execute a systematic data collection process to gather pertinent information from the selected sources. This data is categorized based on the various aspects of the study, including themes, challenges, digital tools, and collaborative strategies.

Analysis and Synthesis

Thematic Analysis: The collected literature undergoes a thematic analysis to identify common themes and essential concepts related to indigenous language preservation. This method allows us to gain a comprehensive understanding of the significance of language preservation, the obstacles encountered, and the role of digital media technology.

Content Synthesis: We synthesize the content from the reviewed literature to construct a cohesive and informative narrative. This synthesis involves combining findings from multiple sources to create a coherent discussion.

Data Presentation

Structured Presentation: The outcomes of the literature review and analysis are presented in an organized manner. The findings are divided into sections, each dedicated to a specific aspect of the research, such as the importance of language preservation, challenges, the role of digital media technology, and collaborative initiatives.

Citing Supporting Evidence: Throughout the presentation, we cite supporting evidence from the reviewed literature to validate the findings. Proper citation and referencing are upheld to maintain academic integrity and acknowledge the original authors' contributions.

Discussion and Implications

Interpretation: The methodology concludes with the discussion and interpretation of the findings. We analyze the data to draw meaningful insights regarding the significance of language preservation, the nature of challenges, the effectiveness of digital media technology, and the importance of collaborative endeavors.

Implications: We explore the broader implications of the study, highlighting how the findings hold significance for indigenous communities, linguists, technology experts, and policymakers. This includes practical applications of the research results in the context of language preservation.

LITERATURE REVIEW

Importance of Indigenous Language Preservation

Indigenous languages are more than just linguistic systems. They are living embodiments of cultural, social, and historical significance for indigenous communities worldwide. The cultural value of these languages lies in their ability to preserve and transmit ancestral knowledge, traditions, and oral histories. For instance, the Aka-Kora language of the Aka people in Central Africa encodes their intricate understanding of the forest ecosystem and their unique hunting techniques (Nettle & Romaine, 2021). Similarly, the Maori language, Te Reo, is a key element of Maori cultural identity, preserving stories, songs, and spiritual connections to the land (Koopu, 2023). Indigenous languages also have a profound social value as they foster community cohesion and identity. In Canada, the revitalization of the Cree language among the Cree Nation of Eeyou Istchee has brought about a renewed sense of pride and connection among community members (Lévesque et al., 2023). The use of the Cree language in everyday interactions strengthens intergenerational bonds and reinforces traditional values within the community.

From a historical perspective, indigenous languages provide vital insights into the histories and experiences of indigenous communities. The Māori language revival movement in New Zealand has revealed previously obscured historical details and helped in reconstructing traditional practices (Berryman, 2020). The Māori language, with its rich vocabulary and concepts, allows researchers to gain a deeper understanding of Māori society before colonization. However, the loss of indigenous languages is a pressing concern. According to UNESCO, approximately 2,500 indigenous languages are endangered and face the risk of disappearing (UNESCO, 2021). With each language loss, valuable cultural and historical knowledge is irrevocably lost. This loss contributes to a sense of cultural erosion and can impact the well-being and self-determination of indigenous communities.

Recognizing the importance of indigenous languages, there are ongoing efforts to revitalize and preserve them. The United Nations Declaration on the Rights of Indigenous Peoples emphasizes the rights of indigenous peoples to maintain, revitalize, and transmit their languages (Metallic, 2023). Initiatives such as language documentation projects, community-led language revitalization programs, and the integration of indigenous languages into educational curricula are making significant strides in language preservation and revitalization efforts (Kral, 2021). Preserving linguistic diversity and preventing language extinction are crucial endeavors that demand our attention and concerted efforts. The world's languages reflect human creativity, cultural richness, and collective heritage. However, linguistic diversity is rapidly diminishing, with many languages facing the risk of extinction.

Language extinction represents the loss of unique worldviews, knowledge systems, and cultural expressions embedded within each language. When a language disappears, a profound loss occurs—a loss of traditional knowledge, ancestral wisdom, and historical insights that cannot be recovered. The impacts are far-reaching, affecting the identity, cultural pride, and well-being of indigenous communities (Harrison, 2019). Furthermore, language loss contributes to the erosion of biodiversity, as indigenous languages often contain detailed ecological knowledge and terminology related to local environments (Gorenflo et al., 2012). Preserving linguistic diversity is not merely an act of conservation; it is an essential element of fostering cultural resilience, social inclusion, and sustainable development. Maintaining diverse languages ensures that future generations can connect with their cultural roots, maintain their cultural identities, and access the wealth of knowledge embedded within their linguistic heritage (González-Ruibal, 2019). It fosters intergenerational bonds, strengthens community cohesion, and promotes a sense of belonging and pride within indigenous communities (Burgess et al., 2021).

Efforts to preserve linguistic diversity require collaboration between communities, governments, researchers, and educational institutions. Community-led language revitalization initiatives play a central role, in empowering indigenous communities to reclaim, teach, and transmit their languages to younger generations (McIvor et al., 2020). Supporting and promoting indigenous languages in education systems, both within indigenous communities and mainstream education, is crucial for language revitalization (Reyhner, 2012a; 2012b). Technology, such as language documentation and digital resources, can also assist in preserving and disseminating endangered languages (Bird et al., 2019). Preventing language extinction goes beyond language preservation—it encompasses the recognition of linguistic rights and the celebration of linguistic diversity as a global asset. Governments and international organizations must establish policies that protect and promote indigenous languages, ensuring their use in public domains, legal systems, and media (UNESCO, 2019). Inclusive language policies and the integration of indigenous languages into digital platforms and technological advancements are also vital for ensuring linguistic diversity thrives in our increasingly interconnected world.

Preserving linguistic diversity and preventing language extinction is not only a matter of cultural heritage but also an ethical responsibility. It is a commitment to valuing and respecting the voices, knowledge, and identities of indigenous communities. By embracing linguistic diversity, we contribute to a more equitable, inclusive, and sustainable world—one that honors the linguistic tapestry that enriches our shared human experience. Language and cultural identity share a deep and inseparable connection. Language serves as a powerful tool for expressing, preserving, and transmitting cultural values, traditions, and collective memories within a community. The intricate relationship between language and cultural identity can be understood through the following aspects:

- Expression of Beliefs and Values: Language enables individuals to articulate their beliefs, values, and worldviews within a cultural framework. It provides a medium for expressing cultural practices, religious ceremonies, and social norms, allowing the transmission of knowledge and wisdom embedded in a community's way of life. For example, the use of the Navajo language among the Navajo Nation in the United

States is intertwined with their cultural identity, including the expression of spiritual beliefs and the preservation of traditional ceremonies (McCarty, 2011).

- Intergenerational Transmission: Language is a crucial tool for the intergenerational transmission of cultural heritage. Through language, older generations can pass on their accumulated wisdom, historical narratives, and ancestral knowledge to younger generations. Indigenous languages, in particular, carry deep cultural significance, acting as a conduit for preserving traditional ecological knowledge, oral histories, and connections to ancestral lands (Smith & Weldon, 2021). When language is lost, there is a risk of severing this vital intergenerational link.
- Sense of Belonging and Identity: Language plays a fundamental role in shaping an individual's sense of belonging and identity within their cultural community. The ability to speak one's native language fosters a connection to ancestral roots and strengthens the bonds of kinship and shared experience. Language serves as a marker of cultural membership, enabling individuals to identify themselves within a broader cultural group. For instance, the Welsh language holds great significance in Welsh culture, representing a vital aspect of Welsh national identity and fostering a sense of community among Welsh speakers (Hodges, 2024).
- Cultural Resilience and Empowerment: Language revitalization efforts have shown that the preservation and revitalization of indigenous languages can contribute to cultural resilience and empowerment within indigenous communities. By reclaiming and revitalizing their languages, communities regain a sense of pride, self-determination, and cultural agency. Indigenous languages become tools for asserting cultural rights, promoting cultural continuity, and challenging the impacts of historical oppression and marginalization (Reyhner & Tennant, 2019).

Preserving linguistic diversity and supporting language revitalization efforts are essential for safeguarding cultural identity. By valuing and revitalizing indigenous languages, we recognize the profound connection between language and cultural heritage, fostering the well-being and cultural resilience of indigenous communities worldwide.

Challenges Faced in Language Preservation

Preserving indigenous languages is a critical endeavor, but it is faced with numerous challenges that contribute to their decline. Factors such as historical events, social dynamics, educational policies, and globalization play significant roles in language loss. Additionally, the transmission of languages across generations presents its own set of difficulties. Furthermore, limited resources and institutional support add to the complexities of language preservation efforts. Let's explore these challenges in more detail:

- Historical Factors: Historical events, such as colonization, forced assimilation, and cultural suppression, have had a profound impact on indigenous languages. Policies implemented by colonial powers often discouraged or banned the use of indigenous languages, resulting in language loss and disruption of intergenerational transmission (Crawford, 1997). The consequences of these historical injustices continue to affect indigenous communities, making language preservation an uphill battle.
- Social Dynamics and Shifts: Social dynamics within indigenous communities can contribute to the decline of indigenous languages. Factors like migration, urbanization, and increased contact with dominant languages can lead to language shifts and reduced language use. The younger generations may prioritize learning and using dominant languages for economic opportunities or social integration, thereby neglecting their indigenous languages (Fishman, 1991). This shift in language preference can result in the marginalization and eventual loss of indigenous languages.
- Educational Policies and Practices: Educational policies often prioritize the teaching of dominant languages, neglecting the importance of indigenous languages in the educational system. The lack of support and resources for indigenous language instruction in schools hinders intergenerational transmission and language revitalization efforts. Inadequate funding, a shortage of qualified teachers, and limited opportunities for language use within the educational context further contribute to language decline (McCarty, 2011).
- Globalization and Language Dominance: Globalization has led to the dominance of a few major languages, making indigenous languages more vulnerable to decline. The widespread use of dominant languages in media, technology, and global communication diminishes the visibility and relevance of indigenous languages. This linguistic imbalance can create a perception of indigenous languages as being less valuable, leading to a decrease in their use and transmission.
- Difficulties in Inter-generational Transmission: Transferring languages across generations can be challenging due to various factors. Geographical dispersion, language proficiency gaps between generations, changing family structures, and limited opportunities for language use in daily life can hinder the transmission of indigenous languages (Grenoble & Whaley, 2006). The weakening of intergenerational bonds and the lack of consistent language exposure pose obstacles to language preservation.

- Limited Resources and Institutional Support: Language preservation efforts often face limited resources and institutional support. Funding for language documentation, revitalization projects, and educational initiatives may be insufficient to meet the diverse needs of indigenous communities. The lack of institutional recognition and support for indigenous languages hampers the preservation and revitalization process, making it more challenging to sustain long-term language preservation efforts.

Addressing these challenges requires a comprehensive and multifaceted approach. It entails raising awareness about the importance of indigenous languages, advocating for supportive language policies, and providing adequate resources for language revitalization programs. Collaboration between indigenous communities, educational institutions, governments, and linguistic experts is crucial for the development and implementation of effective language preservation strategies. Efforts to address limited resources and institutional support involve securing funding, establishing partnerships, and creating networks to facilitate knowledge-sharing and capacity-building. Advocacy for the integration of indigenous languages into educational curricula and the provision of training opportunities for language instructors are essential steps toward strengthening language preservation efforts. By recognizing and addressing these challenges, we can strive to preserve and revitalize indigenous languages, safeguarding cultural heritage, fostering community resilience, and empowering future generations with the knowledge and identity embedded in their linguistic heritage.

Role of Digital Media Technology in Preserving Indigenous Language

Digital media technology plays a significant role in supporting the preservation, documentation, and revitalization of indigenous languages. It offers a range of tools and platforms that can enhance language learning, enable documentation and archiving efforts, and provide wider accessibility to indigenous languages. Let's explore how digital media technology can aid in indigenous language preservation:

- Documentation and Archiving: Digital media technology provides powerful tools for documenting and archiving indigenous languages. Audio and video recording devices, along with digital storage and preservation systems, enable the capture and storage of oral traditions, songs, stories, and other linguistic resources in high-quality formats (Hinton, 2019). Digital archives can ensure the long-term preservation and accessibility of indigenous language materials for future generations, preventing their loss due to physical deterioration or cultural disruption.

- Digitization of Language Resources: Digital media technology allows for the digitization of existing language resources, including printed materials, manuscripts, and linguistic analysis materials. Digitization preserves these resources in a more accessible and shareable format, facilitating their dissemination among researchers, educators, and community members (Bird et al., 2019). Digitized resources can include dictionaries, grammar, language teaching materials, and historical texts, contributing to the overall preservation and revitalization efforts of indigenous languages.
- Language Learning and Teaching: Digital media technology offers innovative approaches to language learning and teaching. Mobile applications, online platforms, and interactive software provide opportunities for self-paced language learning, vocabulary acquisition, and grammar instruction (Austin, 2019). These tools often incorporate multimedia elements, such as audio recordings, video tutorials, and interactive exercises, enhancing engagement and interactivity in the learning process. Digital language learning resources can reach a wider audience, including individuals living in remote areas or outside of indigenous communities
- Social Media and Online Communities: Digital platforms, particularly social media, offer opportunities for language promotion and community engagement. Indigenous language speakers can create online communities, social media groups, and dedicated websites to share language resources, discuss language-related topics, and provide language learning support (Molnar & Chartrand, 2021). These platforms facilitate connections among speakers, learners, and language enthusiasts, fostering a sense of belonging and collective language revitalization efforts.
- Language Revitalization Apps and Tools: Various language revitalization apps and software tools have been developed to support indigenous language preservation. These tools often include features such as pronunciation guides, language games, flashcards, and interactive exercises that engage learners in language practice (Harmon, 2019). Language revitalization apps provide accessible and user-friendly interfaces for individuals to engage with indigenous languages, regardless of their location or language proficiency level.
- Online Language Documentation and Collaborative Projects: Digital media technology enables collaborative language documentation projects. Linguists, community members, and language enthusiasts can collaborate remotely to create digital language resources, transcribe oral recordings, and develop linguistic databases (Gippert & Himmelmann,

2019). Online platforms facilitate collaborative efforts in language documentation, allowing for the pooling of linguistic expertise, cultural knowledge, and community input.

- Language Revitalization in Multimedia Formats: Digital media technology allows for the creation of multimedia materials to revitalize indigenous languages. This includes the production of audiovisual content such as podcasts, videos, and interactive storytelling apps (Dutta et al., 2019). Multimedia formats enhance language learning experiences by incorporating visual and auditory stimuli, making language acquisition more engaging and memorable for learners.
- Language Revitalization through Gamification: Digital media technology offers opportunities for gamifying language learning experiences. Language learning apps and platforms can incorporate game elements such as challenges, rewards, and progress tracking to motivate learners (Beermann & Spreer, 2018). Gamification fosters a playful and interactive environment that encourages language engagement and facilitates knowledge retention.
- Preservation of Indigenous Knowledge: Digital media technology aids in the preservation of indigenous knowledge systems embedded within languages. Through digital platforms, indigenous communities can document and share traditional ecological knowledge, cultural practices, and medicinal plant information (Gippert & Himmelmann, 2019). This preserves and safeguards indigenous knowledge for future generations, contributing to the broader cultural heritage preservation efforts.

The accessibility and reach of digital platforms have revolutionized the promotion of indigenous languages by transcending geographical barriers and making them accessible to a global audience. Through online platforms, language materials, recordings, and learning resources can be disseminated, significantly increasing their visibility and impact. Indigenous communities now can leverage digital media technology to highlight their languages, culture, and traditions, raising awareness and fostering a greater appreciation for linguistic diversity (Dutta et al., 2019). However, it is important to acknowledge the challenges and limitations that come with the use of digital media technology in indigenous language preservation. Issues such as limited access to technology and internet connectivity can hinder the reach and effectiveness of digital resources in certain communities. It is crucial to address these challenges and ensure that efforts are made to bridge the digital divide, making digital resources more accessible to all (Beermann & Spreer, 2018).

Another important consideration is the need for community ownership and control of language resources. Indigenous communities should have the agency to determine how their languages are represented in the digital realm, ensuring cultural protocols and ethical considerations are upheld (McIlraith et al., 2020). This involves actively involving community members in the development and implementation of digital media initiatives, ensuring that they align with the specific needs and goals of the community. Despite these challenges, the integration of digital media technology in indigenous language preservation presents a transformative opportunity to revitalize languages, engage learners, and foster connections within the community. The use of digital tools enables interactive and immersive language-learning experiences, empowering individuals to take ownership of their language-learning journey (Lotherington & Reinhardt, 2019). Digital platforms also facilitate community networking and collaboration, connecting indigenous language speakers, educators, and researchers from different parts of the world, allowing for the exchange of knowledge, resources, and best practices (Scholze-Irrlitz & Struß, 2017).

Digital Tools and Applications for Language Preservation

In recent times, digital tools such as language documentation software, language archiving systems, text analysis software, language learning softwares, language translation software, and various online applications with social media platforms have emerged as influential resources for language preservation, offering new possibilities for documentation, learning, and revitalization efforts. These technological advancements have facilitated language preservation in various ways, making it more accessible and engaging for both linguists and language communities. Mobile apps have become popular tools for language learning, and several of them now offer courses for endangered and indigenous languages. For example, Duolingo, a widely used language learning app, provides courses for languages like Hawaiian, Navajo, and Welsh. These apps use interactive exercises, vocabulary practice, and audio lessons to help learners engage with endangered languages on their mobile devices (Duolingo, n.d.). Online platforms dedicated to language documentation have also emerged, allowing linguists and community members to upload and share audio recordings, dictionaries, and grammar related to endangered languages.

The Endangered Languages Archive (ELAR) and the Archive of the Indigenous Languages of Latin America (AILLA) are two prominent examples of such platforms (ELAR, n.d.; AILLA, n.d.). These platforms ensure the preservation and accessibility of language documentation for research and revitalization purposes. Social media platforms have played a significant role in creating communities around endangered languages. Language-specific pages or channels on platforms like Facebook, Instagram, and YouTube provide spaces where speakers of endangered languages can share content, and stories, and engage with others interested in learning and preserving the language. These online communities foster language practice, cultural exchange, and networking opportunities (Living Tongues Institute, n.d.). Virtual Reality (VR) and augmented reality (AR) technologies have introduced immersive language learning experiences.

Through VR and AR, learners can simulate real-life language scenarios, such as conversations with native speakers or virtual field trips to language-speaking regions. These technologies offer an interactive and engaging environment for learners to practice and engage with endangered languages (Sweller et al., 2019). Online forums, discussion boards, and chat platforms dedicated to specific languages have also become valuable resources. These platforms create virtual communities where language learners and speakers can connect, ask questions, and share resources. Online communities foster language practice, peer support, and networking among individuals interested in preserving endangered languages (Language Communities, n.d.).

Additionally, specific apps like SayMore, ELAN, and FLEx have been developed to assist linguists and researchers in the collection, transcription, and analysis of language data in the field (Living Tongues Institute, n.d.). These apps streamline the documentation process and ensure the preservation of linguistic information for future reference and analysis. Websites like the Living Tongues Institute for Endangered Languages serve as centralized hubs for language preservation efforts. They provide resources, multimedia materials, and information on endangered languages, supporting documentation, revitalization initiatives, and educational efforts (Living Tongues Institute, n.d.). By leveraging these digital tools and applications, successful initiatives have been able to reach broader audiences, engage communities, facilitate language learning, and ensure the long-term preservation of endangered languages. These initiatives exemplify the potential of digital media technology in supporting language preservation efforts.

Collaborative Approaches Toward the Sustainability of Indigenous Language

Collaboration between indigenous communities, linguists, and technology experts is of utmost importance in language preservation efforts. By coming together, these diverse stakeholders bring their unique knowledge and skills, contributing to successful initiatives. Indigenous communities hold invaluable linguistic and cultural knowledge, making their active involvement crucial for accurate language preservation. Linguists, on the other hand, provide expertise in language documentation and analysis, ensuring that languages are properly documented and archived for future generations (UNESCO, 2003). They assist in creating dictionaries, grammar, and teaching materials, facilitating the preservation process. Technology experts play a vital role by leveraging their skills to develop digital tools and applications that aid in language preservation. Their contributions range from creating user-friendly interfaces to designing mobile apps and online platforms for language learning and documentation (Liu et al., 2019). These technological innovations enhance accessibility and engagement with language preservation efforts.

Partnerships between academia, indigenous organizations, and tech companies have yielded successful language preservation projects. Academia provides research expertise, funding opportunities, and access to resources like libraries and archives. Indigenous organizations bring cultural knowledge, community connections, and a deep understanding of the language and its context. Tech companies contribute to technological advancements, resources, and wider reach in terms of user adoption and distribution of language preservation tools (Hinton, 2014). Ensuring community involvement and empowerment is crucial throughout the decision-making processes of language preservation projects. Indigenous communities should actively participate in defining project goals and shaping the direction of initiatives. Their perspectives and priorities should be respected to ensure cultural relevance and sustainability (Reyhner & Lockard, 2009). Community involvement fosters ownership, empowerment, and intergenerational transmission of language knowledge, which strengthens cultural identity and revitalization efforts (McCarty et al., 2017).

DISCUSSION OF FINDINGS

The discussion in this chapter is anchored on looking at the ethical considerations and government policies and support in promoting and preserving indigenous languages using digital media technology.

Ethical Considerations in the Preservation of Indigenous Language

Preserving languages in the digital era presents ethical considerations that require careful attention. These concerns encompass intellectual property, cultural appropriation, and informed consent. One important ethical consideration revolves around safeguarding intellectual property rights. Indigenous languages are the cultural heritage of indigenous communities, and when digitizing and preserving them, it is crucial to respect the community's ownership and control over their language. Obtaining appropriate permissions and implementing safeguards are essential to prevent the exploitation or misuse of their linguistic resources (Cunsolo & Harper, 2014). Cultural appropriation is another significant ethical concern in language preservation. As digital access to linguistic and cultural materials increases, it is vital to handle these resources respectfully and responsibly. They should not be exploited or misrepresented, and measures should be taken to prevent inappropriate commercialization or appropriation that may undermine the cultural significance of the language (Smith, 2012).

Informed consent plays a pivotal role in language preservation projects. Indigenous communities have the right to make informed decisions about the use, dissemination, and accessibility of their language resources in the digital realm. Meaningful dialogue with the community is essential to ensure their understanding of the project's purpose and potential impacts. Obtaining informed consent and involving community members in decision-making processes empower them to have a say in how their language is represented and shared (UNESCO, 2009). To address these ethical concerns, collaboration, and inclusivity are crucial. Establishing partnerships between indigenous communities, academia, and technology companies enables shared decision-making and respects the community's self-determination. Community-led initiatives and input should be prioritized to ensure culturally sensitive and ethically responsible language preservation efforts.

In recent years, there have been notable examples of initiatives that prioritize ethical considerations in language preservation. For instance, the Living Archive of Aboriginal Languages project in Australia collaborates closely with indigenous communities to ensure their language materials are collected, curated, and shared with their informed consent (Parramore, 2021). This approach highlights the significance of community involvement and empowerment in decision-making processes. By addressing these ethical considerations, language preservation efforts in the digital era can uphold the rights and interests of indigenous communities, foster cultural integrity, and contribute to the long-term sustainability of endangered languages. Respecting indigenous knowledge systems and community rights is of paramount importance in language preservation and documentation efforts. Indigenous communities possess rich and unique knowledge systems that are deeply rooted in their cultures, languages, and environments. Recognizing and respecting these knowledge systems is crucial for maintaining the integrity and authenticity of indigenous languages.

Indigenous knowledge systems are holistic and interconnected, encompassing various domains such as language, traditional ecological knowledge, cultural practices, and spirituality. These systems are deeply tied to indigenous languages, as they reflect the intricate relationship between people, land, and identity. Preserving languages without respecting the associated knowledge systems risks stripping them of their cultural context and significance. Respecting community rights is equally essential in language preservation. Indigenous communities have the inherent right to self-determination and to control and protect their languages and cultural heritage. This includes the right to make decisions about how their languages are documented, accessed, and used in the digital era. Community rights also encompass issues of ownership, control, and benefit-sharing. Indigenous communities should have the authority to determine who has access to their language materials and how they are used. This includes addressing concerns about intellectual property rights, preventing exploitation, and ensuring equitable benefits for the community.

By respecting indigenous knowledge systems and community rights, language preservation initiatives can foster cultural empowerment, strengthen community resilience, and contribute to the revitalization and sustainability of indigenous languages. It is crucial to engage in meaningful collaboration with indigenous communities, ensuring their active participation and leadership in all stages of language preservation projects. Respecting indigenous knowledge systems and community rights also aligns with international frameworks and declarations, such as the United Nations Declaration on the Rights of Indigenous Peoples. These instruments emphasize the importance of cultural rights, self-determination, and the preservation of indigenous languages and knowledge.

Government Policies and Support in Promoting and Preserving Indigenous Language Using Digital Media Technology

Governments play a crucial role in promoting and preserving indigenous languages using digital media technology. They have the responsibility to develop policies, allocate funds, and enact legislation that supports and encourages language revitalization efforts, respecting the rights of indigenous communities. Policy initiatives are essential for creating a supportive environment for language preservation. Governments can establish policies that prioritize the documentation and revitalization of indigenous languages using digital tools and platforms. These policies should emphasize the value of linguistic diversity and provide guidelines for integrating technology into language education, cultural initiatives, and community-led projects (Woolard & Bhatt, 2021). Funding opportunities are critical for the sustainability of language preservation projects. Governments can allocate specific funds or create grant programs to support indigenous communities, researchers, and organizations involved in language revitalization.

Financial resources can be utilized for developing digital infrastructure, creating educational resources, training language specialists, and empowering indigenous communities to lead their language preservation efforts (Hinton, 2019). Legislation plays a vital role in protecting indigenous language rights and supporting their revitalization. Governments can enact laws that recognize and safeguard the linguistic and cultural heritage of indigenous communities. This includes provisions for the use of indigenous languages in education, official documents, media, and public services. Additionally, legislation can address issues of intellectual property, ensuring that indigenous communities have control over their language resources and knowledge (Sutherland, 2017). Several countries have implemented successful government-led language revitalization programs.

For instance, New Zealand's Māori Language Strategy focuses on revitalizing the Māori language through various initiatives, including digital resources and technologies (New Zealand Ministry for Culture and Heritage, 2021). In Canada, the Indigenous Languages Act recognizes the significance of indigenous languages and establishes measures to support their preservation, promotion, and revitalization (Graham, 2023). Australia's Aboriginal and Torres Strait Islander Languages Act provides support for the maintenance and revival of indigenous languages (Australian Government, 1991). These examples highlight the positive impact of government involvement in indigenous language preservation through digital media technology. By demonstrating commitment through policies, funding, and legislation, governments can contribute to the revitalization and empowerment of indigenous communities and ensure the preservation of their unique linguistic heritage.

FUTURE PROSPECTS AND CHALLENGES

Emerging technologies such as Artificial Intelligence (AI) and Virtual Reality (VR) hold significant potential for language preservation efforts. These technologies offer innovative ways to enhance language learning, documentation, and cultural immersion, providing new opportunities for indigenous communities. Artificial intelligence can contribute to language preservation by facilitating the development of language learning applications and tools. AI-powered language learning platforms can personalize learning experiences, adapt to individual learners' needs, and provide interactive exercises and feedback. Additionally, AI algorithms can assist in language documentation by analyzing and processing large amounts of linguistic data, helping to create comprehensive language resources and dictionaries (Toutanova et al., 2020).

Virtual reality has the potential to create immersive language learning experiences. It can transport learners to virtual environments where they can interact with native speakers, practice language skills, and experience cultural contexts. VR technology can also be used to digitally preserve cultural heritage sites, traditional practices, and storytelling, providing a means for future generations to engage with their language and culture (García-Peñalvo et al., 2020). However, it is important to acknowledge the challenges that arise in the context of the digital divide and access to technology in indigenous communities. The digital divide refers to unequal access to technology and internet connectivity, which can hinder language preservation efforts. Many indigenous communities, particularly those in remote areas, may face limited infrastructure, lack of internet access, and inadequate technology resources (Dutta et al., 2019).

To address these challenges, it is crucial to ensure equitable access to technology and bridge the digital divide. Governments, organizations, and tech companies can collaborate to provide necessary infrastructure, internet connectivity, and digital devices to indigenous communities. Initiatives should be implemented to promote digital literacy and skills training among community members, empowering them to effectively utilize emerging technologies for language preservation (United Nations, 2021). Furthermore, community involvement and participatory approaches are vital for addressing the challenges related to technology access. Indigenous communities should have a say in the design and implementation of language preservation projects, ensuring that the technologies used align with their cultural values, needs, and preferences. Collaborative partnerships between indigenous communities, researchers, and technology experts can foster culturally sensitive and community-driven approaches (Turin, 2021).

The long-term sustainability of language preservation efforts relies on continuous support from various stakeholders. Language preservation is not a one-time task but a continuous process that requires ongoing commitment and resources. Here, we will discuss the importance of continuous support and the factors contributing to the long-term sustainability of language preservation efforts.

- Funding and Resources: Adequate financial resources are essential for sustaining language preservation initiatives. Governments, philanthropic organizations, and other stakeholders need to allocate funding specifically for language preservation projects. This funding can support activities such as language documentation, curriculum development, technology infrastructure, and community engagement. Sustainable funding ensures the longevity of these initiatives and helps address challenges such as training language experts, developing educational materials, and maintaining digital platforms (Hinton et al., 2016).

- Community Engagement: The active involvement of indigenous communities is crucial for the long-term sustainability of language preservation efforts. Communities should be empowered to take ownership of language preservation initiatives and participate in decision-making processes. Community engagement fosters a sense of ownership, motivates community members to actively contribute to language revitalization, and ensures that preservation efforts align with cultural values and needs. Sustainable language preservation requires ongoing collaboration, communication, and capacity building within indigenous communities (Grenoble & Whaley, 2006).
- Education and Transmission: Language revitalization efforts should focus on education and transmission, particularly among younger generations. Intergenerational language transmission is critical for language sustainability. Initiatives that integrate language preservation into formal and informal educational settings, such as schools, community centers, and digital learning platforms, can ensure the continued transmission of indigenous languages to future generations. Comprehensive language programs that include immersion schools, language nests, and mentorship programs can facilitate language acquisition and use (McCarty et al., 2016).
- Technology and Digital Tools: The integration of technology and digital tools plays a significant role in the long-term sustainability of language preservation efforts. Digital platforms, mobile applications, and online resources provide accessible and interactive ways to learn, practice, and document indigenous languages. These technological tools enable wider dissemination of language materials, facilitate collaboration among linguists and communities, and contribute to the preservation and revitalization of languages in the digital age. Ongoing technological support and adaptation to emerging technologies are crucial for the sustained impact of language preservation efforts (Bird & Simons, 2003).
- Policy and Legal Support: Governments and policymakers play a vital role in creating an enabling environment for language preservation. Developing supportive policies, legislation, and language rights frameworks can ensure the protection and promotion of indigenous languages. Legislative measures can include language recognition, the integration of indigenous languages in education and public services, and the establishment of language preservation institutions. Strong policy frameworks provide a foundation for long-term language sustainability (UNESCO, 2003).

RECOMMENDATIONS

Arising from the discussion in this study, it should be noted that the success of language preservation initiatives relies on collaborative efforts, ethical considerations, and government support. Collaboration among indigenous communities, linguists, technology experts, and various stakeholders is essential for developing culturally appropriate and community-driven language preservation strategies. Specifically, it is recommended that:

- Educational institutions must be proactive in fostering an environment that encourages a profound understanding of the importance of linguistic diversity. It is of paramount importance to acknowledge and emphasize the profound significance of preserving indigenous languages by seamlessly integrating them into educational curricula. This conscious recognition seeks to instill an enduring appreciation for the cultural, historical, and ecological value these languages embody.
- Collaborative engagement with organizations and governments is indispensable in securing sustained funding. The multifaceted challenges intertwined with language preservation necessitate a resolute commitment of substantial resources to indigenous language initiatives. This commitment extends to financial support, the development of robust technological infrastructure, and the establishment of comprehensive training programs. These endeavors aim to equip language enthusiasts with the essential skills required to undertake this monumental task.
- The untapped potential of digital media technology offers an invaluable means of preserving indigenous languages. The imperative here is to meticulously tailor digital platforms, mobile applications, and online resources to cater to the idiosyncratic requirements of each language. The creation of user-friendly interfaces simplifies the intricate processes of language documentation, learning, and sharing within indigenous communities and the broader global audience.
- The adoption of a perpetual evaluation process for digital tools and applications employed in language preservation is a pivotal strategy. Cultivating robust partnerships between linguistic experts, technology developers, and indigenous communities is integral to refining and optimizing these digital resources. The process of customization to meet the specific linguistic needs of each indigenous language is an irreplaceable cornerstone of effective preservation.
- The long-term preservation and sustainability of indigenous languages hinge on the cultivation of collaborative ecosystems. Facilitating robust cooperation among indigenous communities, linguists, technology

experts, and governmental bodies is the key to success. Establishing platforms that promote knowledge sharing and active stakeholder participation is the linchpin in the development and execution of culturally sensitive language preservation strategies.

Incorporating these enriched recommendations into language preservation initiatives will undoubtedly fortify the endeavors to protect and exalt indigenous languages. By duly recognizing their cultural significance, addressing challenges with comprehensive resources, harnessing digital technology, perpetually evaluating digital tools, and promoting collaborative ecosystems, a comprehensive framework is erected to safeguard linguistic diversity and preserve the rich tapestry of cultural heritage.

CONCLUSION AND IMPLICATIONS OF THE STUDY

In the culmination of this study, it becomes evident that the preservation and promotion of indigenous languages bear profound significance not only for the cultural heritage of indigenous communities but also for their overall well-being. These languages serve as reservoirs of invaluable knowledge systems, cultural expressions, and unique worldviews that enrich the tapestry of human diversity. Moreover, in the context of the Fourth Industrial Revolution (4IR), the role of digital media technology in rejuvenating and advocating for indigenous languages stands as a critical and transformative development. The importance of preserving indigenous languages cannot be overstated. These languages are the vessels of traditions, histories, and the collective wisdom of communities that have thrived for generations. They represent a distinct worldview, interwoven with the environment, spirituality, and identity of their speakers. This chapter has reaffirmed that indigenous languages are not relics of the past but living repositories of human understanding and cultural depth.

In the age of the 4IR, digital media technology emerges as the proverbial torchbearer for indigenous language preservation. It offers innovative and powerful tools and platforms that are instrumental in the revitalization and propagation of these languages. Through the lens of digital media, we can witness the creation of digital archives, mobile applications, and online resources that facilitate the documentation, learning, and dissemination of indigenous languages. These technologies transcend barriers and provide accessible and interactive avenues for individuals, whether they belong to indigenous communities or not, to engage with these linguistic treasures. A significant novelty arising from our study is the realization that digital media technology is not just a means of preservation but a powerful catalyst for language revitalization. It empowers learners to delve into these languages in immersive and engaging ways, thereby expanding vocabulary, and fostering cultural immersion experiences. It serves as a bridge connecting generations, ensuring that the wisdom embedded in indigenous languages continues to enrich the lives of future generations.

Furthermore, this chapter has highlighted that digital media technology, through its ability to document languages comprehensively, guarantees the survival of endangered languages. This preservation is not limited to static archives but also extends to dynamic, living repositories of linguistic diversity. These languages are now equipped to thrive, adapt, and evolve in the digital age, thereby securing their place in the cultural tapestry of the future. In conclusion, our research emphasizes the paramount importance of preserving and promoting indigenous languages in the digital age of the 4IR. It underlines the indispensable role of digital media technology in this endeavor, showcasing how it not only safeguards linguistic treasures but also breathes new life into these languages, ensuring that they continue to enrich the world's cultural diversity and understanding.

REFERENCES

AILLA. (n.d.). Archive of the Indigenous Languages of Latin America. Retrieved from https://ailla.utexas.org.

Austin, P. K. (2019). Digital technology and endangered indigenous languages: Challenges and new opportunities. *Language Documentation & Conservation*, 13, 356–382.

Australian Government. (1991). Aboriginal and Torres Strait Islander Languages Act 1991. Retrieved from https://www.legislation.gov.au/Details/C2016C01040.

Bagea, I. (2023). Cultural influences in language learning in a global context. *Indo-MathEdu Intellectuals Journal*, 4(2), 630–645.

Beermann, D., & Spreer, P. (2018). Gamification in language learning: The benefits of specific game features for language revitalization. In Proceedings of the 19th Annual SIGdial Meeting on Discourse and Dialogue (pp. 151–160).

Berryman, M. (2020). Language revitalization and Māori tikanga: Indigenous knowledge, language acquisition and well-being in New Zealand. *International Journal of Wellbeing*, 10(3), 1–20.

Bird, S., & Simons, G. F. (2003). Seven dimensions of portability for language documentation and description. *Language*, 79(3), 557–582.

Bird, S., Shobbrook, K., Flick, D., Carroll, S., Austin, A., & Lim, A. (2019). Technology for Indigenous language revitalization: The state of the field. *Language,* 95(S1), e1–e29.

Burgess, S., Burgess, L., & Miller, P. (2021). Indigenous language revitalization and community engagement: Practices, challenges, and strategies. *Language Documentation & Conservation*, 15, 313–339.

Crawford, J. (1997). At war with diversity: US language policy in an age of anxiety. Multilingual Matters.

Cunsolo, A., & Harper, S. L. (2014). Ecological grief and mourning: The starting point for transformative change. In S. D. O'Connor & C. L. Kuzdas (eds.), Mourning nature: Hope at the heart of ecological loss and grief (pp. 19–35). Routledge.

Duolingo. (n.d.). Learn Navajo with Duolingo. Retrieved from https://www.duolingo .com/course/nv/en/Learn-Navajo.

Dutta, A., Dutta, M. J., Ahmed, S., & Choudhury, S. R. (2019). Mobile technology for indigenous language revitalization: Cases from India and Bangladesh. In Proceedings of the 2019 CHI Conference on Human Factors in Computing Systems (pp. 1–12).

Dutta, U., Anand, N., Chakraborty, S., Bhattacharya, M., & Dutta, S. (2019). Digital technology in preserving the endangered languages: Opportunities and challenges. In J. Mandal & A. Mukhopadhyay (eds.), Disruptive Technology: Concepts, Methodologies, Tools, and Applications (pp. 305–324). IGI Global.

ELAR. (n.d.). Endangered Languages Archive. Retrieved from https://elar.soas.ac.uk/

Fishman, J. A. (1991). Reversing language shift: Theoretical and empirical foundations of assistance to threatened languages. Multilingual Matters.

García-Peñalvo, F. J., Conde, M. Á., Seoane-Pardo, A. M., Fidalgo-Blanco, Á., & Rodríguez-Conde, M. J. (2020). Augmented and virtual reality for the preservation of intangible cultural heritage in indigenous communities. *Sustainability*, 12(6), 2495.

Gippert, J., & Himmelmann, N. P. (2019). Technologies for documenting and revitalizing endangered languages. *Language and Linguistics Compass*, 13(4), e12331.

González-Ruibal, A. (2019). Cultural resilience and heritage ethics in a changing world. *Journal of Contemporary Archaeology*, 6(2), 131–146.

Gorenflo, L. J., Romaine, S., Mittermeier, R. A., & Walker-Painemilla, K. (2012). Co-occurrence of linguistic and biological diversity in biodiversity hotspots and high biodiversity wilderness areas. *Proceedings of the National Academy of Sciences*, 109(21), 8032–8037.

Graham, J. C. (2023). Decolonization through words: Using Indigenous languages to revitalize Indigenous culture in a postcolonial Canada (Doctoral dissertation). Retrieved from http://hdl.handle.net/1946/43927.

Grenoble, L. A., & Whaley, L. J. (2006). Saving languages: An introduction to language revitalization. Cambridge University Press.

Gwerevende, S., & Mthombeni, Z. M. (2023). Safeguarding intangible cultural heritage: Exploring the synergies in the transmission of Indigenous languages, dance and music practices in Southern Africa. *International Journal of Heritage Studies*, 29(5), 398–412.

Harmon, D. (2019). Language revitalization and mobile app development: Opportunities and challenges. *Language Documentation & Conservation*, 13, 546–571.

Harrison, K. D. (2019). When languages die: The extinction of the world's languages and the erosion of human knowledge. Oxford University Press.

Hinton, L. (2014). Language revitalization in the age of new media. *Annual Review of Applied Linguistics, 34*, 197–212.

Hinton, L. (2019). Language revitalization and new technologies: Cultures of electronic mediation and the refiguring of communities. In J. Jaffe, D. Morita, N. D. Vogel, & G. Spolsky (eds.), Language Ideologies and the Globalization of 'Standard' Languages (pp. 244–264). Routledge.

Hinton, L., Huss, L., Roche, G., & Tsosie, E. (2016). Language revitalization in the digital age: Promises and challenges. In L. Hinton, L. Huss, & G. Roche (eds.), The Routledge Handbook of Language Revitalization (pp. 371–384). Routledge.

Hodges, R. (2024). Defiance within the decline? Revisiting new Welsh speakers' language journeys. *Journal of Multilingual and Multicultural Development, 45*(2), 306–322. https://doi.org/10.1080/01434632.2021.1880416.

Koopu, K. M. (2023). Honouring our past, fostering our future: A Kaupapa Māori exploration of identity, Whanaungatanga and how this supports Rangatahi Māori Hauora and well-being (Doctoral dissertation, ResearchSpace@ Auckland). Retrieved from https://researchspace.auckland.ac.nz/docs/uoa-docs/rights.htm.

Kral, I. (2021). Language preservation and revitalization. In The Oxford Handbook of Language and Society (pp. 357–374). Oxford University Press.

Lévesque, M. C., Kutcher, A., Roy, L., Linton, P., Trapper, L., Torrie, J. E., & MacDonald, M. E. (2023). Occupational transaction in support of miyupimaatisiiun (wellness): Eeyou/Eenou community voices. *Journal of Occupational Science, 30*(3), 342–362. https://doi.org/10.1080/14427591.2022.2132999.

Liu, Y., Weng, C., Li, H., & Sanga, G. (2019). Social media-based digital storytelling for preserving oral tradition: A case study in Tibetan culture. *Digital Scholarship in the Humanities, 34*(1), 165–179.

Living Tongues Institute. (n.d.). Language Communities. Retrieved from https://www.livingtongues.org/language-communities.

Lotherington, H., & Reinhardt, J. (2019). Learning with digital media in formal and informal settings. In The Routledge Handbook of Digital Literacies in Early Childhood (pp. 199–214). Routledge.

McCarty, T. L. (2011). Navajo language policy in practice: Reconceptualizing the notion of revitalization. *Journal of American Indian Education, 50*(1), 5–24.

McCarty, T., Nicholas, S. E., & Wyman, L. T. (2016). Language revitalization and technology: New tools, new connections. In L. Hinton, L. Huss, & G. Roche (eds.), The Routledge Handbook of Language Revitalization (pp. 324–339). Routledge.

McCarty, T., Romero-Little, M. E., Warhol, L., & Zepeda, O. (2017). Indigenous language planning, policy, and revitalization in Arizona. In H. K. Cline & J. I. Fernald (eds.), Handbook of Arizona's languages (pp. 93–120). University of Arizona Press.

McIlraith, S., Berkes, F., Kofinas, G., & Humphries, M. (2020). Community engagement, ownership, and the challenge of the 'public' in Indigenous language planning. *Language & Communication, 73*, 45–54.

McIvor, O., Napoleon, A., & Dickie, K. M. (2020). Indigenous youth and language revitalization: An intergenerational approach to language planning. *Journal of Language, Identity & Education,* 19(1), 1–17.

Meighan, P. J. (2023). "What is language for us?" The role of relational technology, strength-based language education, and community-led language planning and policy research to support Indigenous language revitalization and cultural reclamation processes (Doctoral dissertation, McGill University [Canada]).

Metallic, N. W. (2023). Five linguistic methods for revitalizing Indigenous laws. *McGill Law Journal,* 68(1), 47–87. https://doi.org/10.26443/law.v68i1.1191.

Molnar, R., & Chartrand, S. (2021). Decolonizing through Twitter: Indigenous language communities, social media, and language revitalization. *Journal of Sociolinguistics,* 25(1), 21–45.

Montero, M. K., Dénommé-Welch, S., & Henry, S. R. (2022). Indigenous-led, community-based language reclamation and regeneration initiatives. In *A Field Guide to Community Literacy* (pp. 198–211). Routledge.

Nettle, D., & Romaine, S. (2021). Vanishing Voices: The Extinction of the World's Languages. Oxford University Press.

New Zealand Ministry for Culture and Heritage. (2021). Te Maihi Karauna—Crown Māori Language Strategy. Retrieved from https://www.mch.govt.nz/policies-and -programs/te-maihi-karauna.

Onyenankeya, K. (2022). Indigenous language newspapers and the digital media conundrum in Africa. *Information Development,* 38(1), 83–96.

Oosthuizen, J. H., Ungerer, M., & Volschenk, J. (2023). A fourth industrial revolution integrated intelligence taxonomy for top management. *Journal of Contemporary Management,* 20(1), 404–443.

Parramore, M. (2021). The living archive of Aboriginal languages: A digital repository for Indigenous languages in south-eastern Australia. *Language Documentation & Conservation,* 15, 79–100.

Reyhner, J. (2012). American Indian language policy and school success. *Journal of American Indian Education,* 51(3), 13–28.

Reyhner, J. (2012). Indigenous language immersion schools for tribal language revitalization: What do we know and what do we need to know? *Journal of American Indian Education,* 51(3), 61–87.

Reyhner, J., & Lockard, L. N. (2009). Indigenous language immersion in the United States: History, benefits, and other considerations. In N. H. Hornberger (ed.), Indigenous Literacies in the Americas: Language Planning from the Bottom Up (pp. 235–254). Mouton de Gruyter.

Reyhner, J., & Tennant, E. (2019). Revitalizing indigenous languages: A focus on education. In Indigenous Peoples and Language Policy in Canada (pp. 199–214). Springer.

Scholze-Irrlitz, T., & Struß, S. (2017). The role of digital media in supporting language revitalization: Insights from the Pite Saami community. *Language Documentation & Conservation,* 11, 64–84.

Smith, L. T. (2012). Intellectual property rights and the interests of Indigenous peoples. In N. Blomley, D. Delaney, D. McCarthy, & R. C. Blomley (eds.), Indigenous

Peoples and the Law: Comparative and Critical Perspectives (pp. 137–148). Hart Publishing.

Smith, L. T., & Weldon, S. L. (2021). Indigenous worldviews and education: Preserving language, culture, and traditions. In International Handbook on Indigenous Education (pp. 1–19). Springer.

Sutherland, M. (2017). Indigenous languages and law in Australia. *Annual Review of Applied Linguistics*, 37, 81–97.

Sweller, N., Dascalu, M., Ponciano, L., Dascalu, M., & McNamara, D. (2019). Designing virtual reality for indigenous language education. *Educational Technology Research and Development*, 67(1), 171–195.

Toutanova, K., Wu, Y., Li, X., & Sakaguchi, K. (2020). Language technology for under-resourced languages: The case for low-resource language technologies. In Proceedings of the 58th Annual Meeting of the Association for Computational Linguistics (pp. 1576–1590).

Turin, M. (2021). Community-driven digital language preservation. In Proceedings of the Digital Humanities in the Nordic Countries 6th Conference (pp. 277–287).

UNESCO. (2003). Declaration on the Rights of Indigenous Peoples. Retrieved from https://www.un.org/development/desa/indigenouspeoples/declaration-on-the-rights-of-indigenous-peoples.html.

UNESCO. (2003). Universal Declaration on Cultural Diversity. Retrieved from https://unesdoc.unesco.org/ark:/48223/pf0000122526.

UNESCO. (2009). UNESCO Universal Declaration on Cultural Diversity. Retrieved from https://unesdoc.unesco.org/ark:/48223/pf0000183334.

UNESCO. (2019). UNESCO policy guidelines for the development and promotion of indigenous languages. Retrieved from https://unesdoc.unesco.org/ark:/48223/pf0000368650.

UNESCO. (2021). Atlas of the world's languages in danger. Retrieved from https://www.unesco.org/languages-atlas.

United Nations. (2021). Policy brief: Education during COVID-19 and beyond. Retrieved from https://www.un.org/development/desa/dspd/wp-content/uploads/sites/22/2021/02/sg_policy_brief_covid-19_and_education_english.pdf.

Woolard, K. A., & Bhatt, R. M. (2021). Language endangerment and revitalization. *Annual Review of Linguistics*, 7, 25–42.

Chapter 3

Positioning South African Indigenous Languages on Social Media Communication in the Fourth Industrial Revolution

Shumani Eric Madima

In South Africa, indigenous African languages spoken by over 70 percent of the population face degradation and marginalization despite the country's intentions to put them on equal footing with Afrikaans and English (Makatela, 2020). After apartheid was abolished, responsibility was put on the state to take "practical and positive measures" toward increasing the use and status of indigenous languages (Ke Yu & Dumisa, 2015). However, despite these admirable efforts, "nothing of real substance has changed since 1996 regarding the language political state of the African languages [ALs] . . . the ALs are still not being used meaningfully in public life: in parliament, courts of law, universities, schools, and the printed media" (Webb, 2013:179). This chapter addresses the advanced use of South African Indigenous languages in social communication in the Fourth Industrial Revolution (4IR). According to Madima, Makananise, and Malatji (2023), in the South African context, indigenous languages are the original or native languages spoken by the indigenous people. There are nine major indigenous languages recognized as official by the Constitution of South Africa of 1996, namely: IsiNdebele, IsiXhosa, IsiZulu, Sepedi, Sesotho, Siswati, Tshivenda, Xitsonga, Setswana. However, the dominance of English makes it difficult for indigenous languages to be promoted and used in all domains. The marginalization of indigenous languages could be a threat to their existence since they are only used for communication purposes and most commonly by the native speakers regarded as not highly educated.

According to UNESCO, at least 43 percent of the estimated 6,000 languages spoken in the world are endangered. This figure is likely to be low since many languages lack sufficient data to allow for an assessment of their vulnerability (Ebadi, 2018). South African indigenous languages face several vulnerabilities and challenges, which threaten their survival and vitality. These challenges are rooted in historical, social, economic, and political factors. Efforts to address this vulnerability include language revitalization programs, community-based language initiatives, and advocacy for increased recognition and support of indigenous languages in education and media. Increasingly, artificial intelligence (AI) is being used for language learning around the world; major technology companies are making substantial investments in natural language and voice interface platforms. But even as language usage advancements are made in this area, Google's former executive chairman Eric Schmidt acknowledged that languages that are not prevalent are disadvantaged by AI (Ebadi, 2019). These languages are not simply threatened by the declining population of native speakers but also by the technological systems that give preference to the most spoken languages in the world (Ebadi, 2019).

Poor implementation of the language policy in South Africa is another factor blamed for undermining efforts to promote indigenous languages and uphold the principle of "parity of esteem." Implementation failures are said to be due to insufficient consideration of the practicality of the policy intention. For instance, the difficulties in balancing the interests of all twelve official languages (including English, Afrikaans, and the newly added Sign Language); slow progress in linguistic development (including standardization and making them relevant to science, technology, and advanced literature); a low turnover in training teachers who can teach in indigenous languages; and utility of the indigenous languages at higher levels of education, business, and commerce remains low (Ke Yu, 2015).

COLONIAL LEGACY ON LANGUAGES IN DEMOCRATIC SOUTH AFRICA

The colonial legacy in South Africa is a complex and controversial topic that continues to shape the country's political and social landscape. Language imposition is a topic that cannot be ignored when discussing the impact of colonialism on the African continent. The colonizers descended to the African shores with their languages and declared them suitable for education and governance. Even after more than a decade of gaining political independence, South Africa is still struggling to erase the footprints of colonialism from its institutional structures and systems of education. This has resulted in a situation where the South African political elites are still unconsciously adhering to outdated colonial structures of governance, hampering the development of modern institutions (Ebadi, 2019). The legacy of colonialism continues to have far-reaching effects in South Africa and other former colonial territories in Africa. To move beyond the legacy of colonialism, South Africa must confront the deep-seated institutional and structural challenges that were inherited at independence. This will require a concerted effort to reform and modernize governance and educational systems, as well as a commitment to undoing the damage caused by years of colonialism. Only then can South Africa build a truly democratic and prosperous society that is not shackled and poorly administered.

When the Republic of South Africa gained independence from British colonial rule in 1961, the colonial footprint remained visible in many aspects of South African society. Institutional structures and educational systems that were inherited at independence continue to shape governance and education in South Africa, perpetuating the colonial legacy. One of the most significant legacies of colonialism in South Africa is the divide-and-rule strategy that was employed by colonial powers grounded in linguistic imperialism. This strategy involved creating divisions and animosities between different ethnic groups to maintain control and suppress dissent (Mowarin & Tonukari, 2010). Unfortunately, this strategy was perpetuated by African political elites who were unconsciously locked into outdated colonial structures. Despite achieving a democratic government and political independence in 1994, the country's colonial past still looms large in many ways. The institutional structures and educational systems inherited from the colonial era continued to shape the platforms for governance and education. This is particularly evident with the country's political elites, who are often unconsciously locked into the use of English as the lingua franca in all domains and spheres of government (Ebaldi, 2019).

Despite the challenges posed by the country's colonial legacy, there are signs and attempts at progress. The government has taken steps to address the lingering effects of colonialism, such as through initiatives aimed at redressing past injustices promoting multilingualism, and social and economic equality. There is also a growing recognition among South Africans of the need to confront the legacy of colonialism head-on. The continuous use of colonial languages by Africans is another significant aspect of the persistence of colonial footprints in South African societies. The imposition of colonial languages and the suppression of indigenous languages resulted in the marginalization of African cultures (Ebaldi, 2019). Even today, African countries continue to use colonial languages as their official languages, which perpetuates the influence of the colonial past. In many cases, local indigenous languages are not given the same status as colonial languages, which hinders the development of local literature and limits the opportunities for African languages to be used in various fields. This legacy also affects the education system, where students are taught in colonial languages, often at the expense of the local indigenous languages. Therefore, it is essential to recognize the importance of African languages and integrate them into various aspects of society, including governance, education, and social media communication. Only then can we truly begin to move toward a state of political and cultural independence from the shackles of colonialism.

The colonial era saw the suppression of indigenous languages in favor of European languages, which were and are still considered superior. The persistent use of English as the medium of instruction in South African schools and government institutions perpetuates the power dynamics that existed during the colonial era. Politicians still commemorate the 16 June, 1976, student protest every year in South Africa. The same students protested the use of Afrikaans as a medium of instruction in public schools in preference to English instead of their indigenous languages. South Africa is so immersed in English to an extent that those who advocate for the use of indigenous languages are seen as promoting ethnicism and regressing to the Apartheid era (Khan, 2009). This has resulted in a situation where African elites are struggling to create an African identity that is not tainted by the colonial past (Khan, 2009). This has led to a situation where political power is concentrated in the hands of a few elites, who can speak English fluently. Consequently, the African state is designed in such a way that ideas of the state, power, and development are superficially copied from the colonial masters, without a proper understanding of the African context (Khan, 2009). Thus, the colonial legacy has left a lasting impact on African societies, and it will take a concerted effort to overcome the challenges that it has created. South Africa is a multilingual country that is supposed to benefit from its language diversity. As May (2003:128) observes, "the process of the state making the national language is a form of practice, historically contingent and socially embedded." Therefore, government intervention has significance in broadening the linguistic base of state institutions. Jeremy Waldron (2019) states that, fundamentally, in liberalism, "social and political order is illegitimate unless it is rooted in the consent of all those who have to live under it."

Mowarin and Tonukari (2010:78) reinforce the researcher's argument that "government intervention is necessary to rectify the current inadequacies in the use of both foreign and mother-tongue languages." Whether from large-scale or micro-level language planning approaches (Baldauf and Kaplan, 2006), it is argued that the state has a key role to play in redeeming African languages. Social exclusion, information and communication barriers, and low literacy promote a poorly defined national vision and retard opportunities for national consensus building in society (Jenkins, 1991). Cummins (1995) also argues that literacy can be explicitly focused on issues of power, as seen in the work of Paulo Freire (1972), who highlights "the potential of written language as a tool that encourages people to analyze the division of power and resources in their society and to work toward transforming discriminatory structures" (Burnaby & Reyhner, 2002:2).

Competence in a language affords access to information. It helps individuals and organizations scrutinize power and hold it to account. Hence, the right to education should be complemented by the right to be taught in one's language. Balduaf and Kaplan (2006) argue that current language policies in most African countries are driven by market forces, justifying the continuation of colonial trends in educational planning and policies. But even where the language of trade is different from the official language, as in Guinea Bissau and Niger (Hovens, 2003), "bilingual education is a cognitive advantage and not a deficit" (May, 2003:144). Yuka and Omoregbe (2010) prove that even minority African languages, among them Tshivenda in South Africa, have the requisite linguistic structures to accommodate scientific and non-scientific knowledge production.

LANGUAGE USE IN SOCIAL COMMUNICATION

The government of South Africa has committed itself to the preservation of indigenous languages as enshrined in the Constitution of 1996 under Section 6 which specifically emphasizes the need to achieve parity of esteem among eleven official languages. According to Esteron (2021:93),

> English language is said to be the universal language and learning it, means having access to the world, to other people, ideas, ways of thinking, and literature. It is the medium for teaching different subjects in the academy and the medium of knowledge in transferring and sharing certain ideas and feelings.

English is one of the most common means of communication used among people globally in different fields such as government, politics, technology, social media, and so forth. But the major influence on the English language is and has been the media. Language is influenced by many factors such as class, society, developments in science and technology, etc. However, the major influence on the English language is and has been the media (Sharma, 2013). Another factor is modernization, the bloom of different gadgets and machines can influence language, such as the use of social media as a way of communication (Esteron, 2021).

Social media has become one of the most powerful sources for information and news updates through platforms such as Facebook, Blogger, Twitter,

82   *Shumani Eric Madima*

WordPress, LinkedIn, Google+, Tumblr, Myspace, and Instagram. On the other hand, from a linguistic point of view, the impact of social media reflects on new words or expressions like newsfeeds, viral, and hashtags which did not make sense a few years ago but meant something completely different than they do nowadays (Esteron, 2021). Schonfeld (2010), in an article titled "Discourse of Twitter and Social Media," pointed out that Social Networking Sites (SNS) are the most used form of social media wherein millions of people around the world can create and produce millions of different messages.

While AI and other exponential technologies present opportunities for the preservation of language, there are also inherent challenges to using these technologies to meaningfully revitalize these languages. Many indigenous languages are rooted in oral tradition. The act of transcribing them into a written form may alter or fail to capture the full meaning of these languages (Ebadi, 2018). The very act of transcribing these languages and removing them from the contexts and cultures they are embedded in is likely to contribute to a loss in meaning. Language is not simply communicated through written words (Ebadi, 2019); the way people speak, their facial expressions, and the context and environment in which they speak all contribute to the message that is being conveyed. Simply recording indigenous languages and using these recordings to develop AI tools is not enough to safeguard and revitalize indigenous languages. The vast array of knowledge and culture captured by indigenous languages would be lost if we failed to recognize that language is more than a succession of letters and sounds put together.

The languages preferred in international discourse and fora impact the understanding of the issues being discussed. Some researchers have argued that language is important to hegemony, especially as it relates to cultural domination. It is perhaps for this very reason that the residential school system consciously worked to deprive indigenous youth of their language, as a means of control and dominance. In the digital space, the deployment of AI tools that use a select group of languages in their design may replicate colonialism and marginalization (Ebadi, 2019). As it stands, most of the online content is stored in English and Chinese, with the top ten languages representing over 80 percent of all online content (Ebadi, 2019). The absence of indigenous languages in the digital space can contribute to a lack of representation and a loss of indigenous knowledge. As younger generations of indigenous peoples become more actively engaged online and use digital applications that are aligned with knowledge and Western tradition over indigenous languages and culture, their behavior and understanding of the world are likely to be altered. Such an outcome could marginalize indigenous populations around the world by depriving them of their culture and identity. AI's ability to recognize patterns will never be an effective replacement for the holistic and meaningful learning that happens when indigenous elders and leaders pass their language and knowledge down to younger generations. Further, AI tools for the protection and revitalization of indigenous languages must be developed with indigenous involvement and consent (Ebadi, 2019).

Social communication is a vital aspect of human interaction, playing a crucial role in our everyday lives. The language used in social communication is of immense importance, as it facilitates the conveyance of ideas, emotions, and thoughts among individuals in different settings. In recent years, there has been a growing interest in exploring the relationship between indigenous languages and social communication. Studies have shown that the use of indigenous language in social communication can have a positive impact on language revitalization efforts, as it promotes their continued use and documentation. Moreover, the use of indigenous languages in social communication can also facilitate intercultural understanding, leading to increased cultural awareness and appreciation. However, despite the potential benefits of using indigenous languages in social communication, the dominance of major world languages in global communication poses a significant challenge. This further underscores the need to promote and preserve indigenous languages, not only for cultural reasons but also for effective social communication. The use of indigenous language in social communication can promote cultural inclusivity and diversity while fostering intercultural understanding. Thus, efforts should be made to preserve indigenous languages and promote their use in social communication.

Social communication is a complex and dynamic process, and language plays a crucial role in shaping it. The language used in social communication is often influenced by a variety of factors, including cultural norms, social status, and personal preferences (Oldfield, 2022). The use of indigenous languages in social communication is particularly significant, as it reflects the cultural heritage and identity of a community. When examining language use in social communication, it is important to consider the diversity of languages spoken around the world (Oldfield, 2022). While some languages are more widely spoken and understood than others, the use of indigenous languages in social communication is crucial to preserving cultural diversity and promoting inclusivity. Research has shown that the use of indigenous languages in social communication can have a positive impact on individuals and communities (Wijarnako, Andriani & Ernawati, 2023). It can enhance cultural pride and identity, facilitate communication between generations, and foster a sense of community belonging. While the use of indigenous languages in social communication may face challenges such as limited resources and a lack of support, efforts to promote their use should be encouraged. It is important to recognize the value of linguistic diversity and promote multilingualism in social communication (Wijarnako, Andriani & Ernawati, 2023). By doing so, we can help ensure that all individuals and communities can communicate effectively and inclusively.

Social communication involves the use of language in various forms. The language used in social communication can differ based on the context and the individuals involved in the communication process. It is important to understand the nuances of language in social communication to effectively communicate with others and avoid misunderstandings. The language used in social communication can vary depending on the social norms and expectations of the community or group involved. For example, in a formal setting, such as a business meeting or a court hearing, more formal language may be used. On the other hand, in a more casual or informal setting, such as a social gathering or a family dinner, a more relaxed language may be used. Indigenous language can also play a significant role in social communication. These languages may have unique features and nuances that are specific to the culture and customs of the community. Therefore, understanding these languages and their use in social communication can help promote cultural understanding and respect. However, language use in social communication is a complex and dynamic process that requires careful consideration and understanding. Whether it is the language used in formal or informal settings or the use of indigenous languages, it is important to be aware of the cultural context and norms surrounding the language to effectively communicate with others.

Language use in social communication is a complex field of study that encompasses a wide range of linguistic practices utilized in various social contexts. Social communication is the process by which individuals exchange information through verbal and nonverbal means, and the language used in such interactions is a crucial aspect of this process. The use of language in social communication is closely linked to cultural practices, norms, and values, which often dictate the appropriateness of linguistic practices in different social settings. One area of study that is of particular interest in the field of language use in social communication is the use of indigenous languages in social contexts. Indigenous languages are an integral part of many cultures around the world, and how they are used in social interactions can provide insights into the social dynamics of these communities. Studying the use of indigenous languages in social communication can also shed light on how language use is linked to power dynamics and identity construction in these communities. In addition to the study of indigenous languages, research in language use in social communication also encompasses how language is used in different social settings, such as workplaces, schools, and healthcare settings. The language used in these settings can have a significant impact on the outcomes of social interactions, and the study of language use in these contexts is crucial for understanding the social dynamics at play. Overall, the study of language use in social communication is a vital field of study that has far-reaching implications for our understanding of social interactions and cultural practices. By examining the use of language in various social settings, we can gain insights into how language use shapes social relationships and identities and better understand the complex dynamics at play in social interactions.

The language used in social communication is complex and multifaceted. The use of indigenous languages is one aspect that has gained increasing attention in recent years. Its positive impact on social communication and cultural preservation makes it a valuable aspect of language use that should be preserved and promoted. Language use in social communication is a critical aspect of human interaction that deserves attention. The use of indigenous language in social communication can promote cultural inclusivity and diversity while fostering intercultural understanding. Thus, efforts should be made to preserve indigenous languages and promote their use in social communication. Furthermore, language use in social communication is a complex and dynamic process that requires careful consideration and understanding. Whether it is the language used in formal or informal settings or the use of indigenous languages, it is important to be aware of the cultural context and norms surrounding the language to effectively communicate with others.

PRESERVATION OF INDIGENOUS LANGUAGES

Language provides a specific identity to the aspects of indigeneity and is therefore inseparable from them (the primacy of language in articulating indigenous knowledge, practice, and culture). Indigenous languages capture and transmit the knowledge and wisdom of indigenous communities through stories, proverbs, folktales, myths, poetry, and songs that convey meanings about individuals, society, culture, and nature interactions (Manyike & Shava, 2019).

Academics and linguists have been debating the preservation and promotion of indigenous African languages for years. With multilingualism being a defining characteristic of the African continent, it is essential to recognize the importance of language preservation in both local and global spheres. The role of language and media in promoting indigenous languages cannot be overstated. The media has the power to shape public attitudes and perceptions toward these languages and, in turn, promote their use and development (Manyike & Shava, 2019).

The preservation of indigenous African languages is crucial in maintaining the diversity of African culture and heritage. Multilingualism is an essential part of African identity, and the preservation of indigenous languages is necessary to foster a sense of belonging and pride in African communities. In recent years, the importance of language preservation has gained recognition on a global level, and various initiatives have been implemented to preserve and promote African languages. One such initiative is the use of language and media, which has proven to be an effective tool in language preservation. By incorporating indigenous languages into various media platforms, such as television and radio broadcasts, newspapers, and magazines, African communities can feel more connected to their culture and language. Additionally, the use of language AI technology can further facilitate the preservation of indigenous African languages (Manyike & Shava, 2019). However, the preservation of indigenous languages should not be limited to media platforms alone. It is essential to create opportunities for language learning and encourage its use in daily life. Governments and educational institutions can play a significant role in language preservation by including indigenous languages in the curriculum and providing resources for language learning. In conclusion, the preservation of indigenous African languages is vital to preserving the cultural and linguistic diversity of Africa.

In today's world, where multilingualism is celebrated and acknowledged, the preservation of indigenous African languages has emerged as a pressing need. The significance of indigenous languages cannot be overstated, as they are not only integral to the cultural identity of African societies but also contribute significantly to preserving their cultural heritage (Manyike & Shava, 2019). Therefore, promoting indigenous languages has become a vital aspect of African societies. Language and media play a crucial role in creating awareness and encouraging the use of indigenous languages. The media can be a powerful tool in promoting indigenous languages by creating awareness campaigns, developing educational materials, and providing platforms for people to learn and use the language. Furthermore, media can also use the language to disseminate and exchange information, thus creating an environment that fosters multilingualism in societies. It is important to recognize the importance of multilingualism and take proactive steps toward preserving indigenous languages using media, artificial intelligence, and educational initiatives.

Language preservation can be achieved by integrating indigenous languages into the educational system, thereby creating opportunities for students to learn and use the language (Oldfield, 2022). This initiative can also help in the preservation of the language and contribute to the intellectual and cultural development of the community. Moreover, the development of language policies that prioritize the use of indigenous languages in government activities can also encourage the use of these languages. In essence, the preservation of indigenous African languages is essential in preserving cultural heritage and promoting multilingualism. Therefore, African societies must embrace and celebrate their linguistic diversity by promoting the use of indigenous languages through media, education, and language policies. This way, they can create a harmonious and inclusive society that values and recognizes the significance of linguistic diversity.

Language is a vital part of a society's cultural identity, and it is important to promote the use of indigenous languages to preserve and celebrate this identity. The preservation of multilingualism is also crucial for fostering cross-cultural communication and understanding. The media can play a significant role in the preservation of indigenous languages, by incorporating them into their programming and encouraging their use in daily communication. Efforts should be made to raise awareness and encourage the use of indigenous languages in everyday life, from education to business and social interactions. This can be achieved through language preservation campaigns, festivals, and events that celebrate the diversity of languages spoken in Africa. Furthermore, the inclusion of indigenous languages in media outlets such as television, radio, and newspapers can help to bring them to a wider audience and promote their use in daily life. Language and media play an important role in shaping public opinion and attitudes toward different cultures and communities.

Isizulu is second on the list of South African languages on Google Translate. It was added to Google Translate in 2017 at the same time IsiXhosa and Sesotho were added and all three have since been recently added to the offline version. Isizulu is the most spoken language in South Africa and is also spoken in Lesotho, Botswana, Mozambique, Malawi, and Eswatini. Hence, it was added to Google Translate. The next language on the list of South African languages on Google Translate is IsiXhosa. It was added to Google Translate at the same time Isizulu and Sesotho were added in 2017, and like the other two languages has recently been added to the offline version. IsiXhosa is a Bantu language mostly spoken in South Africa and is the second most spoken language there. Lesotho and Botswana also have Xhosa-speaking people. Sesotho was added to the list of South African languages on Google Translate while Isizulu and IsiXhosa were added. It is one of the twelve official languages in South Africa and is also an official language in Lesotho and Zimbabwe. Sesotho has been available on Google Translate since 2017 but only became available on the offline version recently. It is the seventh most spoken language in South Africa and was added to Google Translate first before Northern Sotho (Sepedi) which is the fifth most spoken language in South Africa because of its high prevalence in Lesotho and Zimbabwe (Nkoala, 2022), while Northern Sotho is only spoken in South Africa. Next on the list of South African languages on Google Translate is Sepedi or Northern Sotho. It has been recently added to Google Translate with twenty-three other languages. This recent addition happened in May 2022 (Nkoala, 2022). Last on the list of South African languages on Google Translate is Xitsonga. Xitsonga is a Nguni-Tsonga sub-language, next to IsiXhosa, Isizulu, Siswati, and IsiNdebele, though these four languages are only considered to be Nguni sub-languages. It was added to Google Translate in May 2022, along with Sepedi. The minority languages that are not included in Google are Tshivenda and IsiNdebele, apart from being official languages of the Republic of South Africa. It is unfortunate at this point to find that these two official languages are not enjoying parity of respect as other South African official languages and are still marginalized in the democratic setup.

INDIGENOUS LANGUAGES AND THE FOURTH INDUSTRIAL REVOLUTION

Language questions in South Africa remains unresolved almost three decades after democracy, with debates about mother tongue education raging without any end in sight (Lee, 2022). Against the backdrop of constraining global forces, and Africa's internal problems (wars, repression, and general economic misery), this chapter argues that African languages could be the most critical element for Africa's survival, and cultural, educational, and economic development. For this to happen, however, Africa must invest in this sector of the "cultural economy" as much as it should do in the "material economy" since both spheres are interrelated and impact each other (Negash, 2005).

The usage of digital technology in the Fourth Industrial Revolution (4IR) is a threat to the preservation of the indigenous languages of South Africa. As a result, the South African indigenous languages are among those at risk of a serious decline due to the increasing use of digital technologies. Nkoala (2022) estimates that only 5 percent of the world's languages are likely to survive online usage. South African universities, as the hub of knowledge generation, have an essential role in ensuring this doesn't happen. When democracy came into place in South Africa in 1994, multilingualism was seen as imperative to ensure that all the country's twelve official languages were esteemed and promoted (Nkoala (2022). Universities could play a role in the preservation of indigenous languages in high-status functions like teaching, learning, and research. The adoption of remote (online) education during the height of the COVID-19 pandemic in 2020 and 2021 widened the situation further since English is the dominant language in online engagement in the South African language context.

The latest report on the investigation conducted by the Commission for the Preservation for the Rights of Cultural, Religious and Linguistic Communities (CRL Rights Commission) on marginalized languages and the need to elevate them revealed that indigenous languages are not enjoying parity in the South African departments. The usage of indigenous languages, especially in government departments, is still not equitable after twenty-seven years since SA declared them as official languages, hence English is still the dominant language (Bambalele, 2023). The findings of the report show that even though government departments have adopted two or three official languages as per the Language Act, English was still predominantly used at the expense of other languages. According to Bambalele (2023), the investigation in the report found that the obstacles for all official languages to enjoy parity of esteem are caused by a lack of budget and skilled personnel. In its recommendation, the CRL Right Commission highlighted that all government departments, enterprises, and entities should establish functional language service centers. It further called on the Department of Higher Education to identify a pool of teachers who will teach mathematics, science, and technology in their mother tongue. The usage of indigenous languages in government departments and education could be the right direction for the preservation of these languages.

Makananise, Malatji, and Madima (2023) concur that indigenous languages are important to media users to an extent that whether through analogue or digital, they cannot successfully transmit information or messages to receivers, audiences, or consumers without using a specific language that is understood and comprehended by the audience. Therefore, the continuous use of indigenous languages in the 4IR could not be undermined but rather be incorporated into the mainstream of social media communication. The question that needs to be addressed is "How can indigenous languages be utilized as the main languages of communication in social media?" There are several issues and measures to be put in place to address the above question. The most crucial one is to encourage youth who are the main users of social media to advance the use of indigenous languages for communication purposes. But how can they be encouraged to use languages that are not used as media of instruction in their education? This is one of the negative aspects that affect the promotion of indigenous languages in South Africa. These are languages that are used in low-level functions, unlike English, which is dominant and used in high-level functions.

CONCLUSION

The preservation of South African indigenous languages is twofold and most challenging. There is a school of thought that indigenous languages should be promoted and preserved for fear of their becoming extinct. In reality, indigenous languages are not used in higher functions like government, education, science, and technology. Another school of thought is that English should continue to be used as the language of higher functions since it is a neutral, global language. Linguists have written widely about the preservation of indigenous languages but their words seem to be falling on deaf ears since there is no political will on the side of the politicians on this matter. Since the adoption of the South African Constitution of 1996, little has been done toward the preservation of the indigenous languages. These languages are seen by some politicians as a way of promoting divisions among the ethnic groups that have been sown by the colonial mechanism and Apartheid regime. Instead of investing in and using their linguistic, cultural, and human potential, African governments and the elite continue to channel away their resources and energies into learning "imperial" languages that are used by a tiny minority of the population (Negash, 2005).

On the other hand, indigenous languages are seen as not suitable enough to perform high functions in government, education, judiciary, economics, science, and technology. Their preservation in the 4IR is strongly threatened by digital technology which is widely dominated by English terminologies. Some scholars believe that we should embrace the use of English hence using indigenous languages on a local basis for lower functions like churches, funerals, traditional functions, and social gatherings like tribal meetings and family meetings. However, English usage is advancing to the lower functions as well. Churches are now using English for sermons with the assistance of interpreters, even though there may not be any English-speaking people in their congregations. The same applies in local funerals, where programs will be written in English whereas most people are local language speakers. Some members of the bereaved family, especially children of the diseased, deliver their speeches in English as a sign that they are fluent in it.

Having said all that, we still must find a way of preserving our indigenous languages since they are central to the identity of indigenous peoples, the preservation of cultures, and the expression of self-determination. Scholars should infuse the use of these languages into digital technology. According to the United Nations Forum on Indigenous Issues, the threat to indigenous languages is the direct consequences of colonialism and social practices that resulted in the decimation of indigenous peoples, their cultures, and languages. It further states that through policies of assimilation, dispassion of lands, discriminatory laws, and actions, indigenous languages in all regions face the threat of extinction further exacerbated by globalization. Article 13 of the United Nations Declaration of the Rights of Indigenous Peoples states that indigenous peoples have the right to revitalize, use, develop, and transmit to future generations their languages, oral traditions, writing systems, and literature. Furthermore, it provides that states shall take effective measures to protect this right, including through interpretation in political, legal, and administrative proceedings (UN Forum of Indigenous Issues, n.d.).

In 2007, two researchers in Tanzania investigated the differences between teaching a topic in English and then in Kiswahili. The researchers gathered the data using both qualitative and quantitative methods (Mberia, 2015). The researchers found out that, in every case, the students taught the same topic by the same teacher, performed better when the teaching was conducted in Kiswahili than in English or when code-switching was used. The research demonstrated that students learn better when they are taught in a language, they are very familiar with (Mberia, 2015). Although the Tanzanian experiment involved secondary school students, the results have implications for the use of mother tongues as media of instruction at the lower levels of formal education (Mberia, 2015). The results showed that an indigenous language does not impede learning. On the contrary, mother tongues facilitate understanding of the subjects being taught. This advantage to the learner is even more pronounced among younger learners than among the secondary school students used in the Tanzanian experiment. Digital technology has been used in education since the outbreak of COVID-19. However, digital technology is dominated by the English language at the expense of indigenous African languages. There is a serious need to consider the use of indigenous languages in schools and institutions of higher learning. This could pave the way for the use of indigenous languages in social media communication.

In response to the indigenous language crisis, the UN Permanent Forum on Indigenous Issues has consistently drawn attention to the threats against the indigenous languages and pushed for actions to promote and preserve them. As early as 2003, the UN Permanent Forum on Indigenous Issues recommended that governments introduce indigenous languages in public administration in indigenous territories, where feasible. In 2005, the Permanent Forum on Indigenous Issues recommended that the UN country offices make efforts to disseminate their published activities in indigenous languages. Over the years, the Permanent Forum on Indigenous Issues also recommended that states support the creation of indigenous language cultural studies centers in universities, and encouraged the United Nations Educational, Scientific and Cultural Organization (UNESCO) to support such initiatives. Furthermore, the 2030 Agenda for Sustainable Development, adopted by the General Assembly in 2015, aims to ensure equal access for indigenous peoples to all levels of education and vocational training under Sustainable Development Goals Target 4.5. The use of indigenous languages in education and training has been strongly put forth as an approach to meet the target.

REFERENCES

Baldauf Jr., R. B., & Kaplan, R. B. (2006). Language policy and planning in Botswana, Malawi, Mozambique and South Africa: Some common issues. Accessed April 30, 2007. eprint.uq.edu.au/archive/00002935/01/AFRICA_1_LPPAfrica.pdf.

Bambalele, P. (2023). Indigenous languages not enjoying parity at state departments. Sowetan Live, May 24, 2023.

Burnaby, B., & Reyhner, J. (2002). *Indigenous languages across the community.* Flagstaff: Northern Arizona University.

Cummins, J. (1995). *Negotiating identities: Education for empowerment in a diverse society.* Los Angeles, CA: Association for Bilingual Education.

Ebadi, B. (2019). Technology alone can't preserve endangered languages. Multimedia. Centre for International Governance Innovation.

Esteron, M. A. S. (2021). Equity in online learning amidst pandemic in the Philippines. *International Journal of English and Social Sciences, 6*(5), 139–151. DOI. 10.22161/ijels.65-23.

Fereira, P. (1972). *Pedagogy of the oppressed.* Harmondsworth: Penguin.

Hovens, M. (2003). Bilingual education in West Africa: Does it work? Accessed March 18, 2023. www.multilingual-matters.net.

Jenkins, J. (1991). R*ethinking history.* London: Routledge Publishers.

Ke Yu., and Dumisa, S. (2015). Community support: The missing link in Indigenous language preservation in South Africa? *A Journal for Language Learning, 31*(1), 60–73.

Khan, M. (2009). Indigenous languages and Africa's development dilemma. *Development in Practice,* 24, 764–776.

Lee, N. (2022). Mother tongue education will produce more literate and intelligent pupils. Sowetan Live, November 16, 2022.

Madima, S. E, Makananise, F. O., & Malatji, E. (2023). Indigenous language newspaper and the deepening of South African democracy. In Abiodun Salawu, Tshepang Bright Molale, Enrique Uribe-Jongbloed, & Mohammad Sahid Ullah (Eds.), *Indigenous language for development communication in the global south* (pp. 191–210). *Lanham, MD*: Lexington Books.

Makalela, L. (2020). African Languages for Sustainable Development. Wits. JHB.

Makananise, F. O., Malatji, E. J., & Madima, S. E. (2023). Indigenous languages, digital media, and the COVID-19 pandemic in the global south: A south African discourse. In Abiodun Salawu, Tshepang Bright Molale, Enrique Uribe-Jongbloed, & Mohammad Sahid Ullah (Eds.), *Indigenous language for for social change communication in the global south* (pp. 75–92). *Lanham, MD*: Lexington Books.

Manyike, V., & Shava, S. (2019). The decolonial role of African indigenous languages and indigenous knowledges in the formal education process. *Indinga African Journal of Indigenous Knowledge Systems, 17(1),* 36–52.

May, S. (2003). "Misconceiving Minority Language Rights: Implications for Liberal Political Theory." In Will Kymlicka & Alan Patten (Eds.), *Language rights and political theory* (pp. 123–168). Oxford: Oxford University Press.

Mberia, K. (2015). The place of Indigenous languages in African development. *International Journal of Languages in African Development, 2(*5), 52–60.

Mowarin, M., & E. Tonukari, E. U. (2010). Language deficit in English and lack of creative education impediments to Nigeria's breakthrough into the knowledge era. *Educational Research and Reviews, 5*(6), 303–308.

Negash, G. (2005). Globalization and the role of African languages for development. *Conference Paper: "Language Communities or Cultural Empires,"* February 9–11, 2005, UC Berkeley.

Nkoala, S. (2022). COVID was a setback for Indigenous languages: South African lecturers on what went wrong. Sowetan Live, September 4, 2022.

Oldfield, J. (2022). Racing neoliberalism and remote indigenous education in the northern territory of Australia: A critical analysis of contemporary Indigenous education language police And practice. *Language And Intercultural Communication, 22*(6), 694–708.

Schonfeld, E. (2010). Languages of the universal: Levinas' (scandalous) doctrine of literature. In Michael, L. & Morgan (Eds.), *The Oxford Handbook of* Levinas (pp. 77–92). Oxford: Oxford University Press.

Sharma, U. (2013). Reforming teacher education for inclusion in developing countries. *Asian Journal of Inclusive Education, 1*(1), 3–16. January 2013

The United Nations Permanent Forum on Indigenous Issues (n.d). United Nations Department of Public Information. UN.ORG/INDIGENOUS.

UNESCO Atlas of the World's Language in Danger. https://unescodoc.unesco.org.

United Nations Forum of Indigenous Issues (n.d.). https://www.un.org.

Waldron, J. 2019. Homelessness and the issue of freedom. *Journal of Constitutional Law,* 1, 27–50.

Watson, J. (2019). The rise and decline of integrity. *Short Version for Conference on Dworkins Later Work Still Rough.* New York University School of Law.

Webb, V. (2013). African languages in post-1994 education in South Africa: Our own Titanic? *Southern African Linguistic and Applied Language Studies,* 31(2), 173–184.

Wijarnako, B., Andriani, A., & Ernawati, A. (2023). Transcendental communication in Indigenous peoples, case study of Kuncen's transcendental communication function with Banokeling spirits for Banokeling Indigenous communities. *Proceedings Series on Social Sciences & Humanities, 8,* 24–33.

Yuka, N. C., & Omoregbe, E. M. (2010). The internal structure of the Edo Verb. *California Linguistic Notes* XXXV (2 spring), 1–19.

Chapter 4

Computational Linguistics and Indigenous Languages

WhatsApp Emoji Use and the Reclamation of Shona and Ndebele Language and Culture

Jennings Joy Chibike

WhatsApp is a popular internet, computer, and smartphone-anchored instant messaging platform. It permits people to communicate through various forms of digital language such as texts, audio, pictures, videos, calls, stickers, and emojis. Particular attention in this chapter is given to WhatsApp emoji use and interpretation in indigenous languages such as Shona and isiNdebele. Emojis are used in casual exchanges between WhatsApp users, and they are vital in enhancing the authors' intended meaning (Hurlburt, 2018), thus they provide a conduit for clear communication. The vitality of emojis in conversation has led to the growth of scholarship in the areas of emoji and communication. Ayan (2020) studied the role of emojis and emoticons as persuasive tools in WhatsApp communication. Swartz (2020), through Twitter emojis, interrogated symbolic representations of behaviour and identity on social media. Koch et al. (2021) examined the use of emoticons and emojis on social media to expose the identity of users in terms of their gender and age. Closely related to this study is Mgogo and Sinoyolo's (2023) scrutiny of the use of Facebook emojis to create new meanings in the African indigenous language, isiXhosa. This brief overview of the literature exposes mature scholarship with respect to emoji use, indigenous languages, and identity articulations. However, there is a dearth of scholarship on how WhatsApp emojis are important in the preservation of Shona and isiNdebele languages

96 *Jennings Joy Chibike*

and culture and how their use aids in mapping out identity. Therefore, this study seizes the opportunity to fill this void through examining how the use, interpretation, and response to WhatsApp emojis in indigenous Shona and isiNdebele when discussing marriage helps in the preservation of the two languages which have been flung down the order of languages in favour of English in contemporary Zimbabwe. Also, the study grapples with how the use, interpretation, and response to the emojis in Shona and isiNdebele is imperative in the imagination of the user's identity and culture. This chapter is important in bringing forth the significance of computational linguistics in preserving indigenous languages, cultures, and identities. Moreover, this chapter is a contribution to the literature on the intersection of the Fourth Industrial Revolution, technocratic symbols, African indigenous languages, and communication—an area which has not been widely explored.

CONTEXT OF THE CHAPTER

The colonial conquest of Africa by the West led to the dehumanization and othering of residents of the Global South. This conquest consequently eradicated the indigenous ways of life culturally, socially, politically, and economically. Of great concern in this chapter is the linguicide and culturecides in Africa spearheaded by colonialists. African languages were rendered barbaric, economically, and politically invalid in favor of English, Portuguese, and French which were dubbed superior and valuable. The British, who colonized Zimbabwe, established English as the supreme and intelligible language in the country. This imposition of English in Zimbabwe led to the subjugation of local official languages such as Shona, isiNdebele, Kalanga, Tonga, Venda, Xhosa, Nambya, and Chewa among others and consequently, local memory, history, culture, and traditions were decapitated (Sibanda, 2019). This has made natives subalterns in their land as their indigenous languages which cascade their humanity and being have been muted. In postcolonial Zimbabwe linguicides have continued to take a toll on indigenous languages under the notion of modernity. Education systems in Zimbabwe have embraced English as the language of instruction, thus rendering local languages ineffective in conveying knowledge in the process of privileging Western histories, identities, and customs (Kubota, 2020). This has seen children being socialized to speak in English in their homes in the process rubbishing proficiency in already endangered local languages and erasing local culture and history. Bearing in mind that this is a media-related chapter, in the media terrain, cultural artifacts are now largely produced in English, a language seen as having economic value (Mpofu, 2013). This exhibits the colonial and postcolonial linguistic challenges that Zimbabwe faces which sees the peripherization and othering of indigenous languages. Against this milieu, this chapter aims to examine the potential of computational linguistics in preserving and resuscitating local languages, cultures, and identities. To do this, it interrogates how WhatsApp users use, interpret, and appropriate meaning in dominant Zimbabwean indigenous languages Shona and Ndebele when discussing important ceremonies, specifically marriage. Ultimately, this chapter progresses literature on the role of technocratic symbols in particular WhatsApp emojis in preserving indigenous languages, culture, and identity in the Fourth Industrial Revolution.

Understanding Emojis

Shigetaka Kurita of Japan's NTT Docomo telecom carrier company is believed to have first introduced emojis in the early 1990s to mobile phones in a bid to help elaborate messaging communication in a playful manner (Moschin, 2016). Alshenqeeti (2016) draws the similarity of current emojis to the pictures drawn by people who lived in past centuries. In this regard, Alshenqeeti (2016:59) posits that there is a relationship between current emojis, and pictures drawn by African cavemen as well as the cuneiform writing system used by the Sumerians in 3300 BC. Hence emojis can be described as forms of computational linguistics in a pictorial form that descend from past non-digitized communications systems. This certainly shows the universality of emojis in the communication processes, making them a good unit of analysis which prompted the researcher to examine how their use and interpretation in African indigenous languages help preserve Shona and isiNdebele and how this offers cues to the identity of users. Charles Darwin stated that facial gestures are universally understood (Alshenqeeti, 2016), hence emojis are also universally understood as they have representations of various facial expressions and objects that transcend geographic, economic, political, social, and cultural borders. Smartphone manufacturing companies have embraced these universal forms of communication and have made it possible for smartphone users to use emojis on their keyboards. This has also facilitated the development of social media applications such as WhatsApp, LinkedIn, Facebook, and Instagram, among others, that embrace a communicative process anchored on the use of emojis. On WhatsApp, there are various types of emojis from those that show the faces and gestures of humans, and represent animals, sports, cars, kitchen utensils, clothes, and flags among others.

LITERATURE REVIEW

Computational Linguistics: Emoji Use and Identity

Computational language is hybrid and does not conform to the offline language systems and rules as it uses a mixture of texts that are not governed by spelling and grammatical rules, audio, videos, pictures, and emojis (Hinnenkamp, 2008), which are the focus of this chapter. Weber (2013) observes that emoji use is not fixed as emojis are used based on the context of the conversation and not on what they mean. Therefore, the essence of this chapter is to examine the use and interpretation of emojis in Shona and isiNdebele by users discussing marriage. The aim here is not to examine the Eurocentric meanings (which are seen as the correct meanings) appropriated to the emojis but the appropriation of meaning to emojis in an African context. Accordingly, the chapter focuses on the epistemically disobedient use and interpretation of emojis in the discussion of African marriage practice and how it aids the reclamation of indigenous language and culture, and offers cues to identity. Emojis are graphical computational symbols that allow meaning to be appropriated to them and play an integral role in the communication process in the digital era where instant messaging is prevalent (Bai et al., 2019). According to Volkel et al. (2019), emojis are important in that they help the communicator communicate issues, thoughts, and emotions that are beyond the confines of written and spoken words. This exhibits the fact that emojis are an important symbolic language which acts as a panacea to unclear and uncomprehensive communication among different parties.

Emojis can be viewed as polysemic meaning they carry varying meanings and can be used in different contexts (Donato and Paggio, 2017). For example, a fire emoji can represent something hot, something dangerous, and in some instances, something likeable and extraordinary. In light of this, Lu et al. (2016) state that emoji use is culturally located. Drawing from this, the chapter examines how emojis are used and interpreted in Shona and isiNdebele, how this is integral in the salvaging of the two languages, and how it offers clues to the identity and culture of users. Shardlow et al. (2022) argue that the use of emojis stems from the desire to clarify communication. Thus, the use of emojis in communication is said to be an act of performance that scholars must pay attention to (Felbo et al., 2017). Therefore, this chapter interrogates the intersection of computational linguistics, African languages, and identity formation. This is important because it extends the scanty literature on how indigenous languages can be preserved through digital technology in the Fourth Industrial Revolution.

Emojis are used to enhance popular and celebrity culture. Stark and Crawford (2015:4) give examples of singers Katy Perry's *Roar* and Beyoncé's

Drunk in Love emoji videos where emojis were used to increase pleasure in the audiences. Consequently, the use of emojis in popular culture is now seen as an extension of fiction as emojis are used to create narratives that are enjoyed by audiences. It then becomes fascinating to examine the potential of the consumption and use of computer-generated fiction in the preservation of Shona and isiNdebele. Research suggests that the use of emojis leaves cues to the identity of users (Jones et al., 2020) about age and gender among other identity variables. According to Olesziewicz et al. (2017) younger users of social media use more emojis than the elderly. This shows that the use of social media emojis gives identity cues about the ages of users. However, in Switzerland, Siebenhaar's (2018) examination of emoji use did not provide cues to the age of users as such concluded that emoji use is not in any way related to the age of users.

Generally, when it comes to gender, it is widely believed that women express themselves more than men, hence, they use more emojis. Through analysis of Facebook, WhatsApp, and internet-based chatrooms, scholars Perez-Sabata (2019), Olesziewicz et al. (2017), and Fullwood et al. (2013) argue that there are significant disparities in the use of emojis about gender as females used more emojis and emoticons than males. This shows that computational linguistics is vital in identity constructions and imagination. In 2016 skin tones were added to emojis. Against this milieu, Barbierri and Camacho-Collados (2018) observed that users were prone to using emojis that had similar skin color to their own. This exhibits that emojis play an integral role in users' identity imaginations based on their skin color.

With regard to emoji use and identity, Mgogo and Sinoyolo (2023) argue that African indigenous languages and cultures are preserved using Facebook emojis. In their seminal work, they posit that users of Facebook emojis in some sections of South Africa interpreted emojis in the Xhosa language. In the process, they used emojis to express Xhosa proverbs and expressions. This shows that indigenous languages were preserved and enhanced through computational language in the Fourth Industrial Revolution. Continuing Mgogo and Sinoyolo's (2023) important work anchored on discourse analysis, this chapter takes a detour and employs digital ethnography and in-depth interviews to examine how the use and interpretation of WhatsApp emojis during a marriage discussion enhances the preservation of isiNdebele and Shona languages in Zimbabwe. The chapter further examines how meaning appropriated to these emojis offers cues to the user's identity. The uniqueness of this study lies in that, first, it focuses on the reclamation of isiNdebele and Shona languages that have not been studied before. Second, it focuses on the decolonial reading of the emojis used in discussing marriage and how this decolonial reading is vital in the preservation of indigenous languages and offering cues to the identity and culture of the users, a research focus which Mpofu et al. (2023) argue has not been interrogated.

THEORETICAL FRAMEWORK

Symbolic Interactionism

This chapter is ingrained within the symbolic interactionism theory which was propounded and George Herbert Mead and developed by Blumer. Its mainstay is that symbols in social interactions shape the social identity, attitude, and behavior of a particular social group (Aksan et al., 2009; Stets and Burke, 2000). Drawing from this, the chapter believes that the use and interpretation of computer-generated communication and symbols such as WhatsApp emojis is an oasis that aids the understanding of the users' social identity and the preservation of language and culture.

According to Korgen and White (2008) and Ashworth (2000), symbols are integral in the communication process and the meaning-making process, thus they help condition the mind to understand communication processes. In the same vein, Swartz (2020) posits that symbolic interactionalism encapsulates how forms of nonverbal communication such as symbols are attributed with a value that enables them to be used in a meaningful conversation. Consequently, meaning is at the epicenter of symbolic interactionism as it allows discussants to understand each other and the symbols used (Tezcan, 2005). Therefore, the chapter aims to examine how WhatsApp users use, interpret, and respond to emojis in African indigenous languages and this stems from the assumption that users give meaning to emojis. Further, it goes on to examine how their responses and interpretations offer cues to their identity and culture.

Critics of this theory question the authenticity of meanings given to symbols such as emojis and whether this leads to a truthful cue to society's identity. In response, this chapter borrows the lenses of Thomas and Thomas (1928), who argues that the key issues are not the accuracy of the interpretation and use of symbols in communication. Berg (2000) corroborates this by stating that it is integral to understand that symbols are polysemic and meaning is socially located. Hence this chapter is not concerned with the accuracy of meaning appropriated to emojis, but it is concerned with the actual meaning, interpretation, and use regardless of accuracy. Symbolic interactionism is important in this chapter because it provides a theoretical standpoint enabling the examination of the appropriation of meaning, consumption, and use of technocratic language, in particular WhatsApp emojis by users.

Decolonial Perspectives on Language

Decoloniality is a concept that questions European power over the globe as first coined by twentieth-century Latin philosopher Anibal Quijano (Salgado et al., 2021). It entails the act of slamming Eurocentric outlooks and conceptualization of the social world to embrace the Global South's epistemologies in the fabrication of facts and sustenance of power (Willems, 2014). Against the milieu that Zimbabwe is a product of coloniality, there is a need for the shaking off of colonial shackles to resuscitate vanquished local knowledges and culture. Language is in this instance a valuable tool for liberation (Sibanda, 2021). Meighan (2022) illustrates the need for the robust use of indigenous languages which are free from imperial undertones to communicate the histories, identity, and culture of the peripherized Global South. In the same vein, McIvor and McCarty (2017) argue that the use of endangered indigenous languages is paramount in the epistemic survival of multiculturalism and multilingualism which were eradicated by the adoption of English as the universal language. Therefore, challenging linguistic imperialism through the adoption of African indigenous languages helps cement the humanness of Africans, their identity, and culture and preserve their conquered languages. Thus, adopting a decolonial trajectory in this chapter is essential in examining decolonial reading, use, and interpretation of WhatsApp emojis in Shona and Ndebele when discussing marriage discourses. Consequently, the chapter interrogates how this reading, interpretation, and use of emojis aid in the imagination of the identity and culture of WhatsApp users.

METHODOLOGY

This qualitative chapter is poised to examine how WhatsApp users use, interpret, and respond to emojis in indigenous languages Shona and Ndebele when discussing marriage cultural practices and how this offers clues about their identity and culture. The qualitative approach according to Johnson and Onwuegbuzie (2004) cited in Chibike (2023) entails the examination of social meaning through individuals' interaction with the world. Therefore, this approach is suitable for this study as it seeks to examine how individuals interact with computational linguistics in particular WhatsApp emojis. Empirical data were gathered through digital ethnography and in-depth interviews. Digital ethnography was conducted in a purposively selected WhatsApp group which the researcher is part of. Digital ethnography entails the study of the social world by examining the lived experiences of people in virtual spaces (Underberg and Zorn, 2013:10). Therefore, ethnography was vital in this study as it allowed the researcher to understand how people appropriate meaning to WhatsApp emojis through examining their emoji centered communications. The researcher followed conversations in the group from February 4, 2023, till February 10, 2023, a period where marriage conversations were prevalent. Mpofu et al. (2023) underscore that there is little research on indigenous language media based on ethnographies. Accordingly, the chapter grabs the opportunity to fill this glaring gap in the study of indigenous language media by employing digital ethnography. The WhatsApp group where digital ethnography was done was selected because it is made up of individuals representing diverse backgrounds, identities, and cultures. What is key here is that these different people respond to emojis in either Ndebele or Shona, the two languages that this study focuses on. Therefore, this discursive space (WhatsApp group) is important in that it helps extract knowledge on how diverse people use, interpret, and respond to emojis in Shona and isiNdebele and how this aids in the imagination of their native identity and culture.

The researcher also conducted in-depth interviews with twelve purposively selected group members resident in Bulawayo from a total of thirty-nine participants. According to Dworkin (2012), it is accepted that five to fifty participants take part in in-depth interviews for academic purposes. It is for those reasons that the researcher opted for twelve participants. The twelve participants were purposively selected because they participated a lot in the group and used a lot of emojis and local languages in their communication. In this chapter, their identities were not revealed particularly their responses. Data were analyzed through thematic analysis anchored on two themes that are related to the objectives of the study. The themes are:

- Users' interpretations of WhatsApp emojis in the isiNdebele and Shona languages.
- WhatsApp emoji use and interpretation: cues to identity.

DISCUSSIONS AND ANALYSIS OF FINDINGS

Overview of the Findings

Empirical data collected through digital ethnography and in-depth interviews hold that users use their semiotic intelligence in using and interpreting WhatsApp emojis in local Shona and isiNdebele languages. Therefore, the findings point to the fact that emojis are interpreted differently in local languages from Eurocentric perspectives in the process of challenging the colonial meaning appropriated to them. Consequently, WhatsApp emojis have been used as a vital tool against cololingualism aiding the reclamation

Computational Linguistics and Indigenous Languages

of African indigenous languages. Gathered data also suggest that the use and interpretation of WhatsApp emojis offer a glimpse into the identity and culture of users thus their gender, skin color, ethnicity, clan, and behavior were fleshed out. This speaks to the fact that emoji use, and interpretation help in the unmasking of African identity and culture. The next section discusses and analyses the findings in detail.

Users' Interpretations of WhatsApp Emojis in isiNdebele and Shona Languages

The researcher observed that in some conversations WhatsApp emojis were interpreted and responded to in indigenous languages. The interpretations and appropriation of meaning in Shona and Ndebele were vital in the preservation of both Ndebele and Shona language and culture. For example, cattle emojis were interpreted in the context of lobola (paying of bride price). One user shared the emoji of the cattle and respondents responded to it with a congratulatory message (Amhlophe in Ndebele and Makorokoto in Shona). Corroborating this was Interviewee 6 who stated that in the Ndebele language, the sharing of cattle emoji is simply interpreted as *inkomo zamalobolo sezingenile ekhaya* (bride price has been paid). This shows that the cattle emoji has been interpreted as a symbol of marriage and this avows Weber's (2013) argument that the use of emojis is not based on their actual meaning but on the context they are located in during a conversation. This shows that emojis have become an avenue for the preservation of native languages relating to the cultural practice of African marriage. Consequently, they have become instrumental in the preservation of African cultural practices such as *lobola*, the paying of bride price in the form of cattle. This therefore shows that decolonial reading of computational linguistics is a breeding ground for African indigenous languages and epistemologies.

The researcher observed that in responding to the cattle emojis group members added ring emojis with the question *takutomirira muchato* meaning we are now waiting for the wedding in Shona language. This fully exhibits that a ring emoji has been interpreted in Shona as a wedding. One participant responded *that' indandatho wena* (take the ring) in Ndebele. Though the exchange of rings is a Western practice, the fact that a ring is interpreted in indigenous languages as a wedding shows that the meaning appropriated to emojis is culturally located (Lu et al., 2016), bearing in mind that we are enveloped in cultural imperialism which sees local people interacting with Western practices and symbols such as wedding rings. Thus, after the payment of bride price (cattle emoji), a couple is expected to wed (ring emoji). Therefore, the appropriation of indigenous meaning in indigenous language explicitly shows the importance of Shona and Ndebele in upholding indigenous knowledge systems. This shows that the reading of emojis in indigenous languages consequently resonates with decolonial overtones which in turn destabilizes the knowledge creation and transmission systems favoring the Global North.

The conversation goes on to be punctuated with emojis of animals precisely an elephant and a lion.

One user writes *maita mhukahuru* (you have done well large animal) and inserts an elephant emoji together with an emoji of a black man wearing a crown while another one says *wenze kahle MaSibanda* (well-done lioness) and inserts a lion emoji and that of a black woman wearing a crown. Commenting on this is interviewee 3 who stated that the elephant emoji was interpreted in Shona as *Nzou* (*mhukahuru* meaning large animal) while the lion was interpreted in Ndebele as *Isilwane* (lion) and these emojis represented the totems of those who were about to wed. The use of these animal emojis was not only to clarify communication as argued by Shardlow et al. (2022) on the totems of the couple, but also to increase the pleasure of texts as using them enticed the WhatsApp audiences. Therefore, in line with the preservation of indigenous languages, animal emojis are being interpreted in a way that helps one to learn animal names in indigenous languages. Thus, the interpretation of animal emojis in indigenous languages becomes a site of learning for those who do not know or would have potentially forgotten animal names in indigenous languages. This is crucial to the youths who did not grow up in circumstances that allow them to interact and understand wild animals unlike the elderly who were raised in rural areas where there is constant interaction with wild animals. Additionally, they convey the importance of totemism in the African culture particularly when giving praise to people who will have been perceived to have done well.

Interestingly, the couple responded to the messages in the native Ndebele and Shona languages respectively saying *ngiyabonga* (thank you) or *tinoteda* (we thank you) coupled with emojis of a red heart, hands clasped together and clapping hands. In response to the red heart, some messages read *lathi siyakuthanda* (we love you too) while to the clapping hands others responded again, with clapping hands. This shows that a red heart is interpreted in the context of love (*uthando*) by WhatsApp users. While upon further inquiry the clapping of hands shows gratitude and respect. In light of this, one participant said: "The clapping of hands is a gesture that shows appreciation, respect and sometimes greeting, kuombera in the Shona culture."

This, therefore, shows that Shona terms such as *kuombera* (clapping) are being preserved and reinvigorated through the use of computational linguistics. Also, the medieval practice of clapping as a sign of appreciation is being reinvigorated through emojis. This ably demonstrates that emojis are vital in resuscitating the endangered African indigenous languages and culture. These

Computational Linguistics and Indigenous Languages   105

findings speak to Swartz's (2020) argument that symbols are appropriated with meaning that allows their use in meaningful conversations in the sense that the red heart and clasped hands emoji are meaningless in their form but WhatsApp users have conditioned their minds and appropriated meaning to them and as such they are interpreted in indigenous languages as love and thankful gestures. This conditioning of the mind and appropriation of meaning is vital in the resurrection of indigenous Shona and Ndebele languages.

One participant in the group asks *kanti kuhamnjwanini e* (when are we going . . .) and inserts an emoji of a thatched round clay house. The emoji is interpreted as *ekhaya* (rural home) in Ndebele language. One user responded with a bow and arrow emoji coupled with a fire emoji and an emoji of a hen and that of meat. In response, another participant wrote *yeye vele inyama siyayifuna* (yes, we want to eat meat). Interviewee 2 stated that the use of a bow and arrow, fire, hen, and cattle emojis means *ukuzingela lokosa kumbe ukupheka inyama* (hunting and cooking the meat). This, therefore, shows that the act of hunting can be depicted in emojis and be interpreted in the indigenous Ndebele language. In continuation of a seemingly celebratory mood, others respond with emojis of watermelons and coconut drinks. One participant quickly responds to the coconut drink *mele sibuhlabe* (we must drink it!). The researcher came to a realization that the coconut drink emoji is interpreted as *umqombothi* (traditional beer). The researcher noted that the champagne emoji was also interpreted as alcohol by some of the participants instead of the coconut drink emoji; they preferred the champagne emoji. The analysis of the use of these emojis brings one to understand the notion that emoji use in the communicative process is an act of performance by Felbo et al. (2017). The use and interpretation of the emojis in this scenario help in the construction of fiction representing the festivities that are associated with weddings. As such, the communicative process in this instance is overloaded with pleaser undertones which excites audiences in the process of promoting indigenous languages and cultures. Therefore, the interpretation and use of emojis in indigenous languages should be done in the context of popular culture and pleasure to entice people in the Fourth Industrial Revolution phase to adopt indigenous languages in the process of immortalizing them.

One participant states that *inindongoda kuzo* (I just want to . . .) then inserts an emoji of a boy dancing. While another participant added an emoji of music notes and a dancing girl. Participant 7 adds *sizagiya*! (we shall dance). Another participant added an emoji of an African drum. Participant 9 sends an emoji of a computer and a dustbin and adds *basa totopedza nhasi*! (we are ending work today). The researcher discovered that the African drum coupled with a music note and a dancing girl is interpreted as a language purporting wedding festivity characterized by music and dance. Thus, the decolonial readings that are parallel to Eurocentric ones of technocratic languages are vital in the preservation of indigenous languages, culture, and identity in the realm of music and merry-making. Given that emojis are interpreted and responded to in indigenous languages and the process of curating indigenous cultural practices at the same time aiding epistemic unlearning the next section explores how this interpretation and use is useful in the imagination of the identity of the users.

WhatsApp Emoji Use and Interpretation: Cues to Identity

Having discussed how WhatsApp users appropriate meaning to emojis in Shona and Ndebele language, this section dwells on how their appropriation of meaning offers cues to their identity. Emojis are essential in identifying one in terms of gender. This is evidenced using an emoji of a male wearing a crown to represent the groom and a female wearing a crown to represent the bride. Therefore, the use of computational linguistics offers glimpses into the identity of users concerning their gender. This argument extends that of Perez-Sabata (2019), Olesziewicz et al., (2017) and Fullwood et al. (2013), whose conclusions on the identification of WhatsApp user's gender based on their use of emojis are entrenched in the frequency of their use and argue that females use more emojis than males. In this chapter, the argument that emojis reveal the gender of the user is based on the actual selection and use of emojis. Females are referred to in reference to female-faced emojis while males are referred to in reference to male-faced emojis. Therefore, emojis should be treated as resources that are vital indicators of being.

In the indigenous African culture, totems are vital in the identification of a people precisely about their behavior, temper, and mannerisms (Mabvurira et al., 2021). The groom was assigned the *Nzou* totem using the elephant emoji and the bride was assigned the *Shumba* totem through the use of emoji. First, the totems help in the imagination of the concerned parties' surnames as some people have surnames which are closely concomitant to their totems. For example, those with a *Ndlovu* or *Zhou* surname have *Nzou* or *Ndlovu* totem and are referred to as elephants. Elephants are known to be steady big animals and as such people with such totems are believed to be calm and collected but potentially powerful and dangerous, while those with lion totems are viewed as proud and who do not shy from showing off their strength and the status that comes with it. These findings dovetail with Aksan et al. (2009) and Stets and Burke's (2000) arguments that symbols play an integral role in understanding the attitudes and behaviors of a people. Therefore, the importance of this chapter is that it is vital in showing how computational linguistics is integral in the erasure of flawed inscriptions of colonial identity for native identity through totems.

Computational Linguistics and Indigenous Languages 107

Ethnicity is vital in the identity of people in poly-racial and multiethnic societies like Zimbabwe. The language used in response to the emoji offers clues to the identity of the participant. Those who responded in the Shona language are likely to be from the Shona ethnic group while those who responded in isiNdebele largely identify as Ndebele people. However, to conclude participants' ethnicity through language is rather reductionist, thus the chapter extends this argument by looking at the gestures they used in the conversations. Those who clapped hands as a way of celebration and showing appreciation coupled with their use of the Shona language are therefore Shonas. This is because, in the physical world, Shonas clap whenever they are showing respect or appreciation. This therefore shows that the plurilogic and decolonial reading of emojis expressing gestures and the language used help in identifying a people (Jones et al., 2020). Consequently, the use, interpretation, and response to WhatsApp emojis in Shona and isiNdebele are integral in rubbishing colonial illusions of Eurocentric identities perversely glued on Africans.

WhatsApp emoji use proved vital in exposing the skin color of the couple. The mere fact that the users opted for brown-skinned showed that the people being talked about were brown-skinned. This ably demonstrates that the choice of emojis used is essential in giving cues to the identity of a person who is being talked about. Though Barbierri and Camacho-Collados (2018) expound that users were prone to using emojis with their skin color this study discovered that users used emojis with skin colors that resonated with those they were talking about and not necessarily their skin color. Hence, this gave an appropriate clue into the complexion of those talked about.

CONCLUSIONS AND RECOMMENDATIONS

What is clear from the empirical data is that computation linguistics, specifically WhatsApp emojis, are integral in the preservation and resuscitation of indigenous languages and cultures. The findings ascertain that they play a huge role in improving Shona and Ndebele's linguistic capital. Their interpretation and use incubated the endangered indigenous Shona and Ndebele languages and potentially shielded them from subjugation. The chapter shows that the use, interpretation, and responses to emojis in an epistemic unlearning trajectory were crucial in cascading, preserving, and resuscitating pristine local languages and cultures in the context of marriage which are now in danger of extinction. This subsequently shows that Shona and Ndebele are as equally important as English in the creation and transmission of knowledge particularly that entailing weddings. Additionally, the chapter fleshes out the importance of the use and interpretation of emojis in the imaginations of the identity of WhatsApp users. Emojis as a form of computational linguistics

108 *Jennings Joy Chibike*

offer cues to the gender, skin color, employment status, behavior, and ethnicity of users discussing marriage. This shows that Western colonial linguistics threats through the use of indigenous language and meaning in understanding emojis provide a relational link between language, identity, and culture. Overall, this chapter has proved that technocratic language is laden with the culture and identity of a people.

There is a need for more studies to carry on this work on the role of computational linguistics in preserving indigenous languages and cultures in the discussion of other indigenous social ceremonies such as funerals. This will help validate the findings of this study. Future studies are encouraged to provide solutions on how to save endangered indigenous languages using technocratic means in Africa. Moreover, leveraging decoloniality as a methodological stance forthcoming study can explore how digital media help resuscitate and preserve African indigenous languages and cultures while at the same time shrugging off the perverse influence of Western cultures in Africa.

REFERENCES

Aksan, N., Kisac, B., Aydrn, M., & Dermibuke, S. (2009). Symbolic interaction theory, *Procedia Social and Behavioral Sciences* 1:902–904.

Alshenqeeti, H. (2016). Are emojis creating a new or old visual language for new generations? A socio-semiotic study, *Advances in Language and Literacy Studies* 7(6): 56–69.

Ashworth, P. D. (2000). *Psychology and 'human nature'*. London: Routledge.

Ayan, E. (2020). Descriptive Analysis of Emoticons/Emoji and Persuasive Digital Language Use in WhatsApp Messages, *Open Journal of Modern Linguistics* 10: 375–389.

Bai, Q., Dan, Q., Mu, Z., & Yang, M. (2019). A systematic review of emoji: Current research and future perspectives, *Frontiers in Psychology* 10: 2221.

Barbierri, F., & Camacho-Collados, J. (2018). *How Gender and Skin Tone Modifiers Affect Emoji Semantics on Twitter.* Proceedings of the Seventh Joint Conference on Lexical and Computational Semantics, 101–106.

Berg, B. L. (2000). *Qualitative research methods for the social sciences.* Boston: Allyn & Bacon.

Chibike, J. J. (2023). Podcasting Covid19 in indigenous languages: Interrogating audio psychology and political anthropomorphism. In Mpofu, P., Fadipe, I. and Tshabangu, T. (eds). *African Language Media*, pp. 112–124. Routledge: London.

Donato, G., & Paggio, P. (2017). *Investigating redundancy in emoji use: Study on Twitter-based corpus.* North American Chapter of the Association of Computational Linguistic Conference, pp. 118–126. Copenhagen: Denmark.

Dworkin, S. L. (2012). Sample size policy for qualitative studies using in-depth interviews, *Archives of Sexual Behavior* 41: 1319–132.

Computational Linguistics and Indigenous Languages

Felbo, B., Mislove, A., Soogard, A., Rahwan, I., & and Lehmaan, S. (2017). *Using millions of emoji occurrences to learn any domain representations for detecting sentiment, emotion and sarcasm.* In Proceedings of the 2017 conference of empirical methods in natural language processing. Copenhagen: Denmark.

Fullwood, C., Orchard, L. J., & Floyd, S. A. (2013). Emoticon convergence in Internet chat rooms, *Social Semiotics* 23(5): 648–662.

Hinnenkamp, V. (2008). Deutsch, Doyc or Doitsch? Chatters as Languages—The Case of a German-Turkish Chat Room, *International Journal of Multilinguistic* 5: 253–275.

Hurlburt, G. (2018). Emoji Lingua Franac or passing fancy, *IT Professional* 20: 14–16.

Jones, L. L., Wurm, L. H., Norville, G. A., & Mullins, K. L. (2020). Sex differences in emoji use, familiarity, and valence, *Computers in Human Behavior* 108: 106305.

Koch, T. K., Romero, P., & Stachl, C. (2021). Age and gender in language, emoji and emoticon usage in instant messaging, *Computers in Human behavior* 126: 1–12.

Korgen, K., & White, J. M. (2008). *Engaged sociologist: Connecting the classroom to the community.* Carlifonia: Pine Forge Press.

Kubota, R (2020). Confronting epistemological racism, decolonizing colonial knowledge: Race and gender in applied linguistics, *Applied Linguistics* 41(5): 712–732.

Lu, X., Wang, N., Huang, G., & Mei, Q. (2016). Learning from the ubiquitous language: An empirical analysis of emojis usage of smartphone users, *ACM*: 770–780.

Mabvira, V., Muchinako, G. A., & Smit, E. I. (2021). Shona traditional religion and sustainable environmental management: An Afrocentric perspective, *African Journal of Social Work* 11(3): 111–118.

McIvor, O., & McCarty, T. L. (2017). Indigenous bilingual and revitalization-immersion education in Canada and the USA. In García, O., Lin, A.M.Y. and May, S. (eds.). *Bilingual and multilingual education.* Springer International Publishing. 421–438.

Meighan, P. J. (2022). Colonialingualism: Colonial legacies, imperial mindsets, and inequitable practices in English language education. *Diaspora, Indigenous, and Minority* Education 17(209): 1–10.

Mgogo, Q., & Sinoyolo, N. (2023). The use of Facebook emojis to construct new meanings in the isiXhosa language. In Mpofu, P., Fadipe, I. and Tshabangu, T (Eds). *African Language Media*, pp. 79–95. Routledge: London.

Moschin, I. (2016). The "Face with Tears of Joy" Emoji. A Socio-Semiotic and Multimodal Insight into a Japan-America Mash-Up. *HERMES-Journal of Language and Communication in Business* (55): 11–25.

Mpofu, P., Fadipe, I. A., & Tshabangu, T. (2023). Conclusions: Reflections on the future of indigenous language media in Africa. In Mpofu, P., Fadipe, I. and Tshabangu, T. (eds). *African Language Media*, pp. 304–306. Routledge: London.

Mpofu, P. (2013). Multilingualism, localism and the nation: identity politics in the Zimbabwe Broadcasting Corporation. Unpublished PhD Thesis. University of South Africa.

Oleszewicz, A., Karwowski, M., Pisanski, K., Sorokowski, P., Sobrado, B., & Sorokowska, A. (2017). Who uses emoticons? Data from 86 702 Facebook users. *Personality and Individual Differences* 119: 289–295.

Perez-Sabata, C. (2019). Emoticons in relational writing practices on WhatsApp: Some reflections on gender. In P. Bou-Franch, P and Garc´es-Conejos, B. (eds.). *Analyzing digital discourse: New insights and future directions.* Springer International Publishing. 163–189.

Salgado, J. G. G., Garcia-Bravo, M. H., & Benzi, D. (2021). Two decades of Anibal Quijano's coloniality of power, Eurocentrism and Latin America, *Contexto Internacional* 43(1): 199–222.

Sibanda, B. (2019). Zimbabwe language policy: Continuity or radical change? *Journal of Contemporary Issues in Education* 14(2): 2–15.

Sibanda, B. (2021). Language as being in the politics of Ngugi Wa Thiong'o. In Steyn, M. and Mpofu, W (Eds). *Decolonising the mind: reflections from Africa on difference and oppression.* Wits University Press. 143–163.

Siebenhaar, B. (2018). Funktionen von Emojis und Altersabhangigkeit ihres Gebrauchs in der Whatsapp-Kommunikation. In A. Ziegler (Ed.). *Jugendsprachen/ youth languages.* De Gruyter. 749–772.

Shardlow, M., Gerber, L., & Nawaz, R. (2022). One emoji, many meanings: A corpus for the prediction and disambiguation of emoji sense. *Expert systems with applications* 92: 116862.

Stark, L., & Crawford, K. (2015). The conservativism of Emoji: Work, effect and communication. *Social Media and Society* 1: 1–11.

Stets, J. E., & Burke, P. J. (2000). Identity theory and Social identity theory. *Social Psychology Quarterly* 63(3): 224–237.

Swartz, M. (2020). Exploring the symbolic representation of identity and collective behavior in social media: Emoji use on Twitter. PhD Thesis. George Mason University.

Tezcan, M. (2005). *Sosyolojik kuramlarda egitim.* Ankara: Ani Yayincilik.

Thomas, W. I., & Thomas, D. S. (1928). *The child in America: Behavior problems and programs.* New York: Knopf.

Underberg, N. M., & Zorn, E. (2013). *Digital ethnography: Anthropology, narrative, and new media.* Austin: University of Texas Press.

Volkel, S. T., Buschek, D., Pranjic, J., & Hussmann, H. (2019). *Understanding emoji interpretation through user personality and message context.* Proceedings of the 21st International Conference on Human-Computer Interaction with Mobile Devices and Services—MobileHCI, 19, 1–12.

Weber, L. (2013). *I have no words: Emoji and the new visual vernacular.* Available at: https://vimeo.com/83241814 Accessed March 13, 2023.

Willems, W. (2014). Provincialising hegemonic histories of media and communication studies: Towards a genealogy of epistemic resistance in Africa. *Communication Theory* 24(4): 415–434.

PART II

Digital Media Strategies and Indigenous Language Preservation in the Fourth Industrial Revolution

Chapter 5

Global Initiatives for Digital Preservation of Indigenous Languages in the Fourth Industrial Revolution

Adeyinka Tella and Joseph Ngoaketsi

Nearly half of the 6,000 languages spoken worldwide, according to the United Nations, are at risk of extinction. Similarly, according to UNESCO (2019), there are 6,700 languages spoken throughout the world, with 40 percent of them in danger of extinction. However, many indigenous, minority, and low-resource languages are excluded from the advantages and opportunities of the Fourth Industrial Revolution (4IR), even though language is one of the many factors contributing to division, particularly in the continent where there are many developing countries. Indigenous languages continue to be in peril and are at risk of extinction because of colonization and imperialism. Indigenous language learning resources are frequently quite scarce due to a dearth of qualified or experienced teachers. Materials that follow outside standards or Western pedagogies may not be appropriate for local needs. Promoting intergenerational language usage and transmission in a variety of social contexts, including the family, is one common objective of indigenous language revitalization projects. The integration of physical, biological, and digital systems is a key feature of the 4IR, a period of rapid technological development. The practice of preserving digital content in a usable state throughout time is referred to in this sense as "digital preservation." Utilizing technology to conserve and enhance linguistic diversity and cultural legacy is the goal of international projects for the digital preservation of indigenous languages in the 4IR. Indigenous languages are regarded as a significant component of cultural variety since they stand for distinct knowledge systems and ways of living. However, due to a lack of intergenerational transmission and the influence of dominant languages, many indigenous languages are in danger of extinction. By building digital repositories of language and cultural resources that can be accessed and shared by speakers and researchers around the world, digital preservation efforts seek to address this problem.

The critical need for the digital preservation of indigenous languages has drawn a lot of attention lately. The 4IR has increased the use of digital technology, opening new prospects for the preservation of indigenous languages, which are in danger of extinction owing to several socioeconomic, political, and cultural causes. On that note, this chapter looks at international efforts to preserve indigenous languages in the 4IR digitally. This chapter covers 4IR technologies, the digital preservation of indigenous languages, approaches, and strategies for the digital preservation of indigenous languages, opportunities and challenges related to the digital preservation of indigenous languages, and global digital initiatives to preserve indigenous languages.

CONCEPTUAL FRAMEWORK

Global Initiatives

Global initiatives encourage cooperation for sustainable development through content, high-level gatherings, and stakeholder engagement. They tackle some of the biggest problems the world is experiencing by exchanging information and best practices and encouraging all parties to act. It is an appeal for tried-and-true, cost-effective, and scalable solutions that can hasten the process of maintaining indigenous languages and their roles, particularly for languages that are slowly dying out.

Digital Preservation

According to Özer and Nazlı (2018), preservation is the most crucial component of a museum's operations. It speaks about the ongoing preservation and defense of collections. It covers the management and conservation of collections as well as their acquisition. The linkages between the past, present, and future are made possible by preservation (Cloonan, 2007). Erturk (2021, p.102) notes that one of the top issues on museums' agendas continues to be the conservation of tangible, intangible, and digital cultural heritage. Active conservation, preventive conservation, disaster management, and risk management are among the conservation techniques used in museums (Erturk, 2021). If digital content is not structured and consistent enough to be available beyond a certain period, the preservation of items and information

Global Initiatives for Digital Preservation of Indigenous Languages 115

will not be realized (Nakata, 2007, p.104). The critical need for the digital preservation of indigenous languages has drawn a lot of attention lately. The fourth industrial revolution (4IR) has increased the use of digital technology, opening up new prospects for the preservation of indigenous languages, which are in danger of extinction owing to several socioeconomic, political, and cultural causes.

Indigenous Languages

The term "indigenous languages" refers to the tongues used by indigenous peoples, who are the first settlers of a given area or country. The preservation and transfer of traditional knowledge, customs, and values depend heavily on these languages, which are a significant component of the cultural heritage of indigenous groups.

The Fourth Industrial Revolution (4IR)

The manufacturing sector's transition to digitization is being called "Industry 4.0," or the fourth industrial revolution. It is being driven by disruptive innovations such as the growth of data and connectivity, analytics, human-machine interaction, and robotics breakthroughs. How modern people live, and work is changing because of disruptive technologies and trends like the Internet of Things (IoT), robotics, virtual reality (VR), and artificial intelligence (AI). These concepts are germane to the discussion and the focus of this discourse.

Theories of Linguistic Diversity, Cultural Heritage, and Digital Technologies

Global initiatives for the digital preservation of indigenous languages in the 4IR are based on the theoretical and conceptual frameworks of linguistic diversity, cultural heritage, and digital technologies. Linguistic diversity refers to the range of languages spoken by different communities around the world. It is a fundamental aspect of human diversity, reflecting the unique histories, identities, and perspectives of different cultures. However, linguistic diversity is under threat due to factors such as globalization, urbanization, and migration. As a result, many languages are at risk of becoming extinct, including indigenous languages spoken by small communities. Cultural heritage refers to the tangible and intangible expressions of a culture's history, traditions, and values. It includes artifacts, monuments, literature, music, and languages, among other forms of cultural expression. Indigenous languages are a crucial part of cultural heritage, serving as a means of transmitting traditional knowledge, practices, and beliefs across generations.

Digital technologies offer new possibilities for preserving linguistic diversity and cultural heritage. These technologies can be used to create digital archives, develop language learning tools, and facilitate communication across linguistic barriers. Global initiatives for the digital preservation of indigenous languages in the 4IR are based on the recognition of the potential of digital technologies to help preserve linguistic diversity and cultural heritage. Theoretical and conceptual frameworks for these initiatives also incorporate principles of cultural sensitivity, community participation, and sustainability. Preserving indigenous languages requires a deep understanding of the cultures and contexts in which they are spoken, as well as the participation and engagement of indigenous communities themselves. Initiatives must also be sustainable, ensuring that digital resources and tools are accessible and usable over the long term.

Researchers from a wide range of fields have looked at a variety of issues related to the human potential for language and the diversity of the world's languages, from the earliest philosophers to contemporary neuroscientists. Linguists refer to the study of language and languages because of the linkages between these fields. To describe and explain language history, dialect variation, cross-cultural parallels and differences, the neurological processing and production of language, and the evolutionary genesis of language, linguists have produced several theoretical paradigms during the past 150 years. The aim of the several schools of linguistic theory, two of which are formal linguistics and functional linguistics, is to provide a theoretical foundation for linguistic phenomena, particularly those that vary between languages. Such a theoretical study, which is based on a variety of different languages, would be quite dull if it lacked strong empirical support (McGregor, 2002; Rijkhoff, 2003, 2004; Vikner, 2005). The foundation of comparative linguistics is made up of such empirical studies or research in linguistic typology which aims to identify the many types of languages that exist and why some are more common than others.

Formal and functional linguistics are the two categories under which explicit theoretical approaches in formal linguistics fall. In formal linguistics, it is assumed that most human linguistic knowledge is intrinsic and that only a small percentage can be learned. In other words, some aspects of language are due to the structure of the human brain. As a result, these theories also have an intriguing justification for why some traits do not differ between languages: The innate portion of human beings' language knowledge may be the source of universal characteristics and lack of diversity (Vikner, 2001, 2004). Additionally, the communicative function of language is given paramount emphasis by functional linguistics. The purpose of linguistic entities is to transfer information; yet this does not preclude the possibility that they might serve other purposes. The fundamental idea is that language research must be conducted in light of our understanding of how consciousness processes various types of outside impressions, and that linguistic form is critically influenced by our understanding of how others might be able to understand what is being said. According to McGregor (2002) and Rijkhoff (2002; 2003), functional linguistics is thus interested in the interaction between linguistic and non-linguistic cognitive processes as well as the communicative function of language.

Our effort to study language scientifically depends on the multiplicity of languages and our comprehension of linguistic diversity. Similar to this, our comprehension of linguistic typology as well as our capacity to accurately classify languages and reconstruct proto-forms depend on our having access to a wide range of languages. In the past, linguistics and the study of non-Western, non-written languages were closely intertwined. Several widely held theoretical presumptions are called into question by the diversity of morphosyntactic features among human languages. There has been growing concern about the loss of global linguistic diversity and the impending extinction of numerous languages since the 1990s (Crystal, 2000). Additionally, it is acknowledged that numerous lesser-known languages around the world are directly or indirectly threatened by the power of dominant languages such as English.

Since they act as the principal center of human knowledge and culture, minority and less widespread languages are believed to be essential parts of many people's cultural identities and to have enormous intrinsic significance for humanity as a whole (Fishman, 1991; Skutnabb-Kangas 2000). Numerous initiatives have been created to preserve, bolster, safeguard, or advance languages as aspects of this diversity as a result of the growing realization that humanity must save and support languages. Although literacy has many advantages, it also gives speech stiff, artificial patterns and helps languages survive by maintaining their grammatical and lexical fossils.

Many researchers, decision-makers, and representatives of linguistic groups presently view the preservation of linguistic diversity as a critical problem. In other cases, maintaining variety is viewed as a matter of revitalizing languages or making required adjustments to those that have significantly lost their speaker populations. The work of several linguists, notably Rob Amery, in Indigenous Australian, North American, and other environments is also included (Amery, 1988; Schmidt, 1993; Lo Bianco and Rhydwen, 2001), as well as Joshua Fishman's Reversing Language Shift (1991), and other linguists' studies. The documentation of languages that are presumed extinct and are not anticipated to be spoken in the future is a common feature of these latter cases.

ICTs and Diversity in Culture and Language

Two schools of thought since linguistics frequently dismisses technological advancement as "mere engineering," and that it lacks a thorough understanding of technology. The area of computational linguistics is tech-savvy, yet it concentrates on the 1 percent of languages that are currently well-resourced and commercially feasible. Language documentation requires the fusion of general linguistic interest in all languages of the globe with technical expertise in computational linguistics. In response to societal demands, literacy or literacies as social activities have evolved with various priorities and emphases. In today's multicultural, multilingual, and multiliterate society, which is increasingly characterized by the mobility of people, capital, labor, and communications in several languages, it is our responsibility to carefully analyze what the function of literacy can be. This is a result of expanding linguistic and cultural variety as well as modern communications technologies.

The most isolated villages are beginning to experience the information age. Denying the realities of our rapidly changing world or the importance of more widely available knowledge and education will not be beneficial to any traditional civilization. The demise of indigenous knowledge and culture could be accelerated by ICTs. They have two sharp edges. On the other hand, the development of creative, culturally relevant educational resources and environments for indigenous children can be empowered and supported by the new digital technology. Two camps disagree on how ICTs impact linguistic and cultural diversity. One holds that the internet contributes to the homogenization of civilizations, whereas the other has the opposite view. Many indigenous communities view the development to enhance, rather than impede, self-sufficiency, preservation of culture, true sovereignty, and general economic conditions if indigenously developed internet resources and technologies are any indication of indigenous peoples' willingness to embrace the technological era. In sum, linguistic variety, cultural heritage, and digital technology form the theoretical and conceptual foundation of international initiatives for the digital preservation of indigenous languages in the 4IR. In addition to combining the values of cultural sensitivity, community involvement, and sustainability, they want to take advantage of digital technology's potential to promote the survival of indigenous languages.

Global Initiatives on Digital Preservation of Indigenous Languages around the World

Recent years have seen the emergence of international initiatives for the digital preservation of indigenous languages in the 4IR, reflecting the urgency and significance of this issue. The goal of these programs, which frequently involve cooperation between indigenous groups, linguists, and technology specialists, is to create long-term and culturally considerate methods for conserving indigenous languages through the use of digital technologies. A vital effort is being made to conserve the linguistic diversity and cultural history of indigenous peoples through global initiatives for the digital preservation of indigenous languages in the 4IR. These projects seek to guarantee that indigenous languages continue to flourish and contribute to the global cultural landscape by using the power of modern technologies.

International organizations, like UNESCO, as well as local community organizations and academic institutions, frequently lead global initiatives for the digital preservation of indigenous languages in the 4IR. With a focus on fostering linguistic and cultural variety, these efforts also acknowledge the value of indigenous languages in maintaining regional knowledge and fostering social cohesion. The global initiatives include but are not limited to:

The Decade of Indigenous Languages

The goal of the International Decade of Indigenous Languages (IDIL) 2022–2032 is to draw attention to how urgently many indigenous languages need to be preserved, revived, and promoted on a worldwide scale. One of the major accomplishments of the 2019 International Year of Indigenous Languages, for which the United Nations Educational, Scientific, and Cultural Organization (UNESCO) is organizing global activities, is the declaration of an international decade. In collaboration with the UN Department of Economic and Social Affairs (UNDESA) and other pertinent UN Agencies, the organization will continue to act as the primary UN Agency for the execution of the International Decade.

The UNESCO-sponsored International Year of Indigenous Languages (IYIL)

The International Year of Indigenous Languages (IYIL) was established by UNESCO to draw attention to the grave risks facing indigenous languages and indigenous knowledge systems. The program aims to promote indigenous knowledge and broaden access to it.

The support focuses on advancing indigenous knowledge and language use in daily life, including:

- Promotion attempts to mainstream indigenous knowledge, as well as provide better access and empower indigenous speakers.
- Access that maintains indigenous languages and advances education, knowledge, and information about indigenous people.

- Language, communication, and information technologies that are used in conjunction with cultural traditions like games and sports to achieve this goal. The action plan is a timetable of conferences, seminars, and events that will be held as part of the International Year.

Indigenous Language Revitalization (ILR)

According to Huilcán (2002), one objective of ILR programs is to promote language use and transmission between generations. British Columbian indigenous groups are making great efforts to protect their languages. The University of Victoria has spent more than forty-five years supporting local and governmental language revival initiatives. We collaborate with local researchers, elders, instructors, linguists who are proficient in regional languages, and members of indigenous communities. Indigenous language revitalization initiatives aim to produce fresh dictionaries, films, and applications; undertake research; educate future generations; and prepare people to work as teachers and interpreters. They also seek to create workable plans for the continuing existence and advancement of primordial languages.

The 4IR Technologies for Preserving Indigenous Languages

The term "4IR" refers to the present stage of technological development, which is defined by the pervasive application of electronic technologies like the Internet of Things, artificial intelligence, and big data. There are various ways in which these technologies could help preserve indigenous languages, for example:

- *Digital documentation*: Native languages can be preserved using digital technologies in a variety of media types, including text, audio, and video. Digital archives can be used to store this documentation, making it available to future generations.
- *Language revitalization:* Apps, games, and online courses are just a few examples of the language learning resources that may be created using digital technologies. By enhancing their use and appeal to younger generations, these instruments can aid in the rejuvenation of primordial languages.
- *Machine translation:* The accessibility and importance of indigenous languages can be increased in a globalized environment by using machine translation technology to translate them into more widely spoken languages.

- *Online Language Learning Platform*: The survival of these languages depends on an online language learning platform and app (Melloy, 2018). Every system for learning a language online should contain the following three components: (1) a spoken and textual translation tool available online, (2) interactive learning tools like games and flashcards, and (3) submitted tales and video lessons by native language speakers. The primary benefit of this platform is the preservation of regional expertise and knowledge that are indispensable to the language and culture of its users. Users with spotty services can still utilize this platform because many of its features can be accessible without an internet connection. The first languages on this platform might be the Inuit tongues spoken in the United States, Canada, and Greenland.
- *ChatGPT*: By combining the capabilities of natural language processing (NLP) and artificial intelligence (AI), ChatGPT is revolutionizing language diversity and preservation. Users may converse in their local tongue thanks to this groundbreaking technology, protecting the variety of languages spoken around the world. A chatbot platform called ChatGPT enables users to converse in their language. The software makes use of AI to produce answers in the users' languages in response to their inquiries. Additionally, it can identify the user's language and respond in that language. This eliminates the need to learn a new language by enabling users to converse in their home tongue. To assess the user's query and produce a response in the user's native tongue, the platform also makes use of NLP. This preserves the variety of languages spoken around the world. Additionally, it enables users to speak in their mother tongue without learning a foreign language. Additionally, ChatGPT supports the preservation of endangered tongues. ChatGPT aids in the preservation of these languages by offering a forum for people to converse in them. This makes it more likely that these languages will survive and be spoken by future generations.
- *Desktop Technology*: The Wahapu (The Estuary) was one of the first ILR projects to make use of the possibilities of communication and Internet technology. A computer-based communications system called Te Wahapu was created in 1990 with a focus on New Zealand's Maori language revival to "symbolize the integration of high technology with Maori concerns and interests . . . [and] convey the message that 'English has no monopoly when it comes to making use of advanced technology.'" Another illustration is Leoki (Powerful Voice), a 1993-founded electronic bulletin board system that is offered fully in Hawaiian (Warschauer, 1998). Leoki offered "online support for Hawaiian language use in the immersion schools and the broader community" (Warschauer, 1998, p.

142). Leoki contributed to the production of resources that were suitable in terms of both language and culture. During the Web 1.0 period, rejuvenation and reclaiming methods included the production of spoken and written dictionaries as well as audio or video recordings of Elders speaking their primordial languages. FirstVoices, a British Columbia–based online resource, is an illustration of how First Nations communities in Canada have used technology to maintain, archive, and teach indigenous languages using text, sound, and video excerpts (First Peoples' Cultural Foundation, 2003). On the website, which also has an archive, chat options, games, movies, storybooks, and a language teacher, users can still communicate.

- *Interactive CD-ROMs and other types of multimedia*: During the Web 1.0 era, interactive CD-ROMs and other forms of multimedia have also been utilized to preserve primordial languages. The story of "How the Crane Got Blue Eyes" by Cazden (2002) indicates that the Lower Kuskokwim School District in Alaska created a bilingual CD-ROM in English and Yup'ik, which is a central Alaskan language. Speaking maps in Tlingit and English can be found in a computerized collection of historical material in the Tlingit language, which is used by the Tlingit people of Southeast Alaska and western Canada (Cazden, 2002).
- *Indigenous Robots—Skotbots*: Additional language technology that appears to be truly promising includes small, wearable robots called "robots" that were created by Danieller Boer, an Ojibwe engineer from the Sault Ste. These devices aim to introduce native students to STEM occupations in a way that helps them see themselves. These innovative tools simultaneously promote engineering and language. With the use of this technology, the notions that indigenous knowledge and technological advancements cannot coexist, and that rural people have no place in STEM professions are all disproved. People can simultaneously make links between several fields. With all the technology that is readily available now, what people can accomplish independently is simply unparalleled. Undoubtedly, language activists have a role in the process of ensuring that technological advancements happen for languages rather than against them.
- *Online Game*: Text-to-speech (TTSO) has been around for a while, but AI and machine learning have greatly improved the quality and versatility of automated speech and voice products. Many video games now have voices and voices thanks to the same text-to-speech technology that powers them. Superheroes, wizards, and pretend commandos frequently use AI text-to-speech technology to speak. Despite their involvement, actors rarely deliver every phrase in a video game. You might be shocked by how many of the sounds you hear in a video game or a

movie. These days sounds are not being uttered by real people. Instead, we can make any voice or utter any line feasible using a combination of skilled linguists, cutting-edge AI technology, and a few extremely exact recording sessions. Public announcements of railway schedules are no longer made by actual individuals but by the voice created by computer technology. Quietly, and more importantly, any language can become virtually immortal thanks to speaker-to-voice creation technology, which also gives superheroes their characters and allows you to add items to your shopping list by simply speaking to them out loud. This gives any language life, a purpose, and the ability to adapt indefinitely. For instance, these audio and AI technologies are enabling South African schoolchildren to not only read books written in the native isiZulu language but also to hear those books read aloud with a real accent and inflection. Hearing this highly human quality of speech, expressed by native speakers with true accents and in languages that are vulnerable, ignored, or spoken by very tiny groups of people.

- *Video/Audio Game*: Nowadays, many kids are becoming multilingual all over the world, and many people are interested in the idea of expanding their linguistic capabilities. Given that individuals of all ages enjoy playing video games, giving players more language options can improve their gaming experience while also improving their language abilities. The issue is that a lot of video games only offer support for one or two languages. This issue can be rectified by asking game developers to provide more language options. By doing this, both the game developers and language learners can greatly profit. Additionally, game makers can expand their fan base globally and foster closer ties with their users, perhaps increasing customer lifetime retention and generating more income. The best method to do this is to localize games, which entails modifying video games to meet the language and cultural demands of a new audience. The games listed below may help enhance and increase native language skillsets (Dimitriadou, 2023).
- *The in-game content*, including item descriptions, can aid students in expanding their vocabulary and identifying grammatical patterns in the language they are learning.
- *Voice-over for the video game*: When using the shadowing approach, the film helps improve the learners' phonetic understanding skills as well as their pronunciation in addition to improving the players' acoustic experience. The subtitles are: With the extra aid of voice-over, this can help students with all the aforementioned.
- *The visual style of the game*: Learners can use the images and other visual components as contextual cues to determine the meaning of various words and phrases.

- ABRACADABRA (ABRA): The importance of ABRACADABRA (ABRA), a web-based literacy program created at the Centre for the Study of Learning and Performance (CSLP) in Concordia University for the primary school pupils in Hong Kong for maintaining their language cannot be stressed (Cheung et al., 2016).

Digital Preservation of Indigenous Languages

Indigenous knowledge can be documented and digitally conserved in a variety of ways for the benefit of the knowledge's holders and their communities as well as to make it available to future generations. However, it's vital to pose the fundamental query about the significance of indigenous languages. According to the United Nations, the right and freedom of individuals to speak in the language of their choice is crucial for maintaining one's dignity, living in harmony with others, acting in good faith, and ensuring the overall well-being and long-term progress of society.

In all human domains, language serves as a systematic means of communication. It permits the transmission of knowledge, history, worldviews, and traditions from one generation to the next as well as a variety of cultural expressions. The economic value and advantages of language enable the creation of new work possibilities as well as research and development. Languages reflect people's unique methods of thinking, remembering, and expressing themselves as well as their worldviews, memories, and traditional knowledge. However, maybe more significantly, language also aids in the development of one's future.

Because diversity, including linguistic and cultural diversity, is an essential aspect of being human, language is crucial for both individuals and the environment. Regardless of affiliation or location, this diversity can be observed in a variety of ways across diverse economic, political, environmental, social, and cultural sectors as well as historical settings. The freedom to self-determination, unrestricted expression of one's opinions, and dynamic engagement in public life without worry of prejudice are all essential components of inclusion and equality, which are essential requirements for the development of transparent and participatory communities. Applying a wider range of human rights as outlined in international agreements on human rights, such as the Universal Declaration of Human Rights and the United Nations Declaration on Indigenous Languages, is the best method to achieve this.

The global decade of traditional knowledge can also be explained by the fact that several languages are currently threatened with extinction. The structural discrimination that languages, especially indigenous ones, have experienced along with the precarious position of their users (speakers and signers),

Global Initiatives for Digital Preservation of Indigenous Languages 125

whose ability to use their languages in daily life depends on their sociocultural, economic, political, environmental, and demographic circumstances daily, are all factors that contribute to the gradual extinction of languages. Numerous indigenous peoples have experienced historical marginalization; they continue to deal with problems including climate change, uncontrolled industry, forced migration, mandated relocation, educational disadvantage, illiteracy, and paucity of resources, especially those reliant on oral tradition. The worry now is that, practically speaking, parents and elders won't be able to teach their kids indigenous languages and that indigenous languages won't be used regularly.

Therefore, it is crucial to prevent their extinction, rejuvenate, and advance primordial languages globally. This requires comprehending their larger and more significant contributions to fostering peace, advancing responsible governance, protecting the environment, and preserving culture in all of its forms. The declaration of the International Decade of Indigenous Languages was influenced by the observations listed below:

- Languages are disappearing at an alarming rate around the globe. The identities, customs, and sophisticated knowledge systems of people that have developed over thousands of years are embodied in many of those languages, many of which are indigenous.
- People's access to justice, respectable employment, health care, and information, as well as other rights protected by the CERD General Recommendations are all recognized. However, the United Nations Declaration on the Rights of Indigenous Peoples, and the Universal Declaration of Human Rights (1948), are all hampered because people are denied the freedom to use their language.
- People who speak indigenous languages, particularly women, young girls and boys, children, people who are disabled, people who have been displaced, and the elderly, encounter many hindrances that call for an all-encompassing strategy.
- A large number of the languages spoken in the world are physically situated within the planet's hotspots of biodiversity, in addition to the fundamental contribution that languages provide to the preservation of biological diversity. Indigenous traditional environmental knowledge is a crucial source for creating cutting-edge responses to famine, climate change, and biodiversity preservation. Indigenous languages are designed with the preservation of indigenous knowledge systems in mind.

Promoting, preserving, and enhancing indigenous languages while also empowering its users requires cooperation and consistency in policy, resource

126   *Adeyinka Tella and Joseph Ngoaketsi*

allocation, multilateral and multistakeholder dialogues, and meaningful participation by indigenous peoples. This continental strategy can be used to build upon the variety of normative frameworks, policies, and international, regional, national, and local contributions that already exist along with additional input from international forums.

Approaches and Strategies for Digital Preservation of Indigenous Languages

The digital methods and tactics utilized to conserve indigenous languages are another important topic. Numerous such strategies have been revised in literature (such as Chang-Castillo, 2019). However, this chapter talks about some of them.

- *Making Digital Archives*: Making digital archives can contain recordings of oral histories, music, stories, and other cultural expressions, as one method of digital preservation. Information may be easily accessed and disseminated by making these archives accessible online.
- *Language Technology*: The creation of language technology, like software and tools for the acquisition of language and maintenance, is another strategy. By making language resources easier to access for speakers and learners alike, digital dictionaries and language learning apps, for instance, can aid in language revitalization efforts.
- *Recording and printing resources*: Written and audio recordings must be made to preserve the acoustical and social context of various languages. To conserve languages by lasting, physical means, linguists, anthropologists, and concerned individuals work to interview, record, and document languages. Libraries, academic institutions, museums, and cultural centers print and store these items. The Living Tongues Institute for Endangered Languages and National Geographic's Enduring Voices initiative are two noteworthy examples of this.
- *Teaching language classes*: Giving language lessons and participating in language sessions are two highly effective strategies to keep up a language. Elders frequently provide free or low-cost instruction in their local communities. Speaking a language is sufficient to give its words and nuanced meanings—some of which might not be directly transferable to any other language a stronger and greater worth, whether in a formal classroom environment or casual conversation.
- *Use of electronic and social media*: On the one hand, it could appear that these platforms considerably contribute to the extinction of languages, especially given that English is the language that is most prevalent on these platforms. On the other hand, those who favor the survival of

indigenous languages have begun to see their usefulness as a means of communication. They create courses, share idioms that are disappearing from the language, record karaoke versions of popular songs with written lyrics, and affordably maintain a pre-servable record of audio, video, and text in the target language via social media, YouTube, and other platforms.

- *Insistence on Speaking the Local Language*: One of the most crucial things communities, families, and individuals can do is to fight the impulse to communicate in a dominant group's language. Insist on using your original tongue. To ensure that business professionals can interact across linguistic boundaries without ever losing their knowledge of what is being said, experienced interpreters are an excellent tool. Chang-Castillo and Associates' qualified simultaneous interpreters and translators are at your disposal if you need to defend the rights of your overseas connections or your language. Everywhere in the world, they offer platinum-standard language solutions in almost every tongue or dialect.

Use of Artificial Intelligence (AI)

The use of AI for language learning is on the increase globally and major technology companies are substantially investing in systems that leverage voice and natural language interfaces. Eric Schmidt, the former executive chairman of Google, acknowledged that, despite these improvements, AI disadvantages languages that are not widely spoken. In addition to the dwindling number of local speakers, the technical systems that favor the most extensively used languages pose a threat to these languages. Artificial intelligence (AI) has been used in some cases to analyze and compile recordings of endangered Native American languages. The recording and preservation of endangered languages is the focus of Dr. Janet Wiles' study at the ARC Centre of Excellence for the Dynamics of Language (CoEDL). CoEDL has more than 50,000 hours of audio recordings; it would take almost two million hours to transcribe all of this audio using conventional methods. To solve this issue, CoEDL and Google worked together in 2017 to create machine-learning techniques for processing audio recordings. Twelve Australian indigenous languages have so far had AI models built using these data.

In addition to the aforementioned, Gopika et al. (2021) proposed that online communities have evolved into a haven where individuals support one another in resolving a variety of issues. Its main benefit is that it is cost- and easily accessible. Our indigenous languages can be preserved and revived via this platform. The following list is not exhaustive:

- *The website Wattpad* is very well-liked by young readers and aspiring writers. Indigenous language literature is rare and not widely distributed. It is a great idea to revive native languages through literature. If the older generations—those who speak the indigenous languages—are ready to transmit that information to the younger ones, they could do so through writing. Now that a significant number have access to a computer, older generations can start writing about their history, religion, rituals, and even fiction if they teach their grandparents or anybody else who knows about this website. This would promote understanding of various cultures and aid in the revival of indigenous languages.
- *Facebook*—Facebook has a feature called Facebook Community where users may connect, network, and share ideas. People who are fluent in indigenous languages can take the initiative to create a group on Facebook where they can exchange knowledge about traditions and culture. People from the same culture who reside in different nations can use this platform to stay in contact with their roots and community. Additionally, this would close the gap created by globalization. There are already several groups like this for other deities, where members exchange mythological tales, knowledge of antiquated practices, organic remedies, and even ethnic food recipes. But all of this can be expanded upon so that people can support one another in instructing the younger generation.
- *YouTube*—Individuals with knowledge of languages and a desire to keep them alive can post videos that instruct viewers about the language and its culture. YouTube is used often by people of all ages, thus posting content in native languages would interest both the young and elderly. Young people can learn about their culture, and seasoned older people can offer ideas for videos' subject matter. This would be a fantastic addition and draw visitors from all around the world.
- *Duolingo*—Language aficionados love the website and program Duolingo, which is used to learn new languages, and engages users in interactive language learning through a variety of fun activities. When a user enters a language they are already familiar with, the desired language course is adjusted to suit their preferences. Hawaiian and Navajo, two indigenous languages on the verge of extinction, have been added to Duolingo's roster to help them survive. Duolingo Incubator is another alternative that enables the general public to help create the content for the additional languages that are not yet represented on the website. Anyone familiar with indigenous languages is welcome to contribute to the Incubator, and if a language has enough content, it is included in their database.

Opportunities for Using Digital Technologies for Preserving Indigenous Languages

Some indigenous peoples are turning to readily available technology to preserve and revitalize their languages in response to the threat of language loss. Indigenous peoples have noticed that linguistic tools can increase the accessibility of indigenous languages, particularly for young people. Utilizing such technologies is a crucial way to put the indigenous peoples' knowledge to use in protecting priceless marine and terrestrial ecosystems, including forests.

To safeguard and transfer local Peoples' knowledge and to promote the revitalization of primordial languages through technology, it is essential to create partnerships between indigenous peoples and the corporate and public sectors. This will help to progress the SDGs. For instance, the Chickasaw Nation collaborated with language specialists from Rosetta Stone, a platform for language learning, in 2015 to create an instructional application for language acquisition. Together with native Chickasaw speakers, the lessons were created. Citizens of the Chickasaw Nation can use Rosetta Stone without charge. The first app created by a tribe or country was Chickasaw Basic.2. Anyone, not just members of certain indigenous tribes, can receive free basic training and education in indigenous languages online. The promotion of indigenous languages and cultures is backed by some digital companies. For instance, a few indigenous languages are now supported by Google's translation tool. The project to translate Facebook into other languages is the result of a collaboration to encourage community members to speak Inuit regularly.

Challenges Associated with Using Digital Technologies for Preserving Indigenous Languages

Accessibility, availability, and financial constraints: In the first instance, technology can be advantageous; on the other hand, it has little influence if the necessary instruments are not accessible or available due to a lack of financing. It's important to keep in mind that communities with limited resources can obtain a variety of freeware programs from the internet. This does not, however, take away access-related worries. The only places where people may use technology are schools and/or community centers, and often the technology is too outdated. For updates, patches, and technical support, the information technology (IT) team must provide ongoing maintenance and support.

Even though there seems to be less of a digital divide between the older and younger generations of indigenous communities, as well as between teachers and students, the effectiveness is only as good as access to and availability of computers and the internet. Additionally, they should be proficient in their native language and possess the knowledge, abilities, and attitudes needed to use technology effectively (Eisenlohr, 2004).

Training: The user's skill level will have a big impact on how useful the tool is. Straightforward presentations, a storyboard for a multimedia project, a digital tale, a slideshow, or an interactive lesson are just a few of the numerous uses for PowerPoint. Technology-assisted language learning can go beyond the word level, depending on the objective. Anyone may use PowerPoint to construct an interactive multimedia lesson that includes text in Hawaiian, photos, graphics, audio and video files, hyperlinks to the internet, and more. With only a little ingenuity and some time, students can create these courses and disseminate them among the school community for language learning. The creation of these projects encourages self-reflection and self-evaluation (Hartle-Schutte & Nae'ole-Wong, 1998) and provides diverse learners with the opportunity to be successful, creative, and inventive.

Usability: Usability and user-friendliness are crucial factors to consider for communities that use technology. Finding technologies that work for different generations will result in some sort of mentorship, probably between the younger and elder generations. At the first use of technology, it might frequently feel incredibly strange. As time goes on, comfort rather than annoyance should settle in. Only a small portion of people will be inclined to use it if the latter happens. A suggestion to prevent this is to download a trial edition of the program to get a feel for it before paying the full amount for it.

Limited resources: Galla (2016) stated that their inability to employ technology is due to a lack of resources. Accessibility and infrastructure play a part in indigenous groups' reluctance to embrace technology in rural places. The primary barrier to technology adoption in language acquisition is a lack of enthusiasm in the community or its schools. Some communities struggle with a shortage of basic computer hardware, software, and other essentials. Others face more severe obstacles that affect the technical instruments that are accepted and used. Due to the daily and rapid release of new digital technology, it is advantageous to plan upgrades to ensure that users have access to the most recent software or fixes, provide training workshops to assist users, and execute an evaluation of the tool or software. If the tools are outdated, difficult to use, not readily available, or irrelevant, technology has minimal potential for language learners and speakers.

RECOMMENDATIONS

Indigenous groups are using digital technologies as tools to aid in their efforts to revitalize their languages. The usage of such tools can have a good effect on identity. However, this is only possible when the community participates actively in the creation of its language materials. The development of relationships and knowledge of our place about everything around us are fundamental components of indigenous identity. New developments are crucial when talking about revitalizing languages. However, it is important to understand the role of digital technologies as tools that may support speakers in their efforts to revitalize themselves rather than as instruments with agency. When using technology tools to support revitalization initiatives, it is important to consider the impact of identity and the impact on identity as the instruments inside these processes become revitalization tools. In other words, they turn into tools that may be used to preserve our culture and assist in reclaiming our voices. Therefore, even if addressing the issue of identity is not the paper's primary objective, it should be promoted in publications and research on initiatives to revitalize communities using digital means. Furthermore, additional research might examine the viewpoints of the participants in these projects using qualitative techniques to look at how their identities are impacted by the use of digital technology and how they feel their identities are shaped throughout the projects. These studies and reflections on modern indigenous identities may provide new perspectives on existing methods as well as point the way toward new directions for supporting indigenous peoples in the digital age.

CONCLUSION

This chapter looked at international efforts to preserve indigenous languages in digital form. The chapter's discussion was centered on conceptual and theoretical framework related to linguistic diversity, cultural heritage, and digital technologies, digital initiatives to preserve indigenous languages worldwide, 4IR technologies for preserving indigenous languages, digital preservation of indigenous languages, approaches and strategies for digital preservation of indigenous languages, and opportunities and challenges associated with using digital technology. The chapter concluded that efforts to conserve the linguistic diversity and cultural history of indigenous peoples worldwide are vital for the digital preservation of indigenous languages in the 4IR. Therefore, the projects seek to ensure that indigenous languages continue to flourish and contribute to the global cultural landscape by utilizing the potential of digital technologies.

REFERENCES

Amery, R. (2009). Phoenix or Relic? Documentation of Languages with Revitalization in Mind. *Language, Documentation and Conservation.* 3(2), 138–148.

Amery, W. K. (1988). Essential Tremor and Flunarizine. *Cephalalgia.* https://doi.org/10.1046/j.1468-2982.1988.0803227.x.

Bianco, J. Lo and Rhydwen, M. (2001). Is the Extinction of Australia's Indigenous Languages Inevitable?" In J. A. Fishman, *Can Threatened Languages Be Saved?: Reversing Language Shift, Revisited: A 21st Century Perspective.* Bristol: Multilingual Matters. pp. 391–422.

Cazden, C. B. (2002). "Sustaining Indigenous languages in cyberspace." In J. Reyhner, O. Trujillo, R. L. Carrasco, and L. Lockard (Eds.), *Nurturing Native Languages.* Northern Arizona University. pp. 53–57.

Chang-Castillo Worldwide and Associate Language Solution (2019). Language preservation: How countries preserve their languages. Retrieved from: https://ccalanguagesolutions.com/language-preservation-how-countries-preserve-their-languages/. (Accessed 02 July 2023).

Cheung, A., Mak, B., Abrami, P., Wade, A. and Lysenko, L. (2016). The effectiveness of the ABRACADABRA (ABRA) web-based literacy program on primary school students in Hong Kong. Journal of Interactive Learning Research, 27(3), 219–245.

Cloonan, M. V.(2007). The Paradox of Preservation. *Library Trends* 56(1), 133–147. Johns Hopkins University Press.

Crystal, D. (2000). *Language Death.* Cambridge University Press.

DeShaw, N. (2023). Analysis: Indigenous languages and technology—a primer. A tribe Called Greek (ATCG). Retrieved https://atribecalledgeek.com/analysis-indigenous-languages-nd-tech/. (Accessed 2 July 2023).

Dimitriadou, A. (2023). Learning languages with gaming and the implications for game creators. Retrieved from https://www.pangea.global/blog/learning-languages-with-gaming-and-the-implications-for-game-creators/. (Accessed 02 July 2023).

Engel, E. (2019). The new online platform brings coding to Canada's Indigenous youth. SooToday. https://www. sootoday.com/local-news/new-online-platform-bringscoding-to-canada indigenous-youth-1345063. (Accessed 02 July 2023).

Erturk, I. (2021). Economic Ekphrasis: Goldin+Senneby and Art for Business Education. Guillet De Monthoux, P. & Wikberg, E. (eds.). Berlin: Sternberg Press, 13 p. (Stockholm School of Economics Art Initiative series Experiments in Art and Capitalism). Research output: Chapter in Book/Report/Conference proceeding › Chapter › peer-review.

First Peoples' Cultural Foundation. (2003). First voices. www.fpcf.ca/resources/First%20Voices/default.htm. (Accessed 02 July 2023).

Fishman, J. (1991). *Reversing Language Shift: Theory and Practice of Assistance to Threatened Languages.* Clevedon: Multilingual Matters.

Frackiewicz, M. (2023). The impact of ChatGPT on language diversity and preservation, In Artificial Intelligence, ChatGPT TS2 Space. Retrieved from: https://ts2.space/en/the-impact-of-chatgpt-on-language-diversity-and-preservation/ (accessed 2 July 2023).

Harvey, D. R., and Mahard, M. R. (2020). *The preservation management handbook: A 21st-century guide for libraries, archives, and museums*. Lanham, MD: Rowman and Littlefield Publishers.

Galla, C. K. (2013). Indigenous Language Revitalization and Technology from Traditional to Contemporary Domains. Retrieved from https://jan.ucc.nau.edu/~jar /ILR/ILR-13.pdf (accessed 02 July 2023).

Galla, C. (2016). Indigenous language revitalization, promotion, and education: Function of digital technology. *Computer Assisted Language Learning*, 29(7), 1137–1151.

Gopika, S., Agarwal, A. and Soundararajan, S. (2021). Revival of Indigenous Languages: Role of Digital Platform. *International Journal of Creative Research Thoughts (IJCRT)* 9(4), 173–175.

Hartle-Schutte, D., & Nae'ole-Wong, K. (1998). Technology and the revival of the Hawaiian language. Reading Online, (May), np. Retrieved from http://www.read-ingonline.org/.

Huilcán, M. I. (2022). The use of technologies in language revitalisation projects: Exploring identities. *Journal of Global Indigeneity*, 6(1).pp.1–17.

Kroskrity, P., and Reynolds, J. F. (2001). "On using multimedia in language renewal: Observations from making the CD-ROM Taitaduhaan." In L. Hinton and K. Hale (eds.), *The green book of language revitalization in practice*. San Diego: Academic Press. pp. 317–329.

Li, J., Brar, A. and Roihan, N. (2021). The use of digital technology to enhance language and literacy skills for Indigenous people: A systematic literature review. *Computers and Education Open*, 2(Dec.). ttps://doi.org/10.1016/j.caeo.2021.100035. (Accessed 02 July, 2023).

McGregor, William B. (2002). *Verb Classification in Australian Languages*. Mouton de Gruyter. pp. xxvi–531.

Melloy, B. (2018). From threatened to thrive: Using technology to preserve Arctic Indigenous languages. *How an online platform could revitalize Arctic languages threatened with extinction*. Retrieved from https://www.arctictoday.com/threatened -thriving-using-technology-preserve-arctic-indigenous-languages/ (Accessed 02 July 2023).

Nakata, M. (2007). The cultural interface. *The Australian Journal of Indigenous Education*, 36(S1), 7–14.

Özer, S.F. and Nazlı, M. (2018). Sustaining Cultural Heritage Using Museums in an Ever-Changing World, *Gaziantep University Journal of Social Sciences* 17(1), 1–14,

Rijkhoff, J. (2002). On the interaction of Linguistic Typology and Functional Grammar. *Functions of Language* 9(2), 209–237.

Rijkhoff, J. (2003). When can a language have nouns and verbs? *Acta Linguistica Hafniensia 35*. 7–38.

Rijkhoff, J. (2004). *The noun phrase* (expanded paperback edition of 2002 hardback publication). Oxford, UK: Oxford University Press.

Schmidt, R. (1993). Awareness and Second Language Acquisition. *Annual Review of Applied Linguisitics*, *13*, 206–226. http://dx.doi.org/10.1017/S0267190500002476.

Skutnabb-Kangas, T. (2000). Linguistic Genocide in Education—Or Worldwide Diversity and Human Rights. Mahwah, NJ and London: Lawrence Erlbaum Associates.

Skutnabb-Kangas, T. (2013). Today's Indigenous education is a crime against humanity: Mother-tongue-based multilingual education as an alternative? *TESOL in Context*, 23(1/2), 82–1240.

UNESCO (2019). World Atlas of Languages. Retrieved from: https://en.wal.unesco.org/. (accessed 02 July 2023).

Vikner, C. (2004). The semantics of Scandinavian 'when'-clauses. *Nordic Journal of Linguistics*, 27(2), 10.1017/S0332586504001209.

Vikner, S. (2001). *'V?-to-I? Movement and do-Insertion in Optimality Theory*, in G. Legendre, J. Grimshaw, and S. Vikner (eds.), *Optimality-Theoretic Syntax*, Cambridge, MA: MIT Press. pp. 427–464.

Vikner, S. (2005). Immobile complex verbs in Germanic. *Journal of Comparative Germanic Linguistics*, 8(1), 85–117. 10.1007/s10828-004-0726-9.

Warschauer, M. (1998). Technology and Indigenous language revitalization: Analysing the experience of Hawai'i. *Canadian Modern Language Review*, 55(1), 140–161.

Williams, S. (2002). "Ojibway hockey CD ROM in the making." In B. Bumaby and J. Reyhner (eds.), *Indigenous languages across the community*. North Arizona University. pp. 219–223.

Chapter 6

Indigenous Language Development and Preservation in the Age of the Fourth Industrial Revolution

Remah Joyce Lubambo

The value of indigenous languages as cultural assets cannot be underestimated. The significance of belonging, as cultural identity, is regarded as a fundamental aspect of life by any tribe or community (Logan, 2016). It is therefore crucial for native speakers of a language to guard against its extinction as it contains the heritage of the people. Indigenous language development and preservation could assist in preserving the wisdom of our forefathers, traditional knowledge and values, verbal art, and the norms and values embedded in it. "Every language lost is a great loss to humanity" (Mutasa, 2002, p. 240). As a result of the development and preservation of indigenous languages, future generations will be able to identify themselves within a culturally diverse community such as South Africa. The emergence of modern technologies has an impact on the preservation of indigenous languages since it affects how communication is conducted and how information is shared and received.

According to Schwab (2017), industrial revolutions are distinguished by the emergence of modern technologies and novel ways of viewing the world, which cause significant changes in economic systems and society in general. He further maintains that before the Fourth Industrial Revolution (4IR), other revolutions evoked and influenced global functions: As such, the First Industrial Revolution refers to society's transition from an agricultural to a large-scale, machine-powered manufacturing economy. This shift was made possible using new materials like iron and steel, as well as new energy sources like steam. With the invention of new machines, labor structures improved, and the use of science in industrial processes increased (Stearns, 2020). The Second Industrial Revolution began at the end of the nineteenth century when the First Industrial Revolution had left off (Pouspourika, 2019). This era saw more technological advances in manufacturing and production, as well as the widespread use of telegraph systems and railroad networks leading to a greater movement of ideas and people and resulting in a wave of globalization (Engelmann & Von Hohendorff, 2019).

Further technological advancements resulted in the Third Industrial Revolution, also known as the Digital Revolution. The period also saw the widespread adoption of personal computing and advanced communications technology, as well as the widespread use of the Internet. The Third Industrial Revolution, according to Rouse (2014), ushered in the Information Age.

With the advent of the 4IR, the internet has become the primary and most accessible mode of communication, allowing people to connect from all over the world in ways that were previously impossible. As a result, speakers of various indigenous languages are no longer constrained by geographical or cultural boundaries. On the other hand, the digital space has put intense pressure on indigenous languages, and its impact cannot be underestimated. The digital era is a double-edged sword for indigenous languages because the internet is flooded with English as the dominant language. Most of the information available online is also in English which includes apps, and language tools such as translation tools. It is lamentable that indigenous languages are less supported, and this could lead to their extinction in the coming decades as the digital era influences all language groups and all ages. The dominant language has gained power over the indigenous languages. Most indigenous languages may become extinct as a result of the 4IR if they cannot adapt to new language technologies. According to Desai (2001), language has the right to exist as a resource. Many indigenous languages are in danger of extinction in the age of the 4IR, taking with them an irreplaceable part of indigenous traditions, cultural norms, and values of native speakers. Preservation of these languages will maintain their identity and cultural heritage. This chapter seeks to strengthen efforts to combat indigenous language erosion to protect culture, customary practices, and heritage by suggesting strategies to support their development amid the impact of the 4IR.

Given that global changes cannot be avoided or ignored, the chapter will further investigate how to preserve these indigenous languages for future generations without compromising or avoiding the essence of change brought about by the 4IR. With this context in mind, the chapter will present some strategies for preserving and developing indigenous languages and cultural traditions embedded in them.

LITERATURE REVIEW

Even though this chapter focuses on South African indigenous languages, literature from the global, African, and local domain were reviewed. Enaifoghe (2021) conducted a study on the 4IR focusing on the integration of ICT in the South African education system. He contends that ICT has become the primary tool for constructing knowledge in societies and that it has the potential to rethink and redesign educational systems, resulting in quality education for all. His motivation was that, as new technologies rapidly change the world's economies, from cultural to social realities, the question of how prepared the South African education system is for the 4IR remains. Makananise (2022, p. 45) suggested that "during the Fourth Industrial Revolution, digital media platforms are the most preferred means of communication, information sharing, and audience access."

This means that more people than ever before are seeking information through online platforms. Philbeck and Davis (2019) studied the 4IR and dubbed it the "epi-digital" revolution because the technologies involved are "epi-digital," given that we view driving change as establishing a fertile layer of innovation and digital foundations. Robotics, advanced materials and genetics, alterations, the internet, drones, neurotechnology, self-driving cars, artificial intelligence, and machine vision are all intertwined in our physical, social, and political spaces, influencing behaviors, relationships, and meaning. Olaifa (2014) carried out a study on language preservation and development, examining the role of libraries in the preservation and development of languages in any society. He claims that the library is the most important institution for language preservation and promotion. According to Siregar (2022), language conservation efforts must eventually address the intergenerational transmission of mother tongues. This is primarily a matter of family and community. A sole focus on education exacerbates rather than solves the problem of language shift. He goes on to say that language groups that succeed in preserving their language find ways to revitalize and stabilize their speech community. In these cases, schools play a role, but the community is the primary focus of action. Based on the arguments of the scholars above, it is evident that in the process of transformation, African languages are also affected since they are effective tools for communication and information sharing. In Section 6 of the South African Constitution, Act 108 of 1996, it is stated that all languages are protected, and they should enjoy equal opportunities.

The Pan South African Language Board (PanSALB) made some efforts to form language boards for different languages to develop the South African indigenous languages especially those that were formerly marginalized.

138 *Remah Joyce Lubambo*

Previous research focused more on investigating the interface between African languages and the disruption caused by the emerging technologies in the twenty-first century while some had their focus on social media as technological tools for communication (Makamani & Nhemachena, 2021). Little effort has been made to preserve and develop the indigenous languages further for them to survive in the age of the 4IR. Considering that fact, this chapter will investigate how indigenous languages can be developed and preserved for future generations without compromising the fundamentals of change brought about by the 4IR. The chapter will further present some strategies that may be implemented by different stakeholders to limit the chances of their languages becoming extinct due to the challenges brought by the 4IR.

METHODOLOGY

The chapter is qualitative and descriptive in nature, driven by the need to understand the issues surrounding the 4IR and its impact on indigenous languages. Additional strategies will be sought for the development and preservation of these indigenous languages and cultures. The study used both secondary and primary data, with a purposeful sample of eight stakeholders serving as data informants, as well as documents such as language policies, language planning documents, and government gazettes. Descriptive methods were used to analyze the data. The information that emerged from the data was organized into themes for easy analysis. The findings of this study will help language stakeholders such as language speakers, educators, lexicographers, language practitioners, and language developers to rise to the challenge and use the suggested strategies to develop and preserve their language as well as their embedded cultures against the backdrop of the 4IR's challenges.

THEORETICAL FRAMEWORK

This study adopts the Afrocentricity theory which was developed by Asante (2000) according to Reviere and Bakeman (2001). It challenges the Western ideology known as "Eurocentric theory." Afrocentricity is thought to have gained popularity in the United States of America during the Civil Rights Movement (Chawane, 2016; Khokholkova, 2016). According to Chawane (2016), Afrocentrism is an African ideology that prioritizes Africans and their contributions. This theory seeks to address the need for an African approach to African problems by employing a scholarly approach more consistent with African ways of thinking and reasoning.

Indigenous Language Development and Preservation 139

This theory focuses on the culture of African people which must be preserved and opposes Eurocentric ideology which oppresses African people (Reviere & Bakeman, 2001). This suggests that research on language and culture (which are intertwined) should be conducted by African people who know the African languages and their cultures. The researcher is of African origin and is well-versed in the development and preservation of indigenous languages, especially in the digital era. Therefore, the study will contribute to the body of knowledge in such a way that speakers of indigenous languages will be aware of the importance of their indigenous language and be inspired to develop and preserve them as their heritage.

A Brief Overview of the Impact of the Fourth Industrial Revolution on Indigenous Languages

From time to time, global changes occur at either a slow or a fast pace. The introduction of digital changes has both negative and positive consequences, as well as opportunities and challenges. As opportunities present themselves, some languages benefit more than others (Xu, David, & Kim, 2018). In the process of change, domination, adaptation, and adoption occur (Juhary, 2020). The dominant language becomes the language of communication, and it dominates powerful institutions such as government institutions, administrations, and education, and even minority languages. As the practical act of dominance occurs, linguistic and cultural heritage is exchanged in favor of the dominant language. At the end of the day, the dominant languages lose all their philosophies and heritage. There has been a significant paradigm shift in recent years regarding the relationship between technology and language extinction, particularly that of indigenous languages (Abraham, 2020; Jany, 2017). The 4IR has dominated the communication space, and speakers of minority languages may find themselves deprived of the communication platforms and without a language of their own. In reality, digital communication is flexible and convenient because there are no time constraints, and it connects people from all over the world almost instantly regardless of geographical boundaries. Communication media such as the radio, television, video, and various social media platforms dominate the flow of communication (Srinivasan, 2006). Digital media and social networks have changed the status quo and are now viewed as vital tools in language preservation and revitalization endeavors (Jany, 2017). The digital era also gives those with access to technological devices easier and faster access to information. It facilitates education by allowing people to learn a language or any subject of their choice online. Above all, the 4IR plays a key role, as the economy grows rapidly in the digital era owing to easier methods of day-to-day communication as well as new machines developed for industries.

Despite the positive effects of the digital era, it cannot be denied that there are negative effects on indigenous languages as languages of communication, teaching, and learning indigenous people's traditions and heritage. The double-edged sword is observed well in the sense that, while the 4IR may facilitate communication and connect people globally, the language that is spoken becomes dominant, and other languages recede, potentially leading to their extinction. A language that is not spoken is easily forgotten, and its correct grammar and phonetics are lost. The adoption of emerging technologies has far-reaching implications for products that make our lives easier as they reflect a fundamental shift in human behavior identity, as well as a restructuring of how we perceive the world (Philbeck, & Davis, 2019). Modern technology connects people, but it also disconnects indigenous people from their own valued languages, cultures, and philosophy of life. This affects the traditional way of communication that includes demonstrating respect as part of Ubuntu whereby the correct manner of articulation, the tone of the language, and embracing the indigenous language's norms and values are to be upheld.

The 4IR affects people differently and impacts the languages and their cultures in diverse ways (Prisecaru, 2016). The digital era also impacts family ties and the way culture is practiced in marriage, parenting, and worship. The use of technological devices for communication may also create a barrier between parents and their children, denying children the opportunity to learn their language directly from their parents or an adult who speaks the language correctly. As a result, if the indigenous language is not spoken correctly, a non-standard language develops and that language cannot be used in formal and public platforms. Communication in the various technological platforms is dominated by translated words that are not standardized and sometimes the translation is done through Google Translate, which does not recognize all indigenous languages and therefore provides incorrect translation with incorrect meaning and incorrect information. Since interaction with adults is decreasing in the 4IR era, some language concepts and content can be misleading and ruin the language. The following paragraphs will give a brief overview of the development and preservation of languages in the 4IR era:

Language Preservation and Development

Language preservation is an effort to save the growing number of languages that are being lost due to a variety of factors. Languages do not always develop as expected because the development process involves social, political, and psychological factors (Adzer, 2012). Norms and values of a society are handed down through language (Oboko, 2020). The extinction of indigenous languages would result in the loss of priceless human historical records and achievements in which local wisdom is taught and learned from

Indigenous Language Development and Preservation

generation to generation (Prasetyo, 2012). The technological changes brought by the 4IR, especially in communication and access to information, may pose a great problem to indigenous languages, therefore, language development and preservation are critical in this digital age.

In the process of preserving or developing a language, it is the responsibility of the native language speakers to guard against factors that could lead to the failure of their efforts. It is disconcerting that some speakers of African indigenous languages do not use their languages when communicating through the new digital platforms, especially social media platforms (Makananise, Malatji, & Madima, 2023). Proper use of these languages in social media would preserve, develop, and grow them to be popular among other languages. According to Mohochi (2003), language stakeholders should be involved in decision-making and plan implementation. The involvement of indigenous language speakers compels them to be part of the promotion and preservation and eventually own their languages and defend them in times of crisis (Schwab, 2016). Warren (1991) advocates for the preservation of indigenous languages for posterity so that the next generation of speakers should find their expository on social media. This may entail recognizing the language's current state and taking part in preserving the language in different technological platforms. Language specialists and developers are to assess whether the language is stable, and in use, or whether it is in danger of extinction, and create conditions in which it can be spoken and taught. Furthermore, indigenous language speakers carry the obligation to ensure that their languages are protected from outside influences such as those brought about by global changes such as the 4IR (Al-Rodhan, 2015). Outside influences, particularly in a multilingual and multicultural setting, can easily destroy language. Following the influence of other languages, speakers tend to adopt unstandardized languages as well as slang. It is therefore native speakers' responsibility to curb mispronunciations on community radio and television, as well as in other public places.

DISCUSSION AND ANALYSIS OF FINDINGS

South Africa has twelve official languages of which one is sign language while the rest are spoken languages that are still in use. The main problem is that the indigenous languages are pressured or influenced by dominant languages (Barman, 2018). In South Africa, the dominant language is English since it is used in various formal domains. As a result, the use of a dominant language in the digital space causes a decrease in the use of indigenous languages which may result in them becoming extinct. This has a very serious impact on indigenous languages as the most immediate counterpart of the globalization process (Prasetyo, 2012). Indigenous languages must not be overlooked because of digital globalization fears. Stakeholders such as the national language boards, provincial language units, language developers, lexicographers, language teachers, and the general public should all be involved in language development and preservation. The following paragraphs will discuss the findings using the themes that emanated from the collected data.

Adoption and Utilization of Available Digital Tools

Seeing that digital platforms are dominating the communication space; they are the perfect tool to raise awareness about language development and preservation. Despite the pressures brought on by the 4IR, various types of language technologies can be used to preserve and even develop indigenous languages. Native speakers must establish structures to address the issues of adoption, accessibility, affordability, and the application of technologies posed by the 4IR to globalize their languages (Adhikari, 2019). Technological devices are available to people of all ages to preserve both spoken and written versions of indigenous languages. Translation tools, for example, can be used to translate some of the information into the targeted indigenous languages. However, those tools should be used with caution, and quality assurance should be performed by a qualified linguist before they are made available to the general public. Strong quality assurance is necessary especially in translation since digital translating tools typically translate word for word without regard for the syntactic obligations of a specific indigenous language and possible loss of meaning. The researcher believes firmly that the global era has the capability of advancing technology, especially in communication, and has the potential to make even bigger and greater improvements in every aspect of our lives than the first three industrial revolutions together (Xu et al., 2018).

It is therefore crucial for South African language speakers to preserve their languages using widely available communication technologies like podcasts. Video, audio, and podcasts can be used to preserve spoken versions of indigenous languages, allowing elderly people who speak the language to participate. Furthermore, language experts who understand the science of the language can record information such as vocabulary, proverbs, and sayings supported by linguistics that comprises the science of language, such as phonetics, phonology, morphology, syntax, and semantics. With these being recorded, the young, the old, and future generations can benefit from the tool on a variety of devices, including mobile devices, allowing language speakers to access, share, and use the recordings for general information, education, and research.

Nesting, Promoting, and Facilitating Indigenous Language Learning in Formal and Higher Education Institutions

Nesting the language by teaching it in nursery schools is another method of promoting and preserving the language and its cultures among the young. Preschoolers will learn the language through conversation as well as nursery rhymes, games, and game songs (Malobola-Ndlovu, 2018), thereby keeping the language alive in a fun and joyful way. These songs can be made available online and even sent to parents via mobile devices for home practice. To avoid language teaching becoming lost in the stages of teaching and learning, there should be continuity between language use in the different phases of learning including universities. In the teaching process, the language can be preserved if grammar and vocabulary are emphasized as the heartbeat of each language. Importantly, most indigenous languages are tonal, and teaching the indigenous language in this manner will ensure that the perfect tone is used and preserved for the next generation.

Teaching the language to the young and youth will, therefore, promote language development and inspire them to use the language confidently in the face of the 4IR's challenges. This will allow the youth to overcome most social challenges and even enjoy the convenience of online language material. For successful language teaching, preservation, and development, all stakeholders should stand their ground and face the transformation brought by the 4IR regarding which Gleason (2018, p. 3) noted that "it is exciting to live in a time of real change and transformation, and it is also scary." Following on from the above, there is no need to be scared but to go along with the transformation and transform the way we think about our languages and use them in making presentations and sharing them on social media platforms for the betterment and visibility of the languages. The process of language development and promotion is more successful if it begins with parents, teachers, language developers, language bearers, and curriculum implementers, not forgetting society, whose involvement is critical in policy development.

Using the Indigenous Language in Most Communication

Documentation of an indigenous language alone will not suffice to preserve the language. However, language promotion through language speaking will increase the number of people who speak the language. One of the most important indicators of the survival of a language is the community, speech, and speakers. More speakers determine the position and functionality of the language (Siregar, 2022). Speaking the language will entice even non-native speakers to speak and understand it. Some non-native speakers may even learn it as their first or second language in school. This will prevent a situation in which the language has all resources but is on the verge of extinction because native speakers ignore it in favor of the dominant language. In the previous era, it was a punishable offense to be caught speaking indigenous languages on school premises. That alone was one of the contributing factors to native speakers tending to look down upon their languages. African languages are mostly associated with poverty, barbarism, stupidity, inferiority, and backwardness (Madadzhe, & Sepota, 2006).

The negative comments and labeling when one speaks one's language have a significant impact on dragging indigenous languages into the mud. Malatji and Lesame (2019, p. 80) declare that the speakers of African languages should appreciate these languages by constantly using them on different platforms. The reason for speaking the language is that when an oral language is lost, it takes with it all the knowledge that the people possess. When the last speaker dies, there is likely to be no trace at all of their existence" (Riza, 2012). This signifies that an indigenous language is more effective when it is spoken as it signifies an individual's identity that cannot be separated from his/her language. Native speakers of a particular language should bear in mind that when they come across other languages, they should understand that they are there for communication and economic factors. As Alberts (2000, p. 91) observes, language is a vehicle for the transmission of scientific and technical information, as well as a vehicle for the transmission of cultural information. This also applies to the South African context: information is acquired through language, and that is why people have the right to be assisted in their preferred language in public sectors such as government, civic life, and the education system.

While English is widely accepted as a common lingua franca in South Africa, its use excludes those who are not fluent in the language (Rudwick, Sijadu, & Turner, 2021, p. 242). This further suggests that institutions can help to develop indigenous languages by using them in all communications within their various institutions. The government, whether online, on pamphlets, or on billboards, can best serve the purpose of developing languages if the information is written in the languages of the people and distributed to relevant speakers. It will be more understandable, meaningful, and close to their hearts, as stated by Nelson Mandela.

Verbatim Preservation of Indigenous Languages

People's languages serve as veritable tools for preserving and passing down their literature from generation to generation. The norms, values, riddles, idioms, music, oratory, folktales, folklore, incantations, proverbs, poems, and people's way of life are fully expressed through language (Oboko, 2020) and allow native speakers to invest their energy in a fun and enjoyable way while preserving their languages. From lullabies to nursery rhymes, the goal of teaching was to enrich young children with words, vocabulary, and sentences that will be used in the future. Traditional songs, proverbs, and expressions contained in the nursery rhymes form the nucleus of the indigenous language. The narration of an indigenous folktale promotes language use as well as narration and presentation skills (Lubambo, 2019). A critical examination of praise poems reveals the history of the person being praised, including victories and defeats, which is vital in the preservation of indigenous languages to face the challenges brought by the technological era. The same is true for clan praises which provide similar benefits. Whatever the motivation for writing a song, the result supports the preservation of specific language patterns and words, the presentation of historical and institutional language, and the promotion of the language within the community and globally (Wiremu, 2020). Traditional and modern music are both part of verbatim language transmission because they are fully embedded in a society's language use, sayings, history, and philosophy of life. The poetic devices embedded in music such as figurative speech as well as rhyming, and repetition of words, syllables, and sentences that bring about the rhythm of the language may create a love to sing and further the love for the indigenous language. These oral performances can still be used to preserve and develop the language in the age of the 4IR.

Strategies for the Advancement of Language Development

Language development requires mutual agreement among various stakeholders, including language planners. Language planning is regarded as the first step in language development and is defined by UNESCO (2005, p. 5) as a process of intervening in the natural development of a language. Indigenous languages can be developed if carefully planned for the overall benefit of the nation, which leads to the idea that language and society development should include minorities (Magwa, 2006). Language planners, language boards, and policymakers are the primary participants in language development. As primary developers, it is critical to consult with the community and other native language speakers so that those stakeholders can own the language development processes. Depending on the state of the language and the needs of society, various stakeholders must take various actions to advance language development. The following paragraphs will discuss some actions to consider when developing a language.

Empowering and Showcasing Indigenous Languages

Native speakers must empower their language to prevent it from becoming extinct. One of the most crucial factors in language development is promoting the language despite the challenges posed by the 4IR and the existence of a dominant language. Native speakers and language practitioners can play important roles in language promotion (Xu et al., 2018). Teachers may organize language competitions and debates in their indigenous languages. This will encourage further research in which young people will go around seeking correct terminology from elders, language developers, and language specialists. Learners' participation in celebrating and showcasing their languages on special occasions may propel language development forward. The youth can get involved in the sense that they can share their ideas on the development and preservation of terms with the rest of the world via social media (Makananise et al., 2023).

Using Film, Television, and Social Media to Strengthen Indigenous Languages

Formal language is restricted to the classroom. However, for development purposes, languages can be extended from the classroom to the public and the world by producing films and television programs featuring indigenous languages in consultation with elderly people who know the languages and cultures, as well as language specialists who know the science and vocabulary of the languages. This is simple because the 4IR enables the creation of novel systems that integrate physical and digital technologies for an increasingly interconnected population (Nyagadza, Pashapa, Chare, Mazuruse, & Hove, 2022). Films and television shows are popular among people of all ages; watching the shows will make the indigenous languages visible and appealing to viewers.

According to Davis (2016, p.2), the 4IR can be summarized as "the advent of cyber-physical systems," bringing new ways of integrating technology with human life and society as a whole. Social media dominates communication in a variety of information dissemination methods. As previously stated, technology has both positive and negative effects on human activities, but minority languages suffer the most because communication is done in one common language. As a result, the practice of denying the importance and value of local languages and their use serves to deny the rights of that specific language group, namely the ability to speak and be heard (Miller, 2003). It is, therefore, up to native speakers to stand their ground and develop their languages in social media by communicating on all available platforms such as WhatsApp, Twitter, Facebook, and TikTok using their indigenous languages.

There is no doubt that the presence of indigenous languages on social media platforms sparks metalinguistic reflection among users and increases the legitimacy of indigenous languages as relevant, modern modes of communication (Obi-Ani, Anikwenze, & Isiani, 2020, p. 8). Posting audio-visuals on TikTok and other platforms may help to develop the language as followers will end up understanding the language. It may take some time for that language to gain popularity, but consistency will make the language familiar to social media users.

CHALLENGES IN THE DEVELOPMENT AND PRESERVATION OF INDIGENOUS LANGUAGES IN THE 4IR

Attitude Toward Indigenous Languages

The attitude of dominant languages toward African languages plays a significant role in making them unpopular and useless. Rudwick et al. (2021, p. 242) suggests that "although English is widely accepted as a common lingua franca in South Africa, its use excludes those who are not proficient in the language." In some cases, native speakers present negative attitudes toward their languages to the extent that they shun their language and speak the dominant language. Some native speakers even call their language by the colonial name "vernacular" which means "uncivilized language." This results in inferiority complexes, and in the end, native speakers lose their identity in favor of the dominant language. Attitudes toward indigenous languages cause some native people, particularly the elite, to forbid their children to learn an indigenous language. Such parents even forbid their children to speak the language at home, denying their children knowledge of their own identity. Consequently, language attitude can be used to either destroy or build a language. Sibeyan (1991) concurs that language is an emancipator weapon and urges Africans to rally behind their indigenous language in order to be liberated from psychological and scientific blindness. Even in the 4IR era, native language speakers are obliged to change their attitudes toward their languages and adopt what the digital era demands of them. Some attitudes toward indigenous languages may be attributed to global changes brought about by the digital era. In this case, indigenous language speakers should play a key role and be positive in sharing resources in their languages since this will be beneficial for them and non-language speakers especially if the language is used in different domains. Furthermore, the need to decolonize their mind is critical since in the process of decolonization language reintegrates and restores the previously dominated to their culture and human story (wa Thiong'o, 2000).

Digital Literacy in African Perspective

The major problem with the digital era is that it gives those with access to technological devices easier and faster access to information while those who do not have access are disadvantaged. Most adults who are the bearers of information on indigenous languages are not well-versed in digital technology. This poses some problems in getting the information from them. As a result, most of the minority indigenous languages are voiceless on social media (Malatji, 2019). Even though the youth are active on digital platforms digital literacy among adults might hinder the smooth development and preservation of indigenous languages.

CONCLUSION AND RECOMMENDATIONS

This chapter discussed the preservation and development of indigenous languages in the 4IR era. Although there are challenges that affect indigenous languages, there are also positive aspects. The importance of English and the global changes brought about by the 4IR are not denied in the chapter, but the emphasis is on rising above the storms. Though English is the global language of communication it does not mean that native speakers can sit back and watch their languages die. Aside from the impact of the digital era, language speakers have the opportunity to develop and promote their language through the use of digital platforms. Nevertheless, indigenous language speakers should not be concerned about the impact of the 4IR because it is here to stay and will advance as time goes on. Instead, the challenges can be defeated by adopting digital methods such as social media platforms, television, mobile devices, and digitization of language resources for future generations. Furthermore, speaking the language is vital from home to formal institutions, increasing the number of speakers. There are online language development methods that can also be used to empower indigenous languages. Moreover, the digitalization of language resources is significant for the development and preservation of the language. We are indeed living in the digital era, but it is also true that there are opportunities for language development in this age of the Fourth Industrial Revolution.

REFERENCES

Abraham, A. (2020). Impact of digital media on society. *International Journal of Creative Thoughts*, 8(5), 2742–2748.

Adhikari, D. (2019). Status of English language teaching at secondary level under different school interventions. *Journal of NELTA*, 24(1–2), 162–177.

Adzer, V. C. (2012). Factors militating against the development of indigenous languages: The TIV language in perspective. *Journal of Igbo Language & Linguistics*, 5(1), 76–79.

Alberts, M. (2000). Terminology management at the national language service. *Lexikos*, 9 (Series 10), 234–251.

Al-Rodhan, N. (2015). Strategic culture and pragmatic national interest. *Global Policy*, 22.

Asante, M. K. (2000). Afrocentricity, race, and reason. In M. Marable (ed.), *Dispatches from the ebony tower: Intellectuals confront the African American experience* (pp. 195–203). New York: Columbia University Press.

Barman, U. (2018). Automatic processing of code-mixed social media content. Doctoral thesis. Dublin City University, Dublin.

Chawane, M. (2016). The development of Afrocentricity: A historical survey. *Yesterday and Today*, 16, 78–99.

Davis, N. (2016). What is the fourth industrial revolution? *World Economic Forum*, 19 Jan 2016.

Desai, Z. (2001). Multilingualism in South Africa with particular reference to the role of African languages in education. *International Review of Education*, 47, 323–339.

Enaifoghe, A. (2021). The digitalisation of African economies in the Fourth Industrial Revolution: Opportunities for growth and industrialisation. *African Journal of Development Studies*, 11(2), 31.

Engelmann, W., & Von Hohendorff, R. (2019). Regulatory challenges in nanotechnology for sustainable production of biofuel in Brazil. In M. K. Rai & A. P. Ingle (eds.), *Sustainable bioenergy: Advances and impacts* (pp. 367–381). Elsevier.

Gleason, N. W. (Ed.). (2018). *Higher education in the era of the fourth industrial revolution*. Singapore: Springer Nature.

Jany, C. (2017). The role of new technology and social media in reversing language loss. *Speech, Language and Hearing*, 21(2), 73–76.

Juhary, J. (2020). Industrial Revolution 4.0 and its impact on language and cultural studies. *International Journal of Languages, Literature and Linguistics*, 6(1), 65–68.

Khokholkova, N. (2016). Worlds of color. *Asia and Africa Today*, 5, 72–76.

Logan, W. (2016). Cultural diversity, cultural heritage and human rights: Towards heritage management as a human rights-based cultural practice. In S. Ekern, W. Logan, B. Sauge, and A. Sinding-Larsen (eds.), *World heritage management and human rights* (pp. 19–32). Routledge.

Lubambo, R. J. (2019). Manipulation in folklore: A perspective in some siSwati folktales. Doctoral dissertation. University of South Africa, Pretoria.

Madadzhe, R. N., & Sepota, M. M. (2006). The status of African languages in higher education in South Africa: Revitalization or stagnation. In D. E. Mutasa (ed.), *African languages in the 21st century: The main challenges* (pp. 126–149). Pretoria: Simba Guru Publishers.

Magwa, W. (2006). Towards an African renaissance in language planning: A review of strategies to promote the use of indigenous languages as tools for development: The case of Higher Education Sector in Zimbabwe. In D. E. Mutasa (ed.), *African languages in the 21st Century: The main challenges* (pp. 150–175). Pretoria: S. G. Publishers.

Makamani, R., & Nhemachena, A. (Eds.). (2021). *Global Capital's 21st Century Repositioning: Between COVID-19 and the Fourth Industrial Revolution on Africa.* Langaa RPCIG.

Makananise, O. F., Malatji, E. J., & Madima, S. E. (2023). Indigenous languages, digital media, and the COVID-19 pandemic in the Global South: A South African discourse. In A. Salawu, T. B. Molale, E. Uribe-Jongbloed, & M. S. Ulla (eds.), *Indigenous language for social change communication in the Global South* (pp. 75–92). London: Lexington Books.

Makananise, F.O. (2022). Youth Experiences with News Media Consumption: The Pursuit for Newsworthy Information in the Digital Age. *Journal of African Film & Diaspora Studies (JAFDIS)*, 5(2).

Malatji, E., and Lesame, C. (2019). The use of South African languages by youth on social media: The case of Limpopo Province. *Communicare: Journal for Communication Sciences in Southern Africa*, 38(1), 76–95.

Malatji, E. J. (2019). The impact of social media in conserving African languages amongst youth in Limpopo province. Doctoral thesis. University of Limpopo, Polokwane.

Malobola-Ndlovu, J. N. (2018). Functions of children's games and game songs with special reference to isiNdebele: the young adult's reflections Doctoral dissertation. University of South Africa, Pretoria.

Miller, A. P. (2003). Language and power. *Multicultural Perspectives*, 5(3), 33–38.

Mohochi, E. S. (2003). Language choice for development: The case for Swahili in Kenya. *Journal of African Cultural Studies*, 16(1), 85–94.

Mutasa, D. E. (2002). The Renaissance of African languages: An inevitable enterprise? *South African Journal of African Languages*, 22(3), 239–247.

Nyagadza, B., Pashapa, R., Chare, A., Mazuruse, G., & Hove, P. K. (2022). Digital technologies, Fourth Industrial Revolution (4IR) & Global Value Chains (GVCs) nexus with emerging economies' future industrial innovation dynamics. *Cogent Economics & Finance*, 10(1), 2014654, DOI: 10.1080/23322039.2021.2014654.

Obi-Ani, N. A., Anikwenze, C., & Isiani, M. C. (2020). Social media and the Covid-19 pandemic: Observations from Nigeria. *Cogent Arts & Humanities*, 7(1), 1799483.

Oboko, U. G. (2020). Language as a didactic tool and vehicle of cultural preservation: A pragma-sociolinguistic study of selected Igbo proverbs. *International Journal of Society, Culture & Language*, 8(2), 121–136.

Olaifa, T. P. (2014). Language preservation and development: The role of the library. *Journal of Library and Information Sciences*, 2(1), 23–28.

Philbeck, T., & Davis, T. (2019). The fourth industrial revolution. *Journal of International Affairs*, 72(1), 17–22.

Pouspourika, K. (2019). The 4th industrial revolution. Institute of Entrepreneurship Development. Retrieved October 04, 2023, from https://ied.eu/project-updates/the-4-industrial-revolutions.

Prasetyo, H. E. (2012). Preserving indigenous languages through a more integrated national cultural strategy. International Seminar "Language Maintenance and Shift II," July 5–6, 2012. 47. 423–427.

Prisecaru, P. (2016). Challenges of the Fourth Industrial Revolution. *Knowledge Horizons. Economics*, 8(1), 57–62.

Republic of South Africa. 1996. Constitution of the Republic of South Africa, 1996. Pretoria: Government Printer.

Reviere, S. L., & Bakeman, R. (2001). The effects of early trauma on autobiographical memory and schematic self-representation. *Applied Cognitive Psychology*, 15(7), 89–100.

Riza, H. (2012). Indigenous languages of Indonesia: Creating language resources for language preservation. *Proceedings of the IJCNLP-08 workshop on NLP for less privileged languages* (pp. 113–116).

Rouse, M. (2014). What Is Digital Divide? Definition from WhatIs.com.

Rudwick, S., Sijadu, Z., & Turner, I. (2021). Politics of language in COVID-19: Multilingual perspectives from South Africa. *Politikon*, 48(2), 242–259.

Schwab, K. (2017). *The fourth industrial revolution*. Redfern, NSW, Australia: Currency Books. WEF.

Schwab, K. (2016). The Fourth Industrial Revolution. World Economic Forum, Geneva.

Sibeyan, B. P. (1991). *Education and sociolinguistics*. Manila: Manila Publications.

Siregar, I. (2022). Effective and efficient treatment of regional language preservation strategies in the Nusantara. *Journal of Humanities and Social Sciences Studies*, 4(2), 16–22.

Srinivasan, R. (2006). Indigenous, ethnic and cultural articulations of new media. *International Journal of Cultural Studies*, 9(4), 497–518.

Stearns, P. N. (2020). *The industrial revolution in world history*. Routledge.

United Nations Educational, Scientific and Cultural Organization (UNESCO). (2005). *Guidelines for terminology policies*. Vienna: Infoterm.

wa Thiong'o, N. (2000). *Writing for diversity*. In R. Phillipson (ed.), Rights to language, equity, power and education (pp. 101–105). Routledge.

Warren, D. M. (1991). Using indigenous knowledge in agricultural development. *World Bank Discussion Papers*, 127, 35–46. Washington, DC: World Bank.

Wiremu, R. (2020). Language preservation and Māori. *The Choral Journal*, 60(8), 41–46.

Xu, M., David, J. M., & Kim, S. H. (2018). The fourth industrial revolution: Opportunities and challenges. *International Journal of Financial Research*, 9(2), 90–95.

Chapter 7

Kivunjo Names and Naming as an Indigenous Language Preservation and Digitization Strategy

Zelda Elisifa

This chapter aimed to identify and classify place names among the Kivunjo-speaking speech community and ultimately create an online repository for them. This is in line with Oluocha's (2015) assertion that toponyms are revered by the people for their cartographic, cultural, ethnographic, social, historical, linguistic, economic, political, spiritual, intellectual, scientific, and geographical significance. The study of place names or toponyms (topos: place and onomia: name) has been a long research tradition among historical and cultural geographers. The signatories of place names demonstrate power relationships between the colonial and colonized, postcolonial nationalistic sentiments, and changing political relationships. The density of street and place names in cities is testimony to the human desire to make landscapes legible, imageable, and orderly for easy navigation. In turn place names become effective bonds between people and places evoking nostalgic reflections and memoirs of personal experiences (Savage, 2009).

Place names or toponyms, asserts Helleland (2012), are inextricably connected with the history of a place. They commemorate the events of the past or the people that inhabited the place. As carriers of the past, toponyms help individuals develop a sense of attachment to places long after these events have happened. Kostansk (2016), cementing that toponyms foster collective and communal identities, points out:

> Events and actions are remembered by place names, in a way similar to buildings and inscriptions on walls. In this way, in their memorialization of actions

and events, communities utilize toponyms as mnemonic devices for their collective identity. (p. 421)

According to Hough (2006), place-name research involves both the close analysis of individual toponyms, tracing the earliest historical spellings to establish an etymology, and the comparison of corpora from different areas and periods. Tattoni (2019) opines that the names given to places are a legacy of the past distribution of animal and plant species. Studies about the geographical distribution of toponyms are common in historical, archaeological, and linguistic research (Cox et al. 2002) and have been used to reconstruct the displacement of human populations in the past, according to the fragments of the different languages that are still present in the names.

On the linguistic front, toponyms too, conserve aspects of past languages, and, thus, are valuable in the study of the history of languages. Toponyms preserve linguistic elements of the language(s) once spoken in the locality (Særheim 2011; Hedquist et al. 2014; Endo 2021) and because they retain parts of languages that might have disappeared elsewhere, "permit historical inferences about languages and the people who spoke them" (Campbell 2013:436). The toponyms referring to nature are labelled as phyto-toponyms when they refer to plants, and zoo-toponyms in the case of animals. Plant common names used in toponyms also depict the usage of the species as food, medicine, fabric, or for other activities (Gruezo 1999; Fagúndez and Izco 2016). Place names related to nature are not only a legacy of the former presence of species but also provide insights into the traditional usage and interaction with the environment. According to Fagúndez and Izco (2016), toponyms are: "stable, spatially-explicit elements that may be used as indicators of bio-cultural diversity," revealing the socioeconomic value given to nature over time and therefore should be considered an important part of cultural heritage.

Grace (2020a) observes that toponyms are distinguished by spatial granularity, referring to fine-grained locations such as individual buildings and street intersections, or coarse-grained locations such as municipalities, regions, and countries. The granularity of toponyms in crisis social media creates opportunities for social media use in crisis response: fine-grained toponyms can support emergency response, while course-grained coarse-grained (and fine-grained) toponyms can inform, for example, impact assessments in emergency management. The previous empirical studies on toponymy have been on language use in indigenous communities including in Abui society (Gin and Cacciafoco 2021), in S'ncamtho in Zimbabwe (Ndlovu, 2018), and Maasai in Kenya (Kihara 2020). In the area of digital media, there are studies by Grace (2020a, 2020b), Middleton et al. (2014), and Giraut (2020). These studies show that the area of toponymy is complex, multifaced, and eclectic.

In addition, it has been widely studied in various settings. However, studies on toponyms in Tanzania are scanty (save for Mtavangu, 2020; Buberwa, 2012; Alphonce and Sane, 2019) and none in Kivunjo-speaking area. This chapter, therefore, sought to analyze Kivunjo place names as an indigenous language preservation and digitization strategy.

EMPIRICAL STUDIES AND THEORETICAL FRAMEWORK

Review of Empirical Studies

Scholars in toponymy have significantly contributed to empirical evidence for the use of local languages in naming various native places. For example, Raper (2019) recorded at the Cape from the beginning of the seventeenth century, and components of these names are compared phonologically and orthographically with Nama, Korana, Griqua and Bushman equivalents. Cognizance is taken of orthographic devices employed by early writers to represent clicks, click releases, vowel colorings, and other phonological phenomena, and these are compared to standardized symbols. Dutch and Afrikaans names are identified that have proven to be translations of the indigenous names, or to have had the same toponymic motive, or to be folk-etymological interpretations. An indication is provided of the individual Bushman languages with which place name components are compared, and traditional orthographic rules and symbols employed are compared to those of modern Bushman languages. It is pointed out that the identification and preservation of indigenous place names is by United Nations resolutions on geographical names as elements of intangible cultural heritage and in accordance with stipulations of the Constitution of the Republic of South Africa.

The diversity of Bushman languages and the proliferation of orthographic rules applicable to languages preclude the recognition and identification of Bushman equivalents unless the standardized traditional conventions applicable for centuries to the individual extinct languages are employed. Ntuli (2019) examined the extent to which the meaning of selected languages' indigenous place names has been retained or may have gone into extinction due to the influence and hegemony of more influential languages. Data on indigenous place names were collected from the KwaZulu-Natal Provincial Geographic Names Committee (KZN PGNC), the South African Geographical Names Council's (SAGNC) website, interviews, books on onomastics, history, and newspapers. The focus of the study is mainly on KwaZulu-Natal. The study uses the qualitative approach. It also uses language hegemony and semantic theories. The language hegemony theory is utilized to explore the subjugation of one language's place names by another language, while the semantic theory is used to investigate in the main, the meaning of place names and to a lesser degree their origin. The study argues that hegemony on place naming exists within South African or African indigenous languages, contrary to the common belief that language hegemony is usually perpetuated by languages of European origin over African languages. The paper posits that the meaning and origin of place names are usually related. The study of the meaning and origin of place names further reveals that indigenous languages were at some point in time closely intertwined and were not demarcated by current geographical and linguistic boundaries. The then contact among various languages can be observed in the frequent juxtaposition of differing indigenous place names within geographical spaces, predominantly set aside for indigenous languages. The paper utilizes the interpretive paradigm in unpacking views on the meaning and origin of indigenous place names.

Liebenberg (2019) searched for and extracted indigenous names, and toponyms, from primary source VOC Cape archival documents vested in the Western Cape Archives and Records Service (WCARS), covering the governance of the Cape of Good Hope by the VOC (Vereenigde Oost-Indische Compagnie—Dutch East India Company) from 1651 till 1795. The objective was to explore the wealth of indigenous place names thus brought to light, from a historical linguistic perspective with the aid of secondary sources. Although the VOC documents written in seventeenth and eighteenth century Dutch contain invaluable information, the contents remain inaccessible and not available for public use and research if not transcribed. However, by digitizing and transcribing important collections of VOC material (Liebenberg 2017), scholars are now able to follow the tracks of thousands of names of indigenous places and people encapsulated in these documents.

The VOC chronicle of the 1689 expedition into the interior recorded a large number of place names along the route and serves as an excellent example of the value of a geographical description of the landscape and of noting indigenous place and clan names (with/without a Dutch translation). A number of the chronicle's toponyms were complemented by the findings of a modern mapping aid, Garmin Mapsource, which has been applied in this comparative study as it revealed the existence of a large number of indigenous place names not mentioned in the documents. These remnants of the past are still used by local farming communities and descendants of the indigenous peoples alike.

TOPONYM IN DIGITAL MEDIA

In the realm of toponyms in social media, studies have also been conducted, as exemplified below. Grace (2021) examined toponym usage across

22,343 tweets posted during a severe storm in the Northeastern United States. Tweets were qualitatively coded for nineteen types of storm-related information as well as toponym usage, location reference, and granularity. Findings show that users (1) include more geographic information, including toponyms and geotags, in tweets about emergencies than about other topics; (2) report geographically distributed events but tend to include toponyms rather than geotags when reporting local information; and (3) include mostly municipal and regional toponyms in tweets about emergencies but tend to include hyperlocal toponyms and additional municipal or regional markers in reports of infrastructure damage and service disruption. Together these findings offer implications for social sensing applications in emergency response and management. These include more opportunities for course-grained damage assessment than fine-grained situational awareness, and the need for internal and external sources of geographic information to distinguish information about local and remote events. Last, findings suggest opportunities for passive and active sensing approaches responsive to the recipient design of social media: users provide additional geographic context that helps others distinguish local and remote risks within noisy information spaces that emerge during geographically distributed crises.

Grace (2020b) examined toponym usage and granularity across six categories of crisis-related information posted on Twitter during a severe storm. Findings show users often include geographic information in messages describing local and remote storm events but do so rarely when discussing other topics, more often use toponyms than geotags when describing local events, and tend to include fine-grained toponyms in reports of infrastructure damage and service disruption and course-grained toponyms in other kinds of storm-related messages. These findings present requirements for hyperlocal geoparsing techniques and suggest that social media monitoring presents more immediate affordances for course-grained damage assessment than fine-grained situational awareness during a crisis.

Middleton et al. (2014) used event-related keywords to collect 92,300 tweets posted after a 2013 tornado struck Moore, Oklahoma, of which 42,434, or 46 percent, were found to contain some kind of location reference. Similarly, Avvenuti et al. (2016) observe that 35–58 percent of crisis-related tweets posted during two Italian disasters contain at least one toponym. Giraut (2020) investigated the many and diverse toponymic situations where usages, cartography, and nomenclatures reveal a multiplicity of sometimes conflicting denominations, that function according to different registers. These frequent and rich situations can be interpreted in light of political and cultural geography as indicators of a plurality of representations and practices, but also of historical relations to space and potential claims on these spaces. Such plural denominations have so far attracted the attention of researchers when they manifest competing territorial claims and form part of geopolitical conflicts.

Gin and Cacciafoco (2021) analyzed features of Abui society through Abui toponyms collected using Field Linguistics and Language Documentation methods. It finds that, because place names communicate valuable information on peoples and territories, Abui toponyms reflect the agrarian lifestyle of Abui speakers and, more broadly, the close relationship that the people have with their landscape. Furthermore, Abui toponyms express positive traits in the Abui culture like kinship ties and bravery. Notwithstanding, like other pre-literate and indigenous societies, oral stories are commonly used to explain how places are named. This chapter augments the existing Abui toponymic studies on the connection between names and the places they name and provides a deeper understanding of the Abui language, culture, and society.

Similar studies in Africa include Njoh (2017), who analyzed toponymic inscription, the exercise of street/place naming, as a tool for articulating power in Anglophone and Francophone Africa. The focus was on Dakar, Senegal, and Nairobi, Kenya, which were respectively indispensable for the colonial projects of France and Britain in Africa. Dakar was for France's West African Federation and Nairobi was for Britain's colonial East Africa. It is shown that toponymic inscription was used with equal zeal by French and British colonial authorities to express power in built space. Thus, both authorities used the occasion to christen streets and places as an opportunity to project Western power in Africa. With the demise of colonialism, indigenous authorities in Kenya inherited the Western vocabulary of spatiality but speedily moved to supplant Eurocentric with Afrocentric street/place names. In contrast, postcolonial authorities in Senegal remain wedded to the colonial tradition of drawing the most important street and place names from the Eurocentric cultural lexicon. Consequently, although the vocabulary of spatiality in Nairobi projects African nationalism and power, that of Dakar continues to express mainly Western power.

Also in Africa is a study by Zuvalinyenga and Bigon (2021) that explored the present-day problem of gender-biased street names as prevalent in sub-Saharan Africa's cityscapes. That is the abundance of masculine street names as opposed to feminine ones in the urban environments of this region. The article first provides a comparative view of the scope of this toponymic phenomenon in other geographic regions of sub-Saharan Africa. It also identifies a few decisive factors in the creation of gender-biased urban landscapes in sub-Saharan Africa. These factors consist of recent tendencies in critical toponymy studies; colonial and postcolonial cultures of governmentality; and inadequate urban planning legislation and vision as pertained by postcolonial states. This toponymic problem is then exemplified in a site-specific analysis of the city of Bindura in northeastern Zimbabwe.

In Kenya, Daniel and Mátyás (2023) examined the toponymic heritage used in Kenya's Authoritative Geographic Information (AGI) toponyms database of 26,600 gazetteer records through documentation and characterization of meanings of place names in topographic mapping. A comparison was carried out between AGI and GeoNames and between AGI and OpenStreetMap (OSM) volunteered records. A total of 15,000 toponymic matchings were found. Out of these, 1567 toponyms were then extracted for further scrutiny using AGI data in the historical records and from respondents on toponyms' meanings. Experts in toponymy assisted in verifying these data. From the questionnaire responses, 235 names occurred in more than one place while AGI data had 284. The elements used to characterize the toponyms included historical perceptions of heritage evident in toponyms in their localities, and ethnographic, toponymical, and morphology studies on Kenya's dialects. There was no significant relationship established between the same place name usage among dialects as indicated by a positive weak correlation r $(438), \square = \square 0.166, p \square < \square 0.001$ based on the effect of using the related places and the distance between related places.

Also, in Kenya, Kihara (2020) examined place names named by the Maasai based on environmental conditions, physical features, fauna, and flora, as well as social functions. The study revealed that place names of Maasai origins reflect the historical migration of the Maasai. In addition, through contact with other ethnic languages as well as English, Maasai place names have been linguistically adapted. Examples include:

- Kileleshwa, is from "oleleishwa," a type of bush in Maa, which means big bush.
- Ilgirgir is a type of common species of acacia tree around this area.
- Loltiyani, which means "place of bamboo" is administratively called Londiani.
- Enkare nanyokie is derived from the nature of the "enkare" (water) found in that place. Nanyokie means "red water."
- Narok-ilmoru, meaning "place of black stones" is situated at the foot of Mount Kenya.

The chapter concludes that Maasai place names remain resourceful records of ethnic as well as a nation's history, a measure of environmental change or degradation. In Zimbabwe, Ndlovu (2018) focused on the characterization of S'ncamtho toponyms in Bulawayo and it goes on to measure the impact of these toponyms on the population of Bulawayo dwellers. S'ncamtho is an urban youth variety that is built on urbanity and streetwise style. The study assumes that, as S'ncamtho is the language of the youth in Bulawayo, people are exposed to S'ncamtho toponyms as the youth are found in all spheres of urban life in Bulawayo, especially the taxi industry which is used by the majority of people in the city. The research collected S'ncamtho verbal toponyms from Godini taxi rank in Bulawayo through undisclosed nonparticipant observations and some from the intuition of the researcher. Intuition and interviews were used to get the etymology of the toponyms and questionnaire tests of familiarity and usage were used to measure the impact of these toponyms on the population. Content analysis is used to characterize and classify S'ncamtho toponyms in Bulawayo and the metaphor comprehension test is used to measure their impact on the population. This assumes that S'ncamtho has its toponyms for locations in the city and that these are popular, especially with the youth, but people across age groups now use them. It was found that the low-density areas are known in S'ncamtho as emasabhabha (suburbs), emakhiweni or ebalungwini (whitemen's area), emakhitshini (kitchens—because blacks who were found there worked as maids), emayadini (yards), emanozini (at those who speak through their nose—meaning whites) and emasaladini (at the salads—the rich eat salads). The review of the literature shows that the area of toponymy is complex, multi-faced, and eclectic. In addition, it has been widely studied in various settings. However, studies on toponyms in Tanzania are scanty and none in Kivunjo speaking area.

THEORETICAL FRAMEWORK

The study was guided by Saul Kripke's (1980) causal theory of reference, also known as the historical chain theory of reference. It is a theory of how terms acquire specific referents based on evidence (in our case from the Kivunjo speech community). According to Kripke (1979), a name's referent is fixed by an original act of naming (also called an "initial baptism") whereupon the name becomes a rigid designator of that object. The uses of the name later on down history succeed in referring to the referent by being linked to that original act via a causal chain. Furthermore, Kripke argued that to use a name successfully to refer to something, one does not have to be acquainted with a uniquely identifying description of that thing. Instead, one's uses of the name need only be caused (in an appropriate way) by the naming of that thing. In short, a name refers rigidly to the bearer to which it is causally connected, regardless of any particular facts about the bearer, and in all possible worlds where the bearer exists.

While originally the theory was meant for onomastics (study of personal names), it is also suitable for toponyms since place names are also unique designators of particular areas. In Kivunjo speaking community, the precolonial inhabitants most likely had unique happenings, activities, or phenomena (natural, supernatural, or human-induced) that "caused" or "triggered" their baptizing the place to beach such names.

METHODOLOGY

Study Design

The study is a case study in design. Being an in-depth study of one person, group, or event and to learn as much as possible about an individual or group (Cherry, 2022), a case study is a valid design for studying a specific speech community. In the context of this study, the case is Kivunjo speaking community in their names and names of places. The study seeks to delve into this phenomenon of naming places and its relation to the sociocultural and socioeconomic aspects of the people.

Study Approach

The study was approached qualitatively. This approach is defined as a process of naturalistic inquiry that seeks an in-depth understanding of social phenomena within their natural setting that relies on the direct experiences of human beings as meaning-making agents in their everyday lives. Rather than by logical and statistical procedures, qualitative researchers use multiple systems of inquiry (in our case, participant observations and interviews) for the study of human phenomena, which in our case is place names and the meaning and criteria of the naming by Kivunjo speaking people.

Population, Sample, and Sampling

The population for the study is Kivunjo native speakers with ages ranging between fifty and eighty. The native aspect of language was a desirable attribute since, following Kaplan (2016), there is some language (largely by native speakers) that heavily influences thought (naming included). As for age, mature adults are believed to be custodians of received wisdom in terms of name-giving and the social semantics emanating from the naming.

The sample for the study included fifteen key informants and they were obtained via convenient sampling. The criterion for their inclusion was their being native speakers of Kivunjo and residents in the Kivunjo area for at least fifty years. The study took place in Mwika North Division in Moshi Rural District, Kilimanjaro region.

Data Collection Methods

Data were collected via participant observation and unstructured interviews. The researcher together with the research assistant paid site visits to various banners, and direction posts that were and took note of the names they saw as well as snapshots of some of such banners and posts. The unstructured interview was mainly to get the meaning of names that were collected via participant observation in the form of site visits. They were asked to recall the etymological meaning of the names and relate the meaning to current cultural schemata or otherwise. When the latter was the case, the place name was deemed to be an arbitrary label.

After the data were collected, they were thematically classified into the relevant thematic categories depending on the criteria for naming that were researcher-tailored, having studied and made sense of the data.

Ethical Concerns

In the current study, three aspects of research ethics were observed. The first was voluntary participation in which the informants were asked to feel free to opt in or out of the study at any point in time in the course of data collection. The second was informed consent by which the informants were made aware of the purpose, of the study (that is had no monetary incentives) before they agreed or declined to volunteer information. The third was administrative in which the researcher sought the consent of ward and village administrators to move around the study place for data collection.

FINDINGS AND DISCUSSIONS

The study had a single objective that sought to identify and classify place names among Kivunjo speaking speech community. This section handles the findings of that objective. The overall findings have shown that a total of 33 place names were identified. These have been organized into five themes based on the criteria for the place names. The criteria are (1) clan or institution, which were 11(33.3%); (2) occupations, which were 6 (18.2%); (3) beliefs, which were 6 (18.2%); (4) weather and climate, the occurrences of which were 8 (24.3%) and (5) violence and warfare, with only two occurrences, like 6 percent of all names. Each of these categories is analytically presented, exemplified, and discussed in detail hereunder.

CLAN/INSTITUTIONAL

Clans, being institutions in the sense of indigenous clan organizations (The Kivunjo speech community included), influenced the naming of places, notably dominant clans. Findings show that the naming of place names falls in line with clans and falls in four inclinations. There was a total of thirteen place names in Kivunjo, following clans/local institutions. These are classified into three categories social mingling, familiar basis, and residence of notable figures. The social mingling was the most dominant in this category, with seven (53%) out of thirteen names in this category. This indicates how the Kivunjo people had a rich and consistent way of social engagement so much so that they named their places of engagement. The names belonging to this category are shown below.

  i. Kisambo—A gathering place for youths who are news mongers and rumour spreaders/con-men
  ii. Lya-ngoyo—Ngoyo's marketplace
  iii. Kisharinyi—Where the clan members meet
  iv. Mengenyi—Where elders meet in the evening for social engagements
  v. Kiruwenyi—Cattle gathering place for elders to assign the herder of the day/week
  vi. Komburu—Goat slaughtering area
  vii. Mbonyi—Place of greetings to one another

Data indicate that meeting for social activities was a more defining criterion in this subcategory as is the case for Kisambo, Kisharini, and Mbonyi, whereas meeting for socioeconomic reasons ranked second, examples being Mengeni and Komburu. Evidence for serving toponyms but without original denotation is Kisambo, which is used here to indicate the location of a Pentecostal church:

Kanisa la Pentekoste,
Mamba Kisambo,
Siku za Ibada.

Some names, in the course of linguistic adaptation due to modernity and language contact lost their original orthographic representation examples Monyi is now written as Mboni, as illustrated in the address below:

Shule ya Sekondari Mboni
161 Mboni

164 *Zelda Elisifa*

Kijiji cha Mboni
25220 Mamba Kaskazini
Moshi

Ranking second in this category is the familial criterion. The names under this category are as indicated below.

1. Kotela—Area where King Tela lived
2. Lole—Land of generous family people
3. Komolo—Place where once lived a person named Komolo
4. Komakundi—An area occupied by the Makundi clan

The third and the least in this category is the category of names defined by residence. Only two names are in this category. These are Ko-mangi, which refers to the King's residential area/palace, and Marera, which refers to Old buildings place. Lole (meaning "land of the generous family") is now used as an arbitrary place name serving as direction to a Lutheran Church parish location. A study by Nwaha (2020) on toponyms among Basaa people revealed that every place has its name that makes a difference from other places around the world. Among the Basaa's people, toponymy gives praises to the people as well as social events, ferocious or wild animals, and so on. Here, the name of a village for example is more often than that of one common ancestor, explaining the affiliation relationship.

Relating to familial and residence criteria for place names, Okpala-Okaka (1995) observes that ancient place names can equally give an idea of the political or administrative influence an area once had on some other areas. It was commonly the practice in the days of yore that the subordinate or servile regions would give names to some places in the language of the ruling (feudal) or overseeing state.

Occupational Criterion

Occupations in terms of where they were taking place were also a criterion for place names origins. These are in the form of cultivation, ironwork, and trade, each of which occurred twice. The findings show an equal distribution of names on the criterion of speech community members' occupation types. The subtypes in this category are as follows:

The cultivational names: These are names the origin of which is where farming was taking place, signaling that, among the Vunjo speakers, the fields were detached from home neighborhoods even though there was a portion within which a home is located known as "kihamba." The names that were found in this study are Kondeni, meaning flat land with cultivation fields

Kivunjo Names and Naming as an Indigenous Language Preservation   165

away from home, and Kondenyi, which refers to a cultivation area far away from home.

Iron work (smiting). The Vunjo people a home to a strong and popular clan called Makundi (also referring to one another as Mocha, which used to specialize in iron smiting. It is from these members of the Makundi that the two place names owe their origin. Examples of such place names are Nganyeni ("Iron Smithery Factory") and Mnganya ("Iron Smithers' homes").

Trade criterion. The Chaga (Kivunjo speakers inclusive) are uniquely business-conscientious people, and they are the most dominant traders (small, mid, and even millionaires) within Kilimanjaro and in the country at large. It is no wonder some place names are biased towards trade. Examples are Kilacha ("Barter trade area/mini market area") and Uuwo ("Liquor smelling or selling place"). The latter, though preserving its original orthography, just as the case for other names, has lost its name-referent semantic literality and is thus an arbitrary label serving located school locations for example, shule ya Msingi Uuwo.

So human activities have a role to play in toponymy, notably in activities that are recurring and peculiar to a speech community. As Algeo and Algeo (2000) observe rightly so, the use of the name is generally central to humans and human activities and the interconnections of onomastics with such disciplines as medicine, anthropology, business, linguistics, folklore, and literature are central. Mandillah (2022) in her study noted that people are honored through naming as a result of their impact on the progress of the community in various fields such as agriculture, education, business, and health. For instance, Wadina (The place of Dina) according to Kakai is named after a prominent female businesswoman in Webuye town called Dina. In this case, the possessive prefix {wa-} means 'owner of' followed by the root {Wangamati} or {Dina.} to derive the place aforementioned place names. One can easily infer that the names are driven by the fact that the person is said to own the place which serves as its distinguishing feature.

In addition, zeroing to trade activities, the South African Geographical Names Council (2002) asserts that toponyms are also necessary for other purposes such as trade and commerce, transportation, communication, regional and environmental planning, science and technology, successful conduct of elections and censuses, provision of social amenities and services, tourism, disaster management, and search and rescue operations.

Beliefs

Kivunjo people (as is the case for the rest of the Chaga clan) are highly religious people (over 90% Christian); such piety was also the case before conversion to Christianity. Thus, there are place names associated with beliefs.

166 *Zelda Elisifa*

These were in the form of religious beliefs and death (and handling of the dead). The findings show that out of six place names in this subcategory, six (66.7%) were related to death or handling of the dead. Since may be attributed to the fact that handling death and the dead is among the most dreadful things among many pre-literate societies. Examples of such names are religious and death/handling of the death.

The current findings concur with Alphonce and Sane's (2019) analysis of the origin and the sociolinguistic meaning of 110 place names around the Hanang' District in Tanzania. The study revealed, inter alia, that place names in Hanang served to describe the people's history and beliefs. Similarly, Anyachonkeya (2014) conducted a linguistic and cultural survey of naming in Igbo land. He noted that personal names reflect people's cultural norms and practices and that naming among the Igbo showcases their fears and aspirations, joys and hates, ideals and values, and cultural and spiritual values. He concludes that Igbo names have social, eschatological, and religious implications.

Kivunjo Related to Toponyms Related to Death

The names and their meanings are as indicated below:

1. Lanzi—A place of flies due to corpses being dumped therein
2. Kilomenyi—At graveyard
3. Komafio—A hospital area where death wailings and lamentations are prominent
4. Ashira—A place smelling of corpses/where human corpuses were dumped

The names referring to death were only two (33.3%), which are: Lyakirumu, which means "a place inhabited by ghosts" and Kirashionyi, which refers to a "Sacrificial place." The name Ashira (meaning "A place smelling of corpses/ where human corpses were dumped"), is now but an arbitrary designator of the place name.

The findings concur with Oha et al. (2017) who, using an interpretative approach to translation, text analysis, and cultural studies, selected one hundred (100) toponyms from different parts of India and Nigeria and analyzed them to show the development of place names in both countries in the new millennium. In Nigeria, the influence of British English is everywhere in the names of cities, towns, villages, streets, tourist centers, and rivers, including "Douglas Road," "Wetheral Road," "Owerri" instead of "Owere," "Awka" instead of "Oka," "Warri" instead of "Wori," among others. In India, however, we see indigenized naming forms such as "Tilak Nagar," "Mahavir

Kivunjo Names and Naming as an Indigenous Language Preservation 167

Nagar," "Rama Krishna Ashram Marg," and "Rajiv Chowk." Similarly, Namunguba and Ong'nda (2022), in their study of place names of Luburusu place names in Kenya, found that Lubukusu toponyms remain important cultural sources and spatial records of past generations. Therefore, toponyms play a significant role in preserving the identity of the local population and as such, they are also an important part of the cultural heritage.

Weather/Climate

Weather and climate also define events in terms of waterbodies, landforms, and fauna. The place names under weather and climate were variously distributed as water bodies had the most recurring names at the frequency of five, which equals 71.4 percent of all eight names of the category, followed by water bodies which were only 2 (28.5%) while the fauna toponymy occurred only once (14.3%). Room (1996) classifies this kind of classification as hydronyms, in other words, proper names of various bodies of water.

The data show that most place names related to water bodies derived their designation from rivers and springs rather than from rainy phenomena. This might be explained by the fact that the water bodies on the ground/habitat are tied to daily perennial livelihood activities such as water fetching, laundry, and irrigation while the rainy phenomena are related to seasonality. However, the water bodies earlier on referred to are no longer there as exemplified in Shokonyi ("a place of water spring") and which, due to modernity and language contact, has undergone orthographic adaptation, serve only as place name designator for government institutions such as primary school.

In connection to naming water bodies According to Hudson (2013: 16) "In naming waterfalls the milieu must be in the naming because that place marked the point of its creation." Thus, the names reflect the place-names inhabiting the historical monuments." In addition, in a study by Levshin, (1832) on the naming of water bodies, it was noted that the name of Alakol Lake, located in the south-east of Kazakhstan (called "Gurge-nor") is a translation from Mongolian, which, means "lake with a bridge." Furthermore, Sacelux (1939) noted that semantic extension is found in some of the names derived from geographical features, like rivers such as Hurumuzi, which is a narrow waterway in Iran well known worldwide for the passage of vessels, and Pangani, a city situated on the left bank of the river Pangani in Tanzania from which it derives its name.

In the current study, the two names that originated from landforms are Kilemawaka, which means "a place so difficult and steep" and Fumvunyi, meaning "hilly place." Only a single name was found that is related to fauna. This is Ngurungi, which means "In the forest." Moreover, in a study by Sane (2019) on place names in Hanang District, Tanzania, it was established that

168 *Zelda Elisifa*

the names have informative content deriving from landscape features, plants, people, animals, and names of birds, events, activities, and the behavior of some objects in the place. This is to say that marked geographical features and events in a particular place characterize the place in Hanang. This also is the case in the present study.

Warfare and Violence

The Kivunjo people, like any strong chiefdoms of precolonial Africa, had warfare activities for defense and even aggression among clans or against neighboring communities such as Shirombo and Machami. There were place names that originated from such warfare and violent activities. Examples of such place names are Mbakonyi, meaning "a dangerous bloodshed area" and Lekura, which means "a place of trouble-making people."

Meiring (2010) in his investigation of place names related to violence in South Africa observes that aspects of violence in names reflect the ordeals and suffering of people who were exposed to wars and other forms of violence like natural disasters and environmental dangers. In this article, a few examples are shown to illustrate that toponyms are not meaningless but are rich in historical data that is often overlooked when the names of these villages, settlements, towns, historical sites, post offices, etc., are used in everyday communication. Examples in the study are Bloedrivier/Blood River (named after the battle between 12000 Zulus and 460 Voortrekkers), Aggeneys (a Khoe name for "place of slaughter/blood"), Emfabantu (mountain), which is isiXhosa name for "the death of the people," and Ingogo (site/ (river) (<an isiZulu name for "river/place of corpses/carcasses").

Lawal (1992: 17), studying toponyms in Nigeria concludes that "Place-names that are used in the lore of Nigerian society have historical significance. They remind people of the places passed through during the period of migration. In land disputes, place names have been very useful in finding solutions to entitlement to land."

CONCLUSION

The chapter has shown that the Kivunjo speech community has rich and diverse means of naming places. Most of these names have their origin in pre-colonial Tanzania and reflect the socioeconomic and religio-cultural aspects then. In other words, what the place names suggest is that the Kinvunjo speech community were crop cultivators, iron smelters, and traders, had chiefdoms, and strong beliefs and taboos. The place names, while they are but arbitrary designators of habitats in the modern Kivunjo community, do tell a lot about their historical past. They behave like an unwritten anthropological encyclopedia of the history of the Kivunjo people. Even when the names are now homes to modern institutions and religious houses, they still bear witness to relics of the non-perishability of cultures (spiritual and material) of Kivunjo's past. They are being digitalized in modern media via online retrieval means is a contribution to the African rich cultural past, made known by Kivunjo toponymy.

REFERENCES

Algeo, J., & Algeo, K. (2000). Onomastics as an interdisciplinary study. *Names*, *48*(3/4), 265–274.

Alphonce, C., & Sane, E. (201). Toponyms and identity in Hanang District: Their origin and meaning. *Ethnologia Actualis*, *19*(1), 106–116.

Anyachonkeya, N. (2014). Naming in Igbo Land: A linguistic and cultural study. *Mediterranean Journal of Social Sciences*, *5*(17), 113–122.

Avvenuti, M., Cresci, S., Del Vigna, F., & Tesconi, M. (2016). Impromptu crisis mapping to prioritize emergency response, *Computer*, *49*(5), 28–37. https://doi.org/10.1109/MC.2016.134

Buberwa, A. (2012). Sociolinguistic meaning of Bantu place names: The case of Ruhaya in north-western Tanzania. *Journal for Studies in Humanities and Social Sciences*, *1*(2), 111–120.

Campbell, L. (2013). *Historical linguistics: An introduction.* 3rd ed. Edinburgh: Edinburgh University Press.

Cherry, B. (2022). What is a case study? An in-depth study of one person, group, or event. Accessed from https://www.verywellmind.com/how-to-write-a-psychology-case-study-2795722 on 20th September 2022.

Cox, J. J., Maehr, D. S., & Larkin, J. L. (2002). The biogeography of faunal place names in the United States. *Conservation Biology* 16(4), 1143–1150. https://doi.org/10.1046/j.1523- 1739.2002.01202.x

Daniel, N., & Mátyás, G. (2023). Citizen science characterization of meanings of toponyms of Kenya: a shared heritage. *GeoJournal* 88, 767–788. https://doi.org/10.1007/s10708-022-10640-5

Endo, M. (2021). Geographical distribution of certain toponyms in the SamgukSagi. *Anthropological Science*, *129*(1), 35–44.

Fagúndez, J., & Izco, J. (2016) Diversity patterns of plant place names reveal connections with environmental and social factors. *Applied Geography (Sevenoaks, England)* 74, 23–29. https://doi.org/10.1016/j.apgeog.2016.06.012

Gin, S. L. T., & Cacciafoco, F.P. (2021). Toponyms as a gateway to society: An Abui case study. *Old World: Journal of Ancient Africa and Eurasia*, 1–8 (Brill).

Giraut, F. (2020). Plural toponyms: When place names coexist. choGéo, 53,1–8 DOI: https://doi.org/10.4000/echogeo.20760

Grace, R. (2020a). Hyperlocal toponym usage in storm-related social media. WiP Paper—Social Media for Disaster Response and Resilience Proceedings of the 17th ISCRAM Conference—Blacksburg, VA, USA May 2020.

Grace, R. (2020b). Toponym usage in social media in emergencies, *International Journal of Disaster Risk Reduction, 52,* 2212–4209, https://doi.org/10.1016/j.ijdrr.2020.101923

Gruezo, W. S. (1999) Of Philippine plants and places: An ethnobotanical memoir. *Asia Life Sciences* 8, 15–47.

Hedquist, S. L, Koyiyumptewa, S. B, Whiteley, P. M, Kuwanwisiwma, L. J, Hill, K. C., & Ferguson, T. J. (2014). Recording toponyms to document the Endangered Hopi language. *American Anthropologist, 116*(2), 324–331.

Helleland, B. (2012). Place names and identities. *Oslo Studies in Language, 4*(2), 95–116.

Hough, C. (2006). "Place Names," In Keith Brown (ed.), *Encyclopedia of language and linguistics* (Second Edition), 613–620. Amsterdam: Elsevier.

Hudson, B. J. (2013). The naming of waterfalls, *Geographical Research, 51*(1), 85–93.

Kaplan, A. (2016). Women talk more than men: . . . and other myths about language explained. Cambridge: Cambridge University Press. doi:10.1017/cbo9781316027141.011. ISBN 978-1-316-02714-1.

Kihara, C. P. (2020). Maasai toponymy in Kenya. *Language in Africa, 1*(2), 30–47. doi 10.37892/2686-8946-2020-1-2-30-47

Kostanski, L. (2016). Toponymic attachment. In C. Hough (ed.), *The Oxford handbook of names and naming.* Oxford: Oxford University Press, 412–426.

Kripke, S. (1980). *Naming and necessity.* Cambridge, MA: Harvard University Press.

Lawal, A. A. (1992). *The traditional methods of preserving history and culture.* Lagos: Nigerian National Commission for UNESCO.

Levshin, A. (1832). Description Kirghiz-Kazhakh or Kirghiz Kaisak hordes and steppes. Proceedings of the geographical. St. Petersburg, 1: 264.

Liebenberg H. C. (2017). Die beskikbaarstelling van argiefmateriaal. *Afrikaanskollokwium,* 16-17 Augustus 2017, University of Pretoria, South Africa.

Liebenberg, H. (2019). Recognition, Regulation, Revitalisation Place Names and Indigenous Languages. Proceedings of the 5th International Symposium on Place Names 2019 jointly organised by the Joint IGU/ICS Commission on Toponymy and the UFS Clarens, South Africa, 18–20 September 2019.

Mandillah, L. (2022). A morphosyntactic and semantic analysis of toponyms among the Luhya: A case of Bungoma County. *Journal of Languages, Linguistics and Literary Studies, 2*(1), 28–35.

Meiring, B. (2010). Aspects of violence are reflected in South African geographical names. *Werkwinkel, 5*(2), 95–112.

Middleton, S. E., Middleton, L., & Modafferi, S. (2014). Real-time crisis mapping of natural disasters using social media. *IEEE Intelligent Systems, 29*(2), 9–17. https://doi.org/10.1109/MIS.2013.126

Mtavangu, N. (2020). Place names as reservoirs of rare linguistic data: The Bantu locative prefix i- in Southwest Tanzanian toponyms. *Utafiti, 14*(2), 315–338. https://doi.org/10.1163/26836408–14010018

Namunguba, M. N., & Ong'onda. A. N. (2022). The role of toponyms in cultural heritage preservation: A case of Lubukusu toponyms in Kimilili Sub County, Bungoma County. *International Journal of Social Science and Human Research, 5*(9), 4177–4183, DOI: 10.47191/ijsshr/v5-i9-27.

Ndlovu, S. (2018). "Characterisation and social impact of urban youth languages on urban toponymy: S'ncamtho toponomastics in Bulawayo," Literator, *39*(1), 1373. ttps://doi.org/10.4102/lit.v39i1.1373

Njoh, A. J. (2017). Toponymic inscription as an instrument of power in Africa: The case of colonial and post-colonial Dakar and Nairobi. *Journal of Asian and African Studies, 52*(8), 1174–1192. https://doi.org/10.1177/0021909616651295

Ntuli, S. (2019). Reflection on Place Names in Indigenous Languages. Proceedings of the 5th International Symposium on Place Names 2019 jointly organised by the Joint IGU/ICS Commission on Toponymy and the UFS Clarens, South Africa, 18–20 September 2019.

Nwaha, S. (2020). "The toponyms and their meanings among the Basa'a people: Towards a preservation of cultural and ancestral heritage," *International Journal of Development Research, 10*(07), 37649–3765.

Oha, A. C. I., Kumar, B., Anyanwu, B., & Omoera, O. S. (2017). On Nigerian and Indian toponyms: Socio-cultural divergence and development. *World Scientific News, 80*, 268–283.

Okpala-Okaka, C. (1995). Changes in geographical names: A case study of some local government areas in south-eastern Nigeria (Part 1). Proceedings of the 17th annual conference of the Nigerian Cartographic Association, Minna, October 31—November 4 (pp. 84–88). Lagos: Nigerian Cartographic Association.

Oluocha, N. O. (2015). Decolonizing place-names: Strategic imperative for preserving indigenous cartography in post-colonial Africa. *African Journal of History and Culture, 7*(9), 180–192, DOI: 10.5897/AJHC2015.0279

Raper, P. E. (2019). Place Names in the Cape Colony from the Beginning of the 17th Century: A Comparative Study of Onomastic Components with Nama, Korana, Griqua and Bushman Equivalents. *Journal of Southern African Studies, 45*(4), 773–789.

Room, A. (1996). An alphabetical guide to the language of the name Studies. Lanham, MD: The Scarecrow Press. ISBN 9780810831698.

Sacleux, C. (1939). Dictionnaire Swahili-Français. Paris. Institut d'Ethnologie.

Særheim, I. (2011). Toponyms and language history—some methodological challenges. In Proceedings of the 24th International Congress of onomastic sciences, Barcelona: Onomàstica Biblioteca Tècnica de Política Lingüística, p 1403–1408.

Sane, C. A. (2019). Toponyms and Identity in Hanang' District: Their origin and meaning. *Ethnologia Actualis, 19*(1), 106–116. DOI: 10.2478/eas-2019-0012

Savage, V. R. (2009). Place Names. *International encyclopedia of human geography. Amsterdam: Elsevier.*

South African Geographical Names Council (SAGNC). (2002). Handbook on Geographical Names. Pretoria: Department of Arts, Culture, Science and Technology.

Tattoni, C. (2019). Nomen omen. Toponyms predict recolonization and extinction patterns for large carnivores. *Nature Conservation, 37*: 1–16. https://doi.org/10.3897/natureconservation.37.38279

Zuvalinyenga, D., & Bigon, L. (2021). Gender-biased street naming in urban Sub-Saharan Africa: Influential factors, features and future recommendations. *Journal of Asian and African Studies, 56*(3), 589–609. https://doi.org/10.1177/0021909620934825

PART III

Endangered Language Revitalization, Social Media Language Prospects, and Media Training

Chapter 8

Using Social Media to Promote Indigenous Languages

Reality or Delusion: A Critical Review of Shona Facebook Television

Memory Mabika

Over the years many studies have been carried out on the importance of using, revitalizing and the preservation of indigenous languages globally (Tierney et al., 1927; Ruiz, 1958; Reyhner, 1999; McCarty, 2003; Mabika & Salawu, 2014; Grenoble & Whaley, 2021; Sipeyiye, 2023). Indigenous languages are an integral facet of development since they make interaction between various sectors of government and the people effective. Therefore, consistent and continual use of indigenous languages can facilitate development globally, and in Africa, in particular, where meaningful development has not been taking place and is unlikely to do so in the foreseeable future. Indigenous language researchers have never challenged the common thread that unites works produced from the 1920s to 2023 predicting the slow but natural disappearance of indigenous languages globally. The typical indigenous language rhetoric is that there is an imminent danger facing indigenous languages that could result in their loss over the years; it propagates language preservation, revitalization and passing on to future generations. Indigenous languages are vital for transmitting and preserving a people's cultural heritage, unique identities and beliefs, traditions, and indigenous knowledge systems (Gwerevende & Mthombeni, 2023).

Language, being a fundamental element of human communication, plays a crucial role in reflecting social realities. Thus, language is the backbone of our humanness and has ideological implications, particularly when it comes to the often marginalized and endangered indigenous languages in the face of dominant global languages (Mezhoud, 2023). Global languages that are more widely spoken, such as English and French, are more likely to be preserved while most other indigenous languages that are only spoken by their speakers are likely to disappear with time (Alfataftah & Jarrar, 2018). The longevity of a language depends on its continued use so that it can continue to be passed on from generation to generation. Thus, the effective preservation of languages though centered on their usage by their speakers is essential to expand its use from the normal day-to-day interactions to other local institutions such as the government departments, the education system, and the media (Albayrak, & Badam, 2023; Dan, Kovács, Bacskai, Ceglédi & Pusztai, 2023).

Studies have confirmed that a sizable number of people globally, but mostly from developing nations prefer learning English and in English to their languages which pose great danger to various indigenous languages (Mabika & Salawu, 2014). For instance, in Zimbabwe, the fear of exclusion has led some parents to invest significant amounts of money to enroll their children in English-speaking schools, renowned for their higher academic performance compared to ordinary schools. The perception is that attending these schools provides better educational opportunities and increases the chances of success for their children. This emphasis on English schools highlights the value placed on English language proficiency and the belief that it can open doors to future opportunities. Parents' willingness to invest in these schools reflects the importance of education and the desire to secure a better future for their children within the context of Zimbabwean society without considering the threats this causes to their mother tongue (Al-Qahtani & Al Zumor, 2016; Edwards & Tisdell, 1989). Therefore, it is essential to maintain a balance between indigenous languages and English (Liando & Tatipang, 2022). On the contrary, Mpofu (2023) maintains that the use of English and code-mixing African language in the media and education system results from Eurocentric influence, where people perceive English as prestigious and sophisticated. Thus, code mixing is criticized as a corruption of language and a betrayal of the noble struggle to elevate African languages and resist linguistic imperialism.

Nevertheless, the task of addressing the widespread impact of English on the native languages of developing nations has become increasingly difficult due to various factors that contribute to its global popularity, further eroding our mother tongues. Recent studies reveal that the preference for English over indigenous languages stems from various factors. Global English dominance in international communication and commerce makes it attractive. Diverse nations with multiple languages often choose English due to personal interests. English's use as the medium of instruction in prestigious schools and its media dominance reinforce its appeal. Additionally, many use it for teaching technical subjects, particularly in most developing countries, enhancing its position. People believe English improves job prospects and alleviates poverty, contributing to its widespread adoption (Eli & Hamou, 2022; Liando & Tatipang, 2022; Katukula, Set, & Nyambe, 2023).

These factors motivate increased efforts to find spaces for local languages in a globalized world where the usage of universalized languages is essential and inevitable. For this reason, the significance of promoting the use of indigenous languages in public spaces, such as the rapidly expanding social media platforms like Facebook, is imperative to empower linguistic minorities and advance linguistic diversity rather than exclusion (Lapum et al., 2022). Facebook among other social media platforms provides a lifeline for marginalized languages, sparking scholarly debates (Cassels, 2019; Fadipe & Salawu, 2021; Ligidima & Makananise, 2020; Mabika & Moffat, 2023). Advocates see social media as vital for preserving endangered languages, fostering diversity, and empowering linguistic minorities, while concerns persist about potential cultural dilution in the digital sphere (Alfataftah & Jarrar, 2018; Cladis, 2020). Balancing digital language promotion and cultural preservation remains a contentious issue in a multilingual context.

However, Mpofu and Salawu (2018) argue that social media is aiding in addressing ethnocultural hegemony in Zimbabwe, where the Ndebele and Shona groups compete. Minority communities, like the Kalanga Language and Cultural Development Association, and Ndau' Rekete Ndau: Leave a Legacy use Facebook groups to promote their languages and foster discussions, highlighting the importance of their languages in addressing contemporary issues. The primary objective of this chapter is to examine whether the rise of native language mobile television stations on Facebook is a mere deception or if it genuinely presents tangible opportunities for the Shona language to encourage linguistic diversity in Zimbabwe. The following section provides a brief historical overview of the study location to contextualize the study.

A BRIEF HISTORICAL BACKGROUND OF ZIMBABWE

Zimbabwe had a population of 15,178,979 people as of April 20, 2022 (UNFPA, 2022). The name "Zimbabwe" originated from the largest stone-built complex in southern Africa—the Rozwi Shona dynasty also known as the Great Zimbabwe. The monumental *"Dzimba dzemabwe"* was a significant center of political and commercial activity for the world for over 350 years (Sinamai, 2018; Shenjere-Nyabezi & Pwiti, 2021). Zimbabwe inherited an economy viewed as impressively diversified and sophisticated compared to other economies in Africa at independence. However, it is important to note

178 *Memory Mabika*

that this economic growth was not necessarily accompanied by a development in the quality of life for the majority of the country's population. Although at independence, the newly elected government had its post-independence political woes (Bond, 2000).

The new country inherited debts that were taken out by the white government to buy weapons for its side during the war, and those debts are seemingly odious. However, the country's debts also grew substantially in the following decades as it borrowed for development, and then took out further loans just to service existing debts. This ballooning debt failed to bring prosperity to Zimbabwe. (Padgett Walsh & Lewiston, 2022, p. 1)

Therefore, the newly elected Mugabe-led government's socioeconomic policy served a twofold purpose: firstly, to address the socioeconomic disparities that persisted since independence in 1980, and secondly, to foster inclusive economic growth (Kavila, 2022). Issues concerning indigenous language preservation and media freedoms and development though remaining on the agenda became far-fetched issues as the nation grappled with providing its populace necessities such as food, water, shelter, and electricity, among others (Chambwera, 2020). This killed the morale of a once vibrant populace and drove a multitude of people out of the country in search of greener pastures, a trend which has continued to date.

Although Zimbabwe is still wallowing in political and socioeconomic distress, the ongoing global new information communication technologies wave powered by the Fourth Industrial Revolution (4IR) has also swept through Zimbabwe. This technological hype has led to the introduction of Facebook television handles, also known as mobile television stations. This chapter is interested in assessing the impact of online televisions in preserving the Shona language in Zimbabwe. The following section provides an overview of the Zimbabwe film industry.

Overview of Zimbabwe's Mainstream TV landscape

Zimbabwe's TV landscape is dominated by government control, with the Zimbabwe Broadcasting Corporation (ZBC) playing a central role. This control, reminiscent of colonial times, affects media diversity and freedom of expression (Mpondi, 2018). Post-independence television broadcasting has remained a preserve of the state-controlled broadcaster, the Zimbabwe Television (ZTV) with one national station ZTV. From 1986 to 1997 a second channel, ZTV2, which operated like a community television station covering only the capital city of Harare, was launched. The channel later named Joy TV was rented out to Munhumutapa African Broadcasting Corporation (MABC), which operated it from 1998–2002 but was subsequently removed

Using Social Media to Promote Indigenous Languages 179

in 2002 due to alleged non-payment of ZBC fees (Gwaze, 2013). The ZBC monopoly was restored and continued.

Throughout history, radio and television broadcasters and journalists have faced censorship and limited dissent due to media-centralized control. For example, during the Mugabe era, the government used the police and army to enforce laws like the 2002 Access to Information and Protection of Privacy Act (AIPPA) and the Public Order and Security Act (POSA), previously the Law-and-Order Maintenance Act (LOMA) to suppress opposition (Tsarwe, 2020). The controversial media regulations, supposedly promoting media democratization, suppress democracy by targeting dissenting voices and criminalizing content deemed abusive, indecent, obscene, or false. These laws pressured broadcasting journalists to adhere to specific government agendas.

Over the years, ZTV uncritically accepted and reproduced every aspect of ZANU-PF's policies and discussed its history, mission, and position in the media landscape, reducing the public broadcaster to government cheerleaders (Manganga, 2012). This can be pinned to the not-so-covert way the current regime torments and suppresses the media industry, both public and independent. However, the Zimbabwean indigenous language online television industry has established a glimmer of hope thanks to the development of new information technologies and social media platforms (Vennard, 2002). The emergence of digital platforms and online distribution channels has also provided avenues for digital productions such as Facebook indigenous language television handles to reach a broader audience beyond traditional media audiences who were geographically selected and easily controlled by politicians as is the case with ZTV programming. The various social media platforms have started and continue to dish out not just local short and long films online but also disseminate news, music, reality content, satire, etc., in indigenous languages covering contemporary relevant content to the local audience in and outside the country and continent (Mabika & Moffat, 2023).

The Importance of Indigenous Languages in the Fourth Industrial Revolution

According to Davis, the Fourth Industrial Revolution, dubbed 4IR, simply refers to

> the advent of "cyber-physical systems" involving entirely new capabilities for people and machines. While these capabilities are reliant on the technologies and infrastructure of the Third Industrial Revolution, the Fourth Industrial Revolution represents entirely new ways in which technology becomes embedded within societies and even our human bodies. (2016, p. 11)

Indigenous languages play a vital role in 4IR by preserving cultural heritage, promoting inclusivity, and enabling meaningful participation in the digital age (Farnadi, 2023). As technology advances, it is crucial to recognize and incorporate the linguistic diversity of indigenous communities. Indeed, the 4IR may help level existing language disparities many have endured for a long time. Davis (2016) argues that the future is here with 4IR. He also warns that 4IR can be the potential driver of increased inequality, worsening existing linguistics discrepancies since increased exposure to unprepared users has its downside. Ensuring that indigenous languages, knowledge, innovation, and perspectives from our communities are not lost but valued and shared as we navigate 4IR spaces driven by robots, high-speed 5G connectivity, and ChatGPT is essential. The success of technology-based language revitalization powered by artificial intelligence depends on the ability of the community to demonstrate a value proposition of their languages from the outset (Camacho & Zevallos, 2020). Finding gaps to embrace linguistic inclusivity fosters a sense of belonging, empowers indigenous peoples to contribute to the 4IR actively, and enriches the overall digital landscape with a wide range of cultural perspectives, ultimately leading to more equitable and sustainable progress (Davis, 2016).

Although the 4IR and its associated advancements are unfamiliar and threatening to many digital migrants they are overwhelming to digital natives. However, it is crucial to recognize that the driving force behind any industrial revolution is ultimately the choice of individuals and society (Farnadi, 2023). By acknowledging our agency in shaping this revolution, we can meet the challenges and make informed decisions that align with our values and purpose. Indigenous language communities must seize this opportunity to find spaces to perpetuate indigenous language preservation and revitalization in this technology-driven globalized world (Davis, 2016).

Using indigenous languages on social media in the context of the fourth industrial revolution (4IR) brings numerous benefits. It enables the integration of diverse linguistic and cultural perspectives into the digital landscape, fostering inclusivity and representation (Imran, 2023). By embracing indigenous languages, the digital sphere reflects the linguistic richness of the global society. Furthermore, it empowers indigenous communities to actively participate in the digital economy, unlocking economic opportunities and promoting sustainable development (Mauyakufa, 2020). Embracing indigenous languages on social media in the 4IR era is not only a celebration of cultural heritage but also a catalyst for innovation, collaboration, and social progress (Imran, 2023).

THEORETICAL FRAMEWORK

The Media Ecology Theory

The media ecology theory developed in the 1970s depends on where one looks (Strate, 1999). The Greek words for "family," "house," and "science," oikos and logia, are where the word "ecology" originates (Laskowska & Marcyński, 2019, p. 55). Ecology is a science that studies the composition and operation of nature. It provides a valuable framework for examining the complex interplay between media technologies, communication processes, and the social and cultural environment in which they are embedded (Lum, 2000). Media ecology exists within a multidisciplinary intellectual framework shaped by diverse scholars who have paved the way for theoretical perspectives on culture, technology, and communication. It draws upon the research of influential scholars worldwide, including Harold Innis, Lewis Mumford, Elizabeth Eisenstein, Jacques Ellul, Walter Ong, Eric Alfred Havelock, Jack Goody, Marshall McLuhan, and Neil Postman who significantly contributed to our understanding of social communication, media, and technology (Laskowska & Marcyński, 2019, p. 55). However, Herbert Marshall McLuhan (1911–1980) is the proponent of interest in this study.

The media ecology theory, developed by Marshall McLuhan, explores how media technologies shape the human perception of reality and influence social interactions. It emphasizes that media technologies are not just tools but also extensions of human senses and capabilities, and they play a significant role in shaping our understanding of the world (Rahm-Skågeby & Rahm, 2022). Applying this theory to the study, which sought to examine the efficacy of using Facebook mobile television to preserve and revitalize the Shona language in Zimbabwe, can help gain insights into how Shona Facebook TV functions within the larger media ecosystem, its impact on the viewers, and the dynamics of engagement within the platform.

METHODOLOGY

This chapter employs a qualitative approach to investigate the possible effects of Zimbabwe's Shona Facebook Television handles on the perceived decline of indigenous languages, as postulated by some scholars (Liando & Tatipang, 2022; Gwerevende & Mthombeni, 2023). The selection process involved identifying and purposively choosing five Shona Facebook television handles. These handles were selected based on their popularity, engagement, and content relevance to the study. Five videos with the highest viewership and user engagement were chosen from each Shona Facebook television platform

182   *Memory Mabika*

spanning April 2020 to February 2023, resulting in a selection of the top five videos.

Using Video Data Analysis (VDA), the analysis process involved systematically examining the videos and user comments to identify patterns, themes, and emerging trends. Additionally, the comments were analyzed to identify the viewers' language choices. Researchers can replay videos in slow motion and capture subtle dynamics of timing, interactions, and impact (Bramsen & Austin, 2022, p. 457). Thus, with VDA, the researcher could capture the nuances of the local language from the videos and the user's interactions on mobile television handles recording data on a code sheet.

The five Shona Facebook mobile television handles were selected deliberately, depending on their popularity and traits. They include Bustop TV—A youth-run Zimbabwean media house; Sly Media TV—An online channel that brings a variety of live events, zoom meetings, and unbiased news coverage; Mhosva TV—Mai Vee is a well-known comedian and socialite; Karanganda TV—An entertainment channel; and Mbingaldo TV—Mainly covering Zimbabwean socialites, politicians, and other rich and famous people. The name Mbingaldo comes from the slang "Mbinga," a term used to refer to the rich and famous people in Zimbabwe.

This chapter examines five videos selected from each sampled TV station to identify the genres that attracted high audience responses, views, likes, and shares. Furthermore, the researcher scanned through the comments left by viewers on the Shona Facebook television handles to determine the language patterns and identify interesting trends in their deliberations. This analysis established the language preference of the viewers in their responses and engagement with other Shona language speakers and Shona TV content. The various indigenous language trends helped the researcher come out with some conclusions about the future of the Shona language on the mobile media booming and expanding its reach due to improved connectivity in this 4IR milieu. The data collection involved playing, replaying, recording, and documenting the relevant information from each video and the audience's comments.

Table 8.1. Shona Facebook Mobile Television Handles

	Station name	Creation date	Main language of broadcasting	#Followers	#Likes
1	Bustop TV	25 November 2014	Shona	384 000	206 000
2	Sly Media TV	13 April 2017	Shona	351 000	171 000
3	Mhosva TV	04 May 2020	Shona	733 000	167 000
4	Mbingaldo TV	09 July 2021	Shona	148 000	-
5	Karanganda TV	25 September 2020	Shona	141 000	10 000

Ethical Considerations

The study adheres to all ethical considerations outlined in the university's guidelines, such as the privacy and anonymity of users who commented on the selected mobile television stations. The collected data were used in this academic publication only. The selected Shona television handles and associated videos were publicly available on Facebook.

RESULTS

Data collected using VDA from the selected Facebook television channels were tabulated in the tables below.

Bustop TV is a Facebook handle targeting youth. English is more popular on the channel although it popped up as a Shona TV on Facebook, the video content was created mainly by Shona while users' comments were in English and Shona (50/50).

Sly Media TV primarily focuses on news and reality TV programming, strongly emphasizing Shona language across all three sections. While the Facebook television station uses English occasionally, Shona is the predominant language Sly TV employs in most cases.

Mai Vee TV is a comedy-focused Facebook TV station featuring Mai Vee, a male actor. The channel uses the Shona language, with occasional English. Mai Vee uses the Ndau dialect, popular in Manicaland and promotes autonomy from Zezuru.

Mbingaldo TV, an indigenous Facebook TV channel, primarily features Zimbabwean celebrities and affluent individuals, despite using Shona in all sections and prioritizing English in all aspects. This aligns with literature suggesting English is associated with wealth, but some participants lack fluency nullifying the assumption that the knowledge of English summons better prospects and future success.

Karanganda TV, a Shona-based station, focuses on entertainment, news, and cultural events, promoting preserving and upholding indigenous languages. The station's indigenous language usage aligns with literature advocating for protecting and preserving indigenous languages and cultures.

DISCUSSION

This study investigates and identifies the issues that Shona Facebook television addresses and the genres that attract more views. It also sought to determine the language in which viewers leave comments on the Shona Facebook

Table 8.2. Showing Bustop TV

Date	Title of Video	Genre	#Comments/ Likes/ views/ Shares	Languages used—Captions & Commentary		Languages used—Video content		Languages used by the audience (Comment		Observations
				Shona	English	Shona	English	Shona	English	
26 April 2020	1) Lockdown series episode 13	Drama Comedy	1k/ 5.3K/ 110K/ 140K	X	✓	✓	x	✓	✓	-The actors used Shona fluently. - Actors used pidgin English. -This video was shared most by users.
12 January 2023	2) Aya maartists varikuita politics @eeg_international	Political advertisement	2.9k/ 1.6k/ 123k/ 40	✓	✓	✓	x	✓	✓	-Most of the comments were insults to the performers in Shona.
03 February 2023	3) Birthday interview with CCC leader Adv. Nelson Chamisa as he turns 45	Political inter-view	19/ 102/ 39k/ 39k	X	✓	x	✓	✓	✓	-Political elements are still hocked to the English language.

Date	Story	Genre	Metrics							Notes
15 February 2023	4) A stranded man gifted $100 for Valentine	Reality	482/ 1.4k/ 27k/ 29	X	□	□	x	□	□	-The title/caption is in English and subsequently, the users' comments were mainly in English.
13 March 2023	5) An unidentified man was found dead inside a Honda Fit.	News	2.4k/ 6.1k/ 368K/ 57K	X	□	□▷	□<	□	□	-The person narrating the story struggled to use English statements. - Users attacked his poor English.

Table 8.3. Showing Sly Media TV

Date	Title of Video	Genre	#Comments/ Likes/ views/ shares	Languages used—Captions & Commentary		Languages used—Video content		Languages used by the audience (Comments)		Observations
				Shona	English	Shona	English	Shona	English	
02 February 2022	1) MDC leader Mwonzora was arrested and appeared at Rotten Court.	Interview	32k/ 42K/ 47K/ 0	x	□	□	□	□	□	-A politician is interviewed in English while others are inter-viewed in Shona.
01 July 2023	2) Mwanakomana anopfeka nekutaura semusi-kana . . . ashungu-rudzwa munharanda nekunzi musa-tanist uye ngochani.	Investigative interview	2.9k/ 3.3k/ 264k/ 0	□	x	□	x	□	□	-Most of the comments were insults to the per-formers in Shona.

Date	Content	Genre	Stats							Comments
03 February 2023	3) ZAOGA Founder Dr Ezekiel Guti awarded automatic heavenly entry	Interview Discussion	15/ 20/ 92k/ 16k	x	▢	▢	▢	▢	▢	-Political elements are still hocked to the English language.
10 July 2023	4) And then . . .	Political campaign	20/ 8/ 2.2k/ 0	x	▢	▢	x	▢	▢	-Whiteman speaking fluent Shona and black applauding him.
11 July 2023	5) Ndibhadhare wakandibvisa humhandara kumashure kwehondafit	Reality Court	8k/ 11/ 70K/ 13K	▢	x	▢	x	▢	▢	-Traditional content attracts indigenous language speakers. -Ma2 thousand was English in all the eight comments. Thus, difficult to completely avoid English.

Table 8.4. Mai Vee TV (Previously Mhosva TV)

Date	Title of Video	Genre	#Comments/ Likes/ views/ shares	Languages used—Captions & Commentary		Languages used—Video content		Languages used by the audience (Comments)		Observations
				Shona	English	Shona	English	Shona	English	
28 December 2022	1) Denga revarume hakuna ooh	Satire	12k/ 36K/ 436K/ 425	✓	x	✓	✓	✓	✓	- Comedy attracts more viewers and comments.
09 February 2023	2) Zimuroyi Ukaita chakanaka wazviitira	Satire	12k/ 36k/ 436k/ 251	✓	x	✓	✓	✓	✓	-Although the producer used Shona for the production English could not be completely excluded.
25 March 2023	3) Ndakuda kut-amba ndega	Comedy	1.7k/ 24k/ 53k/ 97	X	✓	✓	✓	✓	✓	- Languages are not important in comic skits. This comic video doesn't use language but just a beat and dance moves.

Date	Title	Genre	Metrics								Notes
12 May 2023	4) Vaka kurira kumusha can relate	Comedy	3.2k/ 23k/ 509k/ 219	⍰	⍰	⍰	⍰	⍰	⍰		-Captions/ titles of comedy videos use emojis. Thus, nonverbal communication is essential in comedy productions.
14 June 2023	5) Celebrating 1 miriyoni followers in advance Faith moves mountains	Comedy	3.9k/ 24k/ 527K/ 193K	⍰	⍰	⍰	⍰	⍰	⍰		-Audiences are not looking at the word only by also enjoy the concept as long as it is clear and understandable.

Table 8.5. Mbingaldo TV.

Date	Title of Video	Genre		Languages used—Captions & Commentary		Languages used—Video content		Languages used by the audience (Comments)		Observations
				Shona	English	Shona	English	Shona	English	
08 June 2022	1) Amai Daisy Mtukudzi addressing nyaya yekunzi havawirirane nana Selmor.	Interview discussion	1.1k/ 3.2K/ 150K/ 0	☐	☐	☐	☐	☐	☐	-Audience comments on a deep understanding of the Shona language. It shows Shona still has room to survive in this multilingual world used more often and consistently.
23 November 2023	2) Relatives narrating the shocking story yeku Zengeza 3	Biographical documentary	831/ 1.7k/ 110k/ 0	☐	☐	☐	☐	☐	☐	-Most of the comments were insults to the performers in Shona.

Date	Caption	Genre	Metrics							Notes
17 April 2023	3) Talent at its best.	Musical Talent Show	198/ 1.7k 110k/ 39k	x	▢	▢	▢	▢	▢	-Singing is a powerful instrument of communication.
06 May 2023	4) We once shared this gratitude testimony last year.	Biological documentary	930/ 13k/ 256k/ 48	x	▢	▢	▢	▢	▢	-English and pidgin English are not easy to distinguish when one is speaking in Shona as is the case with Nigerian Pidgin.
17 May 2023	5) Mukudzeyi Jah Prayzah and wife Rufaro	Romantic scene	3.7k/ 52k/ 555K/ 242	x	▢	X	▢	▢	▢	-Background Shona's song sets the romantic mood.

Table 8.6. Karanganda TV

Date	Title of Video	Genre	#Comments/ Likes/ views/ Shares	Languages used—Captions & Commentary		Languages used—Video content		Languages used by the audience (Comment		Observations
				Shona	English	Shona	English	Shona	English	
22 January 2022	1) Razaro muka	Reality documentary	2.6k/ 19k/ 953k/ 631	☑	☑	☑	X	☑	☑	-Shona is also spoken in Mozambique.
15 April 2022	2) Ndakisirwa nhengo yechidzimai	Reality Interview	966/ 6.9K/ 473K/ 90	☑	X	☑	X	☑	☑	-Shona speakers use a lot of slang. Slang with time may threaten indigenous languages.
01 January 2023	3) "Vari kurara nezvitunha" Odzi Mutare	Investigative interview	614/ 415k/ 220k/ 69	☑	X	☑	X	☑	☑	-Shona speakers like using slang despite their age group.
11 January 2023	4) Mwari wedu anopindura nyararai kuchema	Reality Interview	6.1k/ 27k/ 738k/ 440	☑	X	☑	X	☑	☑	-Multilingualism can result in marriage between people from different countries.

| 17 January 2023 | 5) Murume wekunyanga anofungidzirwa kuti akauraya mukadzi wake nevana | News Interview | 706/ 3.1k/ 178k/ 37 | ▢ | X | ▢ | X | ▢ | ▢ | -Traditional leaders try to protect and preserve their indigenous languages by using Shona mixed with slang or English. |

TV handles to gauge the current position of Shona in a country where English is the primary official language viewed as the language of government, education, and the media (Mabika & Salawu, 2014). According to the data drawn from the top five videos from each of the five selected Facebook television handles, topics include politics (4), music and dance (4), witchcraft (4), cheating (4), marital problems (3), questionable prophets (2), love (2), and other (2). The followers of the various Shona Facebook TV preferences resonate with the literature. According to Ureke (2021), social media users in Zimbabwe prefer skits that revolve around everyday issues.

The analyzed content reveals various genres used in the selected videos. Satires/comedies received more views, while political genres received more comments and sharing. Mbingaldo TV follows the life of rich Zimbabweans and socialites. The audience enjoy distraction from the struggles of life brought by the interesting lives portrayed by socialites and the "Mbingas." Escapism is attained when victims of painful social reality temporarily focus on something that helps them escape from the challenges for a while (Ezeonwumelu & Okoro, 2021). As a result, Mbingaldo attracts many followers, scoring quite a significant number of likes and views throughout. According to Mabika and Moffat (2023), Zimbabweans prefer sharing comedic content over serious videos because they find laughter a coping mechanism for the various social, political, and economic difficulties they are currently experiencing. Similarly, music is an influential genre that can transcend language barriers and create emotional connections encouraging the use of the Shona language among speakers and non-speakers. A review of cultural/traditional content shows that the video content uses the Shona language, and the producer's captions and comments are also in Shona. The usage of Shona to produce and share cultural and traditional content attracted mainly Shona comments, with a few English words randomly used in some comments. These findings confirm that the efficacy of using the digital media landscape in enhancing indigenous languages lies with the producers of the content. Cultural/traditional content seems to motivate the audience to reciprocate in humility in the language used to share the message.

One key observation is the correlation between the language used in videos and the primary language used by audiences. The findings show that interviews with politicians were predominantly in English, while others were in Shona. However, people in urban areas, such as the man who was an eyewitness of an incident where an unknown man was found dead in a car in Harare near a hospital, faltered by trying to mix Shona and English in his narration, which drew attacks from the audiences. This reflects the societal hierarchy placed on English as a language of authority and prestige. At the same time, Shona is considered more accessible and relatable to the generally unsophisticated population, mainly the rural populace. Resonating with this assertion,

Mangeya & Ngoshi (2021, p. 8) state that the social environment in which languages are spoken endows languages with a specific value, resulting in the hierarchization of languages where some languages are held in high prestige while relegating others as unworthy.

This study also highlights users' tendency to use Shona for insults and English for compliments or praise in online comments. This tendency evades detection by non-native speakers or monitoring systems that detect abusive language (Sazzed, 2021; Yusra, 2022). However, using insults in indigenous languages doesn't necessarily mean that offensive speech is more prevalent in these languages. It may be due to users' emotional attachment and familiarity with their native languages, making it easier to convey emotions (Sazzed, 2021; Yusra, 2022, p. 76). Speaking one's native language has more profound emotional effects than using a foreign language.

The study shows that traditional content attracts comments in indigenous languages more than others. However, it is difficult to completely exclude English due to its widespread usage and the incomplete development of indigenous languages (Ilyosovna, 2020; Lettiah, 2021). This observation underscores the complexity of language dynamics and the challenges of promoting and preserving indigenous languages in a digital era. In most cases, audiences naturally accepted the blending of Shona and English, indicating English's dominance. English's pervasive presence made exclusively maintaining Shona content and comments on these Facebook channels nearly impossible. With a 34.8 percent internet penetration rate in early 2023, the study found that the top five Shona Facebook television channels collectively had 1.8 million followers, a significant number considering Zimbabwe's 5.74 million internet users (Kemp, 2023). It is also noteworthy that Shona speakers only constitute 75 percent of the people in Zimbabwe (Mahohoma, 2020). These results confirm the digital landscape's importance in preserving and revitalizing the Shona language. Thus, Shona Facebook television can significantly promote the Shona language usage, preservation, and revitalization.

CONCLUSIONS AND IMPLICATIONS OF THE STUDY

In conclusion, the study found that although the Shona Facebook television handles have a relatively limited reach, they have the potential to significantly impact the usage, preservation, and revitalization of the language. This finding aligns with the media ecology theory, which suggests that media platforms and technologies play a crucial role in shaping and influencing a society's communication and cultural practices. Despite the reach challenges, these handles serve as valuable tools for promoting the Shona language and creating a digital space for its speakers to connect, share content, and contribute to its ongoing development. These platforms can promote language vitality and aid in the continued growth and relevance of the Shona language in the digital age by allowing the indigenous language to reach its speakers in various locations worldwide and, to a certain extent, leveling the dominance of English on social media. Therefore, while traditional leaders and elders work to protect and preserve the language, the younger generation brings innovation and revitalization. During the Fourth Industrial Revolution (4IR) era, traditional leaders were crucial in protecting and preserving indigenous languages. At the same time, ordinary people, especially the younger generation, can utilize rapidly advancing technologies to contribute to developing new Shona expressions, first known as slang, but adopted over time. Consenting, Mutonga and Mukaro (2021) argue that despite the risk of inappropriate usage, slang adds vibrancy, color, and appeal to speech.

LIMITATIONS AND OPPORTUNITIES FOR FUTURE RESEARCH

This study acknowledges several limitations. The purposive sampling strategy may introduce some bias, as the selection of Shona Facebook Television handles and videos might not fully represent the diversity of content available on the platform. Additionally, analyzing viewers' comments depends on the researcher's discretion after scanning a portion of the comments since it was difficult to browse through all the audience comments manually due to time constraints. Also, other factors that may have influenced the viewers' engagement and perception of the Shona language were not identified. Therefore, future studies may examine factors influencing the viewers of the Shona Facebook channels. Thus, future studies need to expand sources of information from only the videos to include users and Facebook television channel representatives.

REFERENCES

Albayrak, F., & Badam, A. (2023). A bilingual life among the triangle tent and reindeer: Heritage language education and use of Mongolian Dukha children. *Pegem Journal of Education and Instruction, 13*(3), 104–116.

Alfandika, L., & Gwindingwe, G. (2021). The airwaves belong to the people: A critical analysis of radio broadcasting and licensing in Zimbabwe. *Communication: South African Journal of Communication Theory and Research, 47*(2), 44–60.

Alfataftah, G. I., & Jarrar, A. G. (2018). Developing languages to face challenges of globalization and clash of civilizations: Arabic language as an example. *Journal of Education and Learning, 7*(4), 247–253. https://doi.org/10.5539/jel.v7n4p247.

Al-Qahtani, Z., & Al Zumor, A. W. (2016). Saudi parents' attitudes towards using English as a medium of instruction in private primary schools. *International Journal of Applied Linguistics and English Literature, 5*(1), 18–32.

Bond, P. (2000). Zimbabwe's economic crisis: Outwards vs. inwards development strategy for post-nationalist Zimbabwe. *Labour, Capital and Society/Travail, capital et société,* 162–191.

Bramsen, I., & Austin, J. L. (2022). Affects, emotions and interaction: The methodological promise of video data analysis in peace research. *Conflict, Security & Development, 22*(5), 457–473. https://doi.org/10.1080/14678802.2022.2122696.

Camacho, L., & Zevallos, R. (2020, September). Language technology in high schools for the revitalization of endangered languages. In *2020 IEEE XXVII International Conference on Electronics, Electrical Engineering and Computing (INTERCON)* (pp. 1–4). IEEE.

Cassels, M. (2019). Indigenous languages in new media: Opportunities and challenges for language revitalization. *Working Papers of the Linguistics Circle, 29*(1), 25–43.

Chambwera, C. (2020). Financial and Economic News Production Practices in Zimbabwe 1980–2018. Doctoral dissertation, University of Johannesburg, South Africa. Available at: https://www.proquest.com/openview/f27bb51f8234a8e9f31f adba523bc148/1?pq-origsite=gscholar&cbl=2026366&diss=y (Accessed 10 June 2023).

Cladis, A. E. (2020). A shifting paradigm: An evaluation of the pervasive effects of digital technologies on language expression, creativity, critical thinking, political discourse, and interactive processes of human communications. *E-Learning and Digital Media, 17*(5), 341–364.

Dan, B. A., Kovács, K. E., Bacskai, K., Ceglédi, T., & Pusztai, G. (2023). Family–SEN school collaboration and its importance in guiding educational and health-related policies and practices in the Hungarian minority community in Romania. *International Journal of Environmental Research and Public Health, 20*(3), 2054.

Davis, N. (2016) What is the fourth industrial revolution? World economic forum: Geneva, Switzerland, 2016; p. 11. Available at: https://www.weforum.org /agenda/2016/01/what-is-the-fourth-industrial-revolution/ (Accessed on 5 June 2023).

Edwards, G., & Tisdell, C. (1989). The Educational System of Zimbabwe Compared with those of Selected African and Advanced Countries: costs, efficiency and other characteristics. *Comparative Education, 25*(1), 57–76.

Eli, T., & Hamou, L. A. S. (2022). Investigating the factors that influence students of English studies as a major: The case of University of Nouakchott Al Aasriya, Mauritania. *International Journal of Technology, Innovation and Management, 2*(1). https://doi.org/10.54489/ijtim.v2i1.62.

Ellerson, B. (2020). African women on the film festival landscape. *Black Camera*, *12*(1), 59–89.

Ezeonwumelu, V. U., & Okoro, C. C. (2021). Social media engagement and escapism tendencies of adolescent students in Uyo Education Zone. *Journal of the Nigerian Council of Educational Psychologists*, *14*(1), 54–68.

Fadipe, I. A., & Salawu, A. (2021). Influence of African Indigenous language media in COVID-19 digital health messaging. *Catalan Journal of Communication and Cultural Studies*, *13*(2), 267–284.

Farnadi, G. (2023). The AI Industry through the lens of ethics and fairness. *Missing Links in AI Governance*, 27. Available at: https://unesdoc.unesco.org/ark:/48223/pf0000384787. (Accessed 02 July 2023).

Grenoble, L. A., & Whaley, L. J. (2021). Toward a new conceptualisation of language revitalisation. *Journal of Multilingual and Multicultural Development*, *42*(10), 911–926. https://doi.org/10.1080/01434632.2020.1827645.

Gwaze, A. (2013). Free-to-air Zimbabwe: Zimbabwe's 'hidden ' cosmopolitan satellite identity. *Re-visualising Africa: Journal of African Cinema*, *1*(1), 1–32.

Gwerevende, S., & Mthombeni, Z. M. (2023). Safeguarding intangible cultural heritage: Exploring the synergies in the transmission of Indigenous languages, dance and music practices in Southern Africa. *International Journal of Heritage Studies*, *29*(5), 398–412. https://doi.org/10.1080/13527258.2023.2193902.

Ilyosovna, N. A. (2020). The importance of the English language. *International Journal on Orange Technologies*, *2*(1), 22–24.

Imran, A. (2023). Why addressing digital inequality should be a priority. *The Electronic Journal of Information Systems in Developing Countries*, *89*(3), 1–12. https://doi.org/10.1002/isd2.12255.

Ivaz, L., Griffin, K. L., & Duñabeitia, J. A. (2019). Self-bias and the emotionality of foreign languages. *Quarterly Journal of Experimental Psychology*, *72*(1), 76–89.

Katukula, K. M., Set, B., & Nyambe, J. (2023). Language ideologies and the use of mother tongues as the medium of instruction and learning in junior primary schools: A case study of parents and teachers in a Namibian school. *Innovare Academic Sciences*, *11*(4), 70–79. http://hdl.handle.net/11070/3708.

Kavila, W. (2022). Understanding the fiscal deficit and economic performance in Zimbabwe. Reserve bank of Zimbabwe economic research division report. Available at: https://africaportal.org/publication/understanding-fiscal-deficit-and-economic-performance-zimbabwe/. (Accessed 23 June 2023).

Kemp, S. (2023). Digital 2023: Zimbabwe. Available at: https://datareportal.com/reports/digital-2023-zimbabwe#:~:text=There%20were%205.74%20million%20internet,percent%20of%20the%20total%20population. (Accessed 05 October 2023).

Lapum, J., Bailey, A., St-Amant, O., Garmaise-Yee, J., Hughes, M., & Mistry, S. (2022). Equity, diversity, and inclusion in open educational resources: An interpretive description of students' perspectives. *Nurse Education Today*, 116, 105459.

Laskowska, M., & Marcyński, K. (2019). Media ecology–(un) necessary research perspective in communication and media studies. *Mediatization Studies*, (3). 53–68. https://doi.org/10.17951/ms.2019.3.53–68.

Lettiah, G. (2021). Countering the cumbersome: Rethinking the Shona compounding term-creation strategy. *Language and Communication, 76*, 13–22.

Liando, N. V. F., & Tatipang, D. P. (2022). English or Indonesian Language? Parents' Perception Toward Children's Second Language Learning Context. *Jurnal Lingua Idea, 13*(1), 61–75.

Ligidima, M., & Makananise, F. O. (2020). Social media as a communicative platform to promote indigenous African languages by young students at a rural-based university, in South Africa. *Gender and Behaviour, 18*(2), 15824–15832.

Lum, C. M. K. (2000). Introduction: The intellectual roots of media ecology. *The New Jersey Journal of Communication, 8*(1) (Spring 2000): 1–7. https://doi.org/10.1080/15456870009367375.

Mabika, M., & Moffat, B. (2023). Are we there yet? Examining the portrayal of Zimbabwean women in Naiza Boom Shona short comedy films. *African Language Media*, 36–49. http://doi.org/10.4324/9781003350194–5.

Mabika, M., & Salawu, A. (2014). A tale of failure: Indigenous language radio broadcasting in Zimbabwe. *Mediterranean Journal of Social Sciences, 5*(20), 2391. https://doi.org/10.5901/mjss.2014.v5n20p2391.

Mahohoma, T. (2020). Experiencing the sacred. *Studia Historiae Ecclesiasticae, 46*(1), 1–17.

Manganga, K. (2012). The Internet as a public sphere: a Zimbabwean case study (1999–2008). *Africa Development, 37*(1), 103–118.

Mangeya, H., & Ngoshi, H. T. (2021). The discursive construction of blackness on WhatsApp status posts in Zimbabwe. *African Identities*, 1–19.

Mauyakufa, F. T. (2020). Examining the filmmaking process about production management: A case study of Harare, Zimbabwe. University of Johannesburg (South Africa). Available at: https://ujdigispace.uj.ac.za/. (Accessed 17 April 2023).

McCarty, T. L. (2003). Revitalising Indigenous languages in homogenising times. *Comparative education, 39*(2), 147–163. https://doi.org/10.1080/03050060302556.

Mezhoud, S. (2023). They kill languages, don't they? A short chronicle of the planned death of Berber in North Africa. *Endangered Languages in the 21st Century*, 61.

Mhonyera, G., Masunda, S., & Meyer, D. F. (2023). Measuring the pass-through effect of global food price volatility and South Africa's CPI on the headline inflation of Zimbabwe. *Cogent Food and Agriculture, 9*(1), 2212458. https://doi.org/10.1080/23311932.2023.2212458.

Mhute, I., & Campus, M. R. Impact of the Zimbabwean language policy on the Shona language and culture. *Journal of Culture, Society and Development, 12*, 104–107.

Mpondi, D. (2018). 'Opening Up Spaces': The Politics of Black Economic Empowerment and Indigenization in the Telecommunications Industry in Post-Independence Zimbabwe. *Journal of Pan African Studies, 11*(2).

Mpofu, P. (2023). Code Mixing in Kwayedza: Language Subversion and the Existence of African Language Newspapers. *African Journalism Studies*, 1–16. https://doi.org/10.1080/23743670.2023.2179091.

Mpofu, P., & Salawu, A. (2018). Linguistic disenfranchisement, minority resistance and language revitalisation: The contributions of ethnolinguistic online communities in Zimbabwe. *Cogent Arts and Humanities, 5*(1), 1551764.

Mutonga, L., & Mukaro, L. (2021). The Role of Language in Prophetic Movements' advertisements in Harare, Zimbabwe. *Miṣriqiyā*, 1(1), 65–90. doi:10.21608/misj.2020.42642.1002. Available at: https://misj.journals.ekb.eg/article_135839.html. (Accessed 12 June 2023).

Ngoshi, H. T. (2021) Repression, Literary Dissent and the Paradox of Censorship in Zimbabwe, *Journal of Southern African Studies*, *47*(5), 799–815, doi: 10.1080/03057070.2021.1959780.

Nkomazana, F., & Setume, S. D. (2016). Missionary colonial mentality and the expansion of Christianity in Bechuanaland Protectorate, 1800 to 1900. *Journal for the Study of Religion*, *29*(2), 29–55.

Padgett Walsh, K., & Lewiston, J. (2022). Human capabilities and the ethics of debt. *The Journal of Value Inquiry*, *56*(2), 179–199.

Pasipanodya, I. (2020). Examining the evolving representation of female characters in Zimbabwean films: A case study of Neria (1993) and Sinners (2013) (Doctoral dissertation). https://researchspace.ukzn.ac.za/handle/10413/19756.

Rahm-Skågeby, J., & Rahm, L. (2022). HCI and deep time: Toward deep time design thinking. *Human–Computer Interaction*, *37*(1), 15–28. https://doi.org/10.1080/07370024.2021.1902328.

Reyhner, J. (1999). Some Basics of Indigenous Language Revitalization. Available at: https://jan.ucc.nau.edu/~jar/RIL_Intro.html. (Accessed 12 June 2023).

Ruiz, R. E. (1958). Mexico: The Struggle for a National Language. *Social Research*, 346–360.

Sazzed, S. (2021). Identifying vulgarity in Bengali social media textual content. *PeerJ Computer Science*, 7, e665. https://doi.org/10.7717/peerj-cs.665.

Shenjere-Nyabezi, P., & Pwiti, G. (2021). Ancient urban assemblages and complex spatial and socio-political organization in Iron Age archaeological sites from Southern Africa. In *Africa, the Cradle of Human Diversity* (pp. 111–147). Brill.

Sinamai, A. (2018). Memory and cultural landscape at the Khami World Heritage Site, Zimbabwe: An un-inherited past. Routledge.

Sipeyiye, M. (2023). (Re) imagining the Ndau indigenous religion of Zimbabwe in the digital age. African Identities, 1–14. https://doi.org/10.1080/14725843.2023.2227349.

Strate, L. (1999). Understanding MEA. In *Media Res*, *1*(1), 1–2. Available at: http://www.media-ecology.net/publications/In_Medias_Res/imrv1n1.html. (Accessed 20 June 2023).

Tierney, M., Mulcahy, R., Ua Maolchatha, R., Browne, P., Bergin, O., & O Briain, L. (1927). The Revival of the Irish Language [with Comments]. *Studies: An Irish Quarterly Review*, 1–22. https://www.jstor.org/stable/30094023.

Tsarwe, S. (2020). Understanding Zimbabwe's political culture: Media and civil society. In S. J. Ndlovu-Gatsheni & P. Ruhanya (eds), *The history and political transition of Zimbabwe: From Mugabe to Mnangagwa*. London: Palgrave Macmillan. https://doi.org/10.1007/978-3-030-47733-2_5

UNFPA. (2022) Population and Housing Census Preliminary Results. Zimstat. https://zimbabwe.unfpa.org/en/publications/2022-population-and-housing-census-preliminary-results.

Ureke, O. (2021). Zimbabwe: Cinema exhibition and consumption in a shadow economy. *Screen*, *62*(3), 359–374. https://doi.org/10.1093/screen/hjab032.

Vennard, F. C. (2002). Restoring Democratic Governance in Zimbabwe: A Critical Investigation of the Internet as a Possible Means of Creating New Sites of Struggle for Positive Democratic Change by Zimbabwean Media and Activists in Zimbabwe. Doctoral dissertation, Rhodes University.

Yusra, K. (2022). Switching Languages for Political Fear, Power and Anger in Digitally-Surveillanced Multilingual Facebook Interaction in Indonesia. *Linguistik Indonesia*, *40*(2), 179–196.

Chapter 9

Exploring the Role of Indigenous Languages in Journalism and Media Training in the Fourth Industrial Revolution Era

Toyosi Olugbenga Samson Owolabi

The world's more than 6,000 indigenous languages (IL) are under serious threat of extinction, with one language disappearing every fortnight while others are at risk (United Nations Department of Economic and Social Affairs [UNDESA], 2016). In Africa and Nigeria in particular, several ILs are at the peril of disappearing. When indigenous languages are under threat, so too are indigenous peoples themselves (United Nations, 2016). Further from that claim, it can be deduced that saving indigenous languages and solving associated language problems is the right step toward protecting indigenous ethnic groups from going into extinction. Language Planning and Language Policy (LPLP) is an established process to manage and regulate the relationships and functions of languages within one national territory until it therefore becomes germane (Jung, 2019). Ikoba and Jolayemi (2020) have also discovered some factors responsible for this development. These include love for Western culture, prominence of foreign languages especially English and French, a dearth of indigenous language teachers, failure of parents to encourage their children to use local languages, and poor facilities such as language laboratories where ILs can be taught and developed. Other factors include a lack of political will to develop local languages, fear of not getting job opportunities outside the local language-speaking areas, and the multiplicity of languages, among others (Akinkurolere, Akinfenwa and Oluwapelumi, 2018).

Frequent disappearance of ILs, according to Egele (2023), has become a social phenomenon often triggered by their inability to fulfill social needs and not for lack of essential structure as other surviving ones. Other reasons proffer by linguists such as Unaegbu, Obiamalu, & Orji (2023) as responsible for the endangered ILs are discrimination of the expected users (citizens, academics, and journalists inclusive) against their languages; dialectal differences, limited knowledge of some local words, lack of properly trained teachers to teach ILs, the uncomplimentary politics of language and powerplay of the past and present governments, and the burden of adapting to the rapidly changing technologies associated with the Fourth Industrial Revolution (4IR) era. Although there is nothing improper for a journalist to be global in orientation with proficiency in an international language, it will, nevertheless, be incongruous to be unable to communicate with others in their native language.

Against the above assertions, it can be deduced that for indigenous language use to be greatly enhanced and preserved in the 4IR era, there is a practical need to see how indigenous language media can be incorporated into digital technologies to revive and sustain them, and in a more general sense, to appreciate such integration for what roles it performs in enhancing the teaching of journalism and media practice among tertiary institutions in Nigeria. It is disheartening to note that as the first three industrial revolutions have come to a close, and the Fourth Industrial Revolution (4IR) driven by digitization has commenced, African countries such as Nigeria are still struggling with the fundamentals of the previous revolutions, which include electricity, mechanization, and automation.

The 4IR is a term that describes the blurring of boundaries between the physical, digital, and biological worlds. It is a term coined in 2016 by Klaus Schwab, founder and executive chairman of the World Economic Forum (WEF), which is characterized by the convergence and complementarity of emerging technology domains, including nanotechnology, biotechnology, Internet of Things (IoT), Information and Communication Technology (ICT), social media, new materials and advanced digital production (ADP) technologies such as 3D printing, human-machine interfaces (HMIs), and artificial intelligence among others (Lavopa & Delera, 2021).

In Nigeria, it is apparent there is insignificant attention being paid to the development, preservation, and promotion of indigenous languages especially in the 4IR. This is particularly so because our language policies have failed to effectively capture the intellectual, moral, and cultural climate of the present era, as well as adapt to ensure their longevity, development, promotion, and preservation. Nigeria, a country of about 200 million people, is a multilingual community with about 500 indigenous languages (Oloruntola et al, 2018), all of which have not been recognized as business languages for centuries because they are not known for activities that can sustain a society and its environment on a global scale. According to Madingiza (2020), some speakers of those indigenous languages are under the erroneous belief that their languages are less important than those of the Europeans and other developed nations. Recent research has, however, proved the contrary. This is why this chapter seeks to show that by enacting good language policy, ILs in Nigeria and elsewhere can be developed to function in part as the language of business and of education/teaching journalism and media studies and be protected against extinction. It also explores the strategies of integrating indigenous languages into the 4IR as they migrate into the digital public sphere to ward off threats and tap into its inherent opportunities.

HISTORICAL OVERVIEW OF INDIGENOUS LANGUAGE MEDIA

The history of Nigerian mass media cannot be complete without a mention of Reverend Henry Townsend, an Anglican priest who established *Iwe Irohin fun Awon Egba ati Yoruba* in 1859. As a pioneer newspaper, it was established as an indigenous language media in Abeokuta. Its English version was established two years after and subsequently, other IL newspapers were also published in Lagos, Abeokuta, Ibadan and Ogbomoso axis of southwest Nigeria (Owolabi, 2014). Other early IL newspapers according to Owolabi (2019, p. 190) include *Iwe Irohin Eko* (1885), *Eko Akete* (1922), *Yoruba News* (1923), *Eleti Ofe* (1923), *Eko Igbehin* (1925), *Osumare Egba* (1925), *Akede Eko* (1927), *Irohin Yoruba* (1945), *Egbaland Echo* (1947), *Irohin Imole* (1947), and *Irohin Owuro* (1948).

Also, in the south-south Efik-speaking area, two IL newspapers were established by the Church of Scotland Mission. They were *Unwana Efik* (1885) and *Ubukpon* (1886) (Coker, 1968). In the southeast Igbo-speaking region, the pioneer newspapers were *Anyanwu* (1956) and *Onuora* (1957). In the mid-1970s *Ogene* was established, followed by *Oku Ekwe* (1990), *Olu Umu Igbo* (1991), *Akuko Uwa* (2001), and *Ozi* (2004) (Nnabuihe and Ikwubuzo, 2006). In the northern region, *Gasikiya Tafi Kwabo*, founded in 1939, was the pioneer indigenous language newspaper. According to Salawu (2011), other indigenous weekly newspapers were established; these include *Ardo* in the Fulfude language, *Gamzaki* in the Hausa language, *Mwanger U Tiv* in the Tiv language, *Okaki Idoma* in Idoma language, and *Albashir* in Kanuri language.

The post-independence Nigerian media landscape also witnessed some indigenous language newspapers that gained popularity at different times: *Oko Ane Igala, Gboungboun, Isokan, Amana, Udoka, Alaye, Ajoro* and *Kowee*. There was also *Al Mizan* published in the Hausa language and *Alaroye* in the Yoruba language. The two IL newspapers have been published and are famous till date. However, a common characteristic of all the pre-independence and post-independence IL newspapers was that they suffered premature death. The reasons for their quick demise were due to a lack of advertising patronage because of a preference for English-language newspapers to the detriment of IL newspapers.

The history of broadcast media follows a different pattern. The 1932 relay of the British Empire Service from Daventry, England, marked the genesis of broadcasting in Nigeria. In 1936, the first Radio Distribution Service (Re-diffusion) was established in Lagos by the federal government and in 1951, a full-fledged indigenous radio broadcast service was established. This was followed in 1960 by the establishment of another radio station by the then Western regional government, having first founded the pioneer television station in the entire African continent. With the creation of more states (36) out of the then four regions, each state established its own radio and television stations. However, it was observed that all these media houses are located in urban centers with commercial orientation and have English and partially some ILs as their languages of broadcasting (Owolabi 2019). With the advent of private investors into the broadcast media business coupled with the federal government liberalization policy of the sector, some television and FM radio stations have started changing the narratives by giving preference to major ILs such as Hausa, Igbo, Yoruba, Edo, Efik, Tiv, Igala, and Kanuri among others in their broadcast schedule. It is important to note that ILs are gaining acceptance in the broadcast media, especially radio, and then print media. NBC has mandated other media organizations to ensure a ratio of 60:40 of their programs in favor of local content. It is therefore not surprising that in virtually all the thirty-six states and the federal capital territory of Nigeria, there are television and FM radio stations that broadcast in ILs in conformity with the NBC rule (Ojebode 2017).

THEORETICAL ANCHORAGE

The chapter is anchored on social responsibility theory propounded by Siebert, Peterson, and Schramm (1956). The major assumption of the theory is that the freedom and position of eminence that the media enjoy must be socially responsible to society. The media under the social responsibility theory must be socially responsible to the public; and their responsibilities must be based on truth, accuracy, objectivity, and fairness (Owolabi, 2014). The principle also stipulated that the press must be pluralistic in giving equal voice to diverse groupings represented in society. Nigerian society is desirous of regular up-to-date information that is professionally served to satisfy the information quests of the reading and listening public. It is the socially responsible media that can professionally inform every member of society and provide a platform for mutual discourse and constructive criticism of the governance system.

The theory is relevant to this discourse because it emphasizes the need for media to give equal and adequate coverage to issues affecting every section of society. If one reflects on the new world order and the media's role in educating, informing, and mobilizing the citizens for participation in the socioeconomic development of the state, we need to put into perspective the rural–urban information imbalance about Nigeria's linguistic and cultural diversity. If the developing nations are complaining about world information imbalance at the international level, there is a greater need for as much agitation to maintain information balance at the national level. The mass media as postulated by the social responsibility theory need to give voice to every section of society by publishing and broadcasting more in the native language of the rural communities where more than 70 percent of the citizens are resident. If the media could attain this level of professionalism, there would be avoidance of the international episode of rural-urban information lopsidedness.

METHODOLOGY

This is a qualitative study, which relies on in-depth interviews as well as obtaining secondary data from books, journals, and newspapers. In-depth interviews were conducted with a small sample of five faculty members purposively selected from the Department of Yoruba Communication of Lagos State University and five working journalists reporting for indigenous language media. Codes were given to each of the respondents, L1 to L5 for the lecturers and J1-J5 for journalists interviewed for the reason of ethical considerations.

The findings will be outlined, interpreted, and discussed qualitatively to answer the following fundamental questions: which indigenous language out of many in Nigeria can be adopted for teaching and learning journalism skills? Does the government have any role to play in the choice and development of ILs? How can indigenous language journalists be trained, formal or on-the-job training or a combination? In what language will their curriculum be designed and taught? What are the challenges facing the use of ILs for teaching journalism in the 4IR? The excerpts of the respondents to the questions will represent their opinions and thoughts in the discussion.

National Language Policy and Language Survival Strategy during the 4IR Era

Language, irrespective of its status, foreign or indigenous, is the greatest asset of a given ethnic group. Language is integral to the fabric of our daily life. This is because language serves as a means of social and business interactions among the populace. Without language, there can be no cultural protection and continuity. Woods (2016, p. 13) has brought into sharper focus the functional dimension of language as a social practice created and communicated for a certain end. Language matters in society. We are formed by the language we speak. When we lose our language, we lose a vital part of ourselves. The limits of my language are the limits of my mind. All I know is what I have words for (David, 2010; Wittgenstein, 1926).

Despite the above-identified functionality and perception of language, there have been serious concerns about the continuous threat of extinction among ILs in Africa particularly, in Nigeria (Ajepe and Ademowo, 2016). The multilingual nature of Nigeria and the politics of language have constituted great challenges to its 500 ILs in recent times. Inconsistent language policies of successive governments, non-codification of many minority languages and the inability to elevate any of the ILs to the official status among others, are some of the major causes of this crisis. These often lead to contestations over which language, ethnic group, and culture is superior to others.

However, the National Policy on Education (NPE) of 1977 revised in 1981 states in Section 2 Paragraph 7 that "the medium of instruction in pre-primary, primary and secondary schools shall be the language of immediate community." Section 3 Paragraph 15(4) of the NPE further states that the "government will see to it that the medium of instruction in the primary schools is initially the mother tongue or the language of the immediate community and at a later stage English." It is, however, unfortunate that because of the government's lack of disposition to enforce its laws, most schools still use the English language as a medium of teaching at all levels. It is even very bad that in many schools ILs are outrightly outlawed. If this trend is checkmated, Nigeria must emulate countries such as China, Japan, Korea, and India that have deployed their ILs as the language of teaching at all educational levels and have made significant leaps in the area of technology and national development.

In the present 4IR era, which is largely driven by science and digital technologies, many linguists and communication experts have identified the potential of extending the usage of indigenous language to interpersonal communication and for mass propagation of messages. According to Owolabi (2019), indigenous language media ILM have been credited with the ability to protect not only the language but also culture from extinction. However, it is important to note that the media organizations in Nigeria, especially the broadcast media, by their mode of operations rely more on foreign content than local. In other words, the majority of their broadcast contents are largely foreign and disseminated in the English language. Imagine how many Nigerians are being denied access to vital information because of their inability to understand the English language in which the programs are transmitted. Nigeria is a country where the literacy level is still relatively low, at about 61.2 percent (Dataphyte, 2022). It is against this background of incongruity that the National Broadcasting Commission (NBC) mandated all broadcast stations to maintain a 60:40 ratio in favor of local content written in IL. Fulfilling this mandate is a different story as the government did not show signs of seriousness to enforce compliance. It is, therefore, apposite to claim that the national and regional media as presently structured are unable to cater for the information needs of about 60 million of Nigeria's estimated 200 million population. Against this backdrop, the media have been observed to give preference to English language audiences to the neglect of the indigenous population. This will not do the society any social good as this is contrary to the tenet of the social responsibility theory, which says "the media should reflect its society plurality by giving equal voice to diverse groupings represented in the society" (Siebert et al., 1956).

The growth of information and communication technology (ICT) in Nigeria has also contributed greatly to how much the youths of today create and consume information. It has also opened up new media platforms that paved the way for interconnectivity, interactivity, multiplicity, and accessibility using social media and other digital tools. There are examples in Tanzania (*Swahili online news*), Nigeria (*Urhobo Today* and *Alaroye*), Ethiopia (*Amharic*), and South Africa (*Isolezwe*) where indigenous language users have adopted the social media platforms to reach out to their audiences, especially the youths. According to Owiny et al. (2014), studies have shown that since the above strategies have been used to preserve and promote ILs in many communities in East Africa, it can work for Nigeria and serve to enhance the continuation of the community, its knowledge and culture.

UNESCO (2014) has observed that using foreign language media to transmit development messages for example in West African countries where the literacy level is still relatively low, about 61 percent, cannot attain the desired impact. Out of this figure, only about 40 percent are literate enough to use either French or English proficiently, the remaining 60 percent are indigenous language users, most of whom are rural dwellers. This explains why most development messages meant for the local populace often get lost in transit and the people are unable to make any useful meaning from it. In that situation, the communication process will be incomplete as there will be no feedback. The national or regional media disseminating messages in foreign languages have been observed to be incapable of satisfying the information quests of Africa's sharply divergent urban–rural populace in the 4IR era. Most political leaders in Africa are conscious of this information lopsidedness thus, they are encouraging the establishment of indigenous language media that can cater for the information needs of the rural populace.

Evolution of Journalism Education in Nigeria: An Overview

Journalism and media training in its formative stage has for many decades received very little or no attention throughout the continent of Africa either from the colonial government or its native successors. All of them regarded media education as an unnecessary undertaking. There is also the general belief of some elites, though erroneous, that, once an individual successfully graduates from a secondary school and has a flair for reading, writing, and speaking, he/she is good enough to be a broadcaster, reporter, and public relations officer (Akinfeleye, 2010). Perhaps this is one reason why for many years of colonial rule and even post-independence government, most universities in Nigeria did not offer any formal journalism degree and/or diploma program. That also explains why most pioneer journalists and media professionals were despised and portrayed as a bunch of dropouts.

Although journalism practice started in Nigeria in 1859, formal journalism/mass communication education started much later in 1954 with a two-week, on-the-job training for working journalists. Similarly, radio broadcasts started in Nigeria in 1932 by the colonial government, but formal training for radio journalists did not start until 1956 when a two-year in-service training was organized by the Broadcasting Corporation of Nigeria. As for television broadcast, which commenced in 1959, former training began in the form of a Journalism Workshop in 1959, which was sponsored by the United States Information Service (USIS) later in 1960, the International Federation of Journalists also organized another short-term course for practicing journalists (Ojomo, 2015).

Formal journalism education started in 1962 with the University of Nigeria, Nsukka taking a pioneering lead. This was followed by the University of Lagos in 1967 thus, making only two universities in Nigeria which offered courses in journalism/mass communication within that period. At the polytechnic level, in 1978, the Institute of Management Technology (IMT) Enugu was the pioneer in mass communication education. Between 1967 and now, journalism education has witnessed rapid growth with almost all the private and public universities and polytechnics both federal and state-owned running courses in mass communication.

Role of Indigenous Languages in Journalism and Media Training 211

Besides universities and polytechnics, there were other journalism training institutes run by other private bodies. For example, the Daily Times training school, which metamorphosed into the Times Journalism Institute (TJI) in 1965; the Nigeria Broadcasting Corporation Training School now referred to as Federal Radio Corporation of Nigeria (FRCN) training school founded in 1957; the Nigeria Institute of Journalism (NIJ) established in 1971; and the International Institute of Journalism (IIJ) run by the Nigerian Union of Journalists (NUJ) was founded in 1995. The Nigeria Television College was also established in 1980 at Jos to complement the human capacity building of the few journalism schools (Akinfeleye, 2010).

Although journalism and media practice had been entrenched long before Nigeria's independence, the language of disseminating information both in print and electronic was mostly English. There was little or no preference for the native language. Despite the use of English as the language of communication in the media, journalism education in Nigeria when compared with Europe and America, is still far behind, especially given the characteristics of the 4IR where most developing nations are still struggling to find their feet in every area of life. Nevertheless, as a young profession in Nigeria, its phenomenal growth has created an increasing demand for trained journalists. According to the National University Commission (2020), about seventy-four universities are running accredited programs in journalism/mass communication while forty-six polytechnics are accredited, according to the National Board for Technical Education (2022). In the present 4IR era when science and technology have permeated every facet of human lives and development, various interested parties (journalists, linguists, and cultural experts) have expressed concern about the need for qualitative skills in journalism education to be delivered in IL in other to be relevant and preserve the cultures and languages of the local communities.

Teaching Journalism and Media in the 4IR Era: Role of Indigenous Languages

Traditionally, journalism was understood as a set of professional standards and practices involving the skill of reporting (news), writing (features, editorial, analysis), editing, photographing, or broadcasting news or managing any news organization as a business (Akinfeleye, 2010). But with advancements in society as well as information and communication technologies (ICT), journalism has since transmuted beyond the traditional definition, expanding into varied genres and specializations, among which is data journalism (Vos, 2018). Salawu (2019, p. 2) notes that in global journalism training and scholarship especially, in this 4IR age, the primary focus now is on digital media, algorithms, artificial intelligence, datafication and other computational tools that can aid the process of news gathering, processing and dissemination of messages. There have been controversies about whether or not ILs can be used as language of instruction in the teaching and training of journalists in this digital era.

However, Sure and Webb (2010) observe that, although the use of indigenous languages in education constitutes certain problems in a multilingual society, notwithstanding, it has some noticeable benefits. First, the learning and use of indigenous languages for educational instruction at the various levels of educational institutions have been recognized as a potent strategy for preserving indigenous languages among developed and developing countries of the world. China, Japan, India, and Korea among other nations that deployed indigenous languages into teaching and learning have witnessed significant development in every facet of life (Odu, 2015). In Africa, there are also countries where local languages are taught as subjects and are used as the language of instruction from primary to the university level even used for official and administrative purposes. For example, Yoruba, Hausa, and Igbo languages are three major ILs in Nigeria that have been subjects of study at primary, and secondary schools and in universities, and are also used as the language of instruction. Second, learning and receiving educational instruction in the indigenous language is the right of every member of the human race. This consensus is according to the United Nations Declaration on the Rights of Indigenous Peoples (UNDRIP), which states in Article 14 that "Indigenous peoples have the right to establish and control their educational systems by providing education in their languages." Third, as argued by Kembo (2000), intellectual and emotional development occurs more effectively in a mother tongue that the learner knows very well. Fourth, he posited that learning in general (including second language learning) occurs more easily and effectively if the required mental development has already taken place through the use of a first language as a language of learning.

It is pertinent to note at this point that in a plural-ethnic nation like Nigeria especially, where ethnic politics of power and language are prevalent, there are always agitations over which language to be favored. However, the National Policy on Education recommends that each of the three major ethnic groups should develop its language and use it as subject language as well as language of instruction from primary to secondary school levels. Perhaps this is the basis of Ayedun-Aluma & Tijani-Adenle's (2014) concerns which prompted the following questions that are relevant to this study, and for which answers are provided subsequently.

Which Indigenous Language Out of Many Can Nigeria Adopt for the Teaching Journalism/ Mass Communication?

The federal government of Nigeria since the advent of the colonial regime has identified and elevated three major ILs (Hausa, Igbo, and Yoruba) as the languages of education and teaching in primary and some secondary schools. However, despite the government's seeming preference for the three ILs, this has not elevated any of them to official status. This is an unfortunate situation with Nigerian political elites in government who usually take delight in despising their language. A respondent (L3) said, "most political officeholders do not believe in anything indigenous whether clothing materials, food, drinks etc. They and their families fancy everything including culture more than the locals (L3)."

It is therefore not surprising to note that while the English language is made a compulsory subject and a prerequisite for admission into any program in tertiary institutions in Nigeria, the teaching and learning of indigenous languages are downplayed. Another respondent added that: "even many primary and secondary schools (both private and government-owned) are not even offering indigenous language as a subject let alone use it as the language of instruction (L2)."

According to Owolabi (2021), in the May/June 2018 West Africa School Certificate Examination, out of 123,300 students who registered for senior secondary school examination in English, only 1,560 candidates (0.8%) enrolled for Yoruba language. (L4) In his response, he "wonders why the government has strangely become silent and pretended as if it does not know the negative disposition and apathy of most schools to its indigenous language policies." Although the journalism/mass communication curriculum designed by the National Universities Commission (NUC) for Nigerian Universities provides for the teaching of ILs (Hausa, Igbo, and Yoruba) in the local language, it is surprising that the University of Ibadan and Lagos State University are the two institutions with track records of training and awarding degrees and diploma in indigenous language communication. Both the Ministry of Education and its agency, NUC, have not made efforts to find out why other institutions are deliberately contravening government policy without consequences. "The government and its agency are simply showing signs of unseriousness about IL development" (L5).

To What Extent Can the Current Journalism Curriculum in Nigeria Enhance Journalism Students to Be Fully Equipped to Function Efficiently in the 4IR Age?

Looking at the newly prescribed curriculum for universities also known as Benchmarks Minimum Academic Standard (BMAS), a lot of people and institutions have criticized it for lacking the components that can equip journalists with the necessary skills to participate in the development process of the 4IR and still maintain their status as an integrated member of their community. Data-driven skills involving collection, processing, analysis visualization and digitization that can enhance journalistic practice in the present era are lacking. "For Nigeria to benefit from the 4IR, it must seek to incorporate digital transformation, digital skills, and data management in the journalism/communication curriculum of its universities" (L4 & J3). In present-day journalism scholarship and training, the primary emphasis is no more on the old methods of reporting involving straight news, inverted pyramid, and eyewitness accounts, but on the journalism revolution, digital innovation of the media and issues relating to artificial intelligence, big data, and data journalism. The above observations serve to corroborate Ìyínọlákàn's (2022) assertion that lack of digital literacy in the areas of e-commerce, fintech, and online marketing has greatly impacted the economy in the recent past with over 80 million Nigerians being denied digital information access because of inability to use English language proficiently. Through artificial intelligence and machine learning tools, journalists can learn, create, and manage future challenges using local languages and participate in the global ecosystem. According to the respondents (lecturers and journalists), for the media/ communication training curriculum to be good enough to prepare journalists to function efficiently for the benefit of society in this era, there must be a curriculum review that will emphasize digitization while using indigenous language as a medium of instruction.

What Are the Prospects of Engaging Indigenous Language for Training Journalists in the 4IR Period?

On the prospects of using ILs as the language of communication in the mass media as well as the training of journalists, "there are media organizations in Nigeria already publishing or broadcasting in local languages either fully or partially" (J1). "As a matter of fact, there are presently Yoruba newspapers (*Alaroye, Alariya Oodua*) and radio broadcasting stations across Nigeria (Choice FM, Bond FM, Faaji FM, Miliki FM and Radio Lagos) among others that are observed to be doing well in the market" (J2). In addition, (J2) also observes that: "the British Broadcasting Corporation BBC African

Role of Indigenous Languages in Journalism and Media Training 215

service, since three years ago adopted the three ILs in Nigeria as languages of communication to reach their teaming audiences across Nigeria on issues of health, economy, education, politics and social lives among others." For a journalist to function in an organization like BBC in the 4IR era, he/she must not only be versed in local and international events but must be bilingual in the languages understood by the audiences most of whom are migrating to digital space. For journalism education in Nigeria to be perceived as a dependable ally in social integration, ILs must be seen as inevitable in the venture. In this context, it, therefore, becomes mandatory that reporters must be adequately trained to translate foreign news and innovations into local languages and vice versa. (J2) notes that: "The governments, academic/professional regulatory bodies, media technology experts and training institutions must embrace IL use as the language of instruction in the training of journalists reporting for indigenous media."

On whether it is appropriate for indigenous language journalists to be trained formally or on-the-job training or a combination, all the respondents were unanimous in endorsing formal and informal training. "Journalists reporting for indigenous language media, print or electronic can be trained formally by enrolling in any school of communication/journalism or through on-the-job training." For instance, although, (J5) notes that an individual who will practice journalism in the indigenous language media can be trained informally on the job, (L1, L2, L3, & L4) think that formal training is highly essential for IL journalists who will make an impact in the 4IR age. However, all respondents seem to agree with the findings of Ayedun-Aluma and Tijani-Adenle (2014) who found that reporters in IL media must not only be degree-qualified but also must have additional training in journalism, innovation, artificial intelligence, and digitalization up to certificate or diploma level.

In What Language Will Journalism/Communication the Curriculum Be Designed and Taught?

In response to this question, all the respondents affirmed that a journalism curriculum can be designed and delivered in any language. If the curriculum is designed in IL, it can also be taught in the same. They based their declaration on the fact that no language is superior to any other. Salawu also strengthens this claim, "there is yet no convincing proof that the structure of one language is better than others, easier to acquire (as a first language), less ambiguous, more efficient for cognitive processes, or more economical of effort in oral use, let alone more logical, 'expressive' or the like" (2011, p. 7). If indigenous language media (prints and electronic) can efficiently

216 *Toyosi Olugbenga Samson Owolabi*

disseminate messages either local or foreign among its audiences, the curriculum can be written and taught in IL.

Respondents (L1-L5) have also observed that every English word has its Yoruba equivalence, and that is why indigenous language journalists can report for BBC. Language is dynamic and that explains why, according to Cann, Kempson, and Marten (2014), each language easily adapts words that are ethnic, context, and/or time period-specific. Yoruba, like English and other European languages, is alive and it changes rapidly with hundreds of words being added and/or dropped while meanings also change in quick succession.

What Are the Challenges of Teaching Journalism Courses in Indigenous Languages during the 4IR Era?

There have been concerns about journalism teaching and scholarship using indigenous languages as a medium of instruction. To provide an answer to this question, the respondents, both lecturers and practicing journalists, unanimously affirmed that there are concerns though they are not insurmountable. Respondents (L1, L2 and L4) believe that lack of proper and coordinated language policy and language planning (LPLP) on the part of the government and scarcity of indigenous language teachers are two critical challenges facing indigenous language development in Nigeria, while two respondents (L3 and L5) blame the indigenous people for wholesale acceptance and preference for foreign language at the expense their native languages. Respondents (F1, F2, F3, F4 and F5) also identified a multiplicity of indigenous languages, inadequate lexicon, substandard orthography, absence of indigenous language in digital format, inadequate digital literacy skills, and dearth of readable textbooks as challenges contending against the use of indigenous languages for teaching journalism courses. Further from the above three categorizations, the respondents identified eight different challenges confronting indigenous language use for journalism training in tertiary institutions. The first category includes three respondents (L1, L2 and L4), the second comprises two respondents (L3 and L5), while the third consists of five respondents (F1, F2, F3, F4 and F5). In all, the following challenges were identified:

- lack of proper and coordinated language policy and language planning (LPLP) on the part of the government,
- dearth of indigenous language teachers,
- wholesale acceptance and preference for foreign languages as against their native languages,
- multiplicity of indigenous languages competing for attention,
- inadequate lexicon,

Role of Indigenous Languages in Journalism and Media Training   217

- substandard orthography,
- absence of indigenous language in digital format,
- inadequate digital literacy skills,
- dearth of readable textbooks.

OVERCOMING THE CHALLENGES OF USING ILS IN TEACHING JOURNALISM IN THE 4IR AGE

Going by the above discussion of the findings, there is no doubting the fact that ILs can function as the language of instruction in journalism education especially, in this Fourth Industrial Revolution age if there is proper LPLP in place. However, it has been established in this study that there are factors working against the effective functionality of ILs as language of instruction in journalism education. If the Yoruba language will ever survive to serve as the language of journalism education in this digital era, the multifarious challenges identified above must be seriously addressed.

In Nigeria, the problem with the government is not for lack of language policy and language planning; rather, it is the problem of non-implementation of existing policy and plan. The federal and state governments were desirous of solving ethno-linguistic problems which brought about the 1981 revised National Policy on Education. In section 2, paragraph 7 of the policy, it is stated that the medium of instruction in pre-primary schools should be the local language of the immediate community. However, this is not to be as the government is believed to have abdicated its responsibility of implementing the policy by mandating both private and public schools to implement it. The effect of this is that as children pass through the teenage years to adulthood, they learn only the English language, thus they are detached from their native culture because language is a key element of culture. If journalism practice and journalism education are strengthened and the threat of extinction against ILs is checkmated, the indigenous language must be incorporated into the journalism practice and education curriculum.

Now the government should review its stand on ILs in Nigeria by compelling learning and teaching of the native language of the host community at private and public pre-primary and primary school levels. The Ministry of Education, National University Commission (NUC), and the National Board of Technical Education (NBTE) should also give ILs its pride of place in the education industry. Indigenous languages such as Hausa, Igbo, and Yoruba should be taught as subjects and be used as the languages of instruction at the university. A credit pass in the English language is a compulsory requirement for admission into the university so a credit pass in any IL should be a prerequisite. Besides, the NUC could also give recognition to ILs by allowing communication/journalism to be combined with an indigenous language as a course of study as is the case with Lagos State University, where the Yoruba language can be combined with Communication Arts. The Chinese, Japanese, and Korean nations serve as good examples of how a country can develop its native language, education, and other areas of life.

Research in the area of language development is paramount. The government must provide funds for the universities and other language development centers to research various aspects of indigenous African languages, particularly in such areas as lexicon, vocabulary and morphology development, syntax, standard orthography, translation, and production of teaching material with the intent that some of the indigenous languages will develop to the level of functioning as instructional languages.

The government, universities, and language research centers should collaborate to identify and target some indigenous languages on a regional basis that could be developed and made to function as subjects of study and language of instruction in higher institutions particularly, in journalism training and innovation, artificial intelligence and digital journalism.

Each university should be required to identify an indigenous Nigerian language of its choice for development as a medium of instruction. Where there is more than one institution in a particular region, those institutions could collaborate to specialize in a definite aspect of a language to standardize orthography and make it develop as a medium of instruction in journalism courses. Language planners must give the foreign languages and indigenous languages equal functional status. If indigenous languages are used in teaching and as language of study, they will gain prestige, which will increase the need to study them seriously.

Indigenous media organizations should also enter into partnerships with multinational media organizations such as the BBC, VOA, and Radio Mosco as is presently in operation between BBC World Service and many AM/FM frequencies in Africa. Examples are *Alaroye* Yoruba newspaper, Radio Lagos 107.5FM, Ray Power 100.5, and Choice FM 93.3 stations in Lagos and Benue states respectively. According to reporters from these stations, the BBC has assisted them in many ways. They provide media equipment and assist in manpower development. Specifically, they taught them how to investigate and report corruption; and they introduced them to "Paperless Newsroom" with regular follow-up visits to ascertain the continuity and effectiveness of their efforts. With constant training and investment in technology and digital innovation, it is therefore not surprising that these purely indigenous media organizations are visible in the global public space to satisfy the information quests of their diaspora audiences.

CONCLUSION

For journalism and communication education in Nigeria to be seen as contributing to the cultural and socioeconomic development of Nigeria in the present 4IR age, the indigenous language must be seen as a compulsory undertaking. Although it has been established that no language is superior or inferior to another because of its structure, ease of acquisition (as a first language), less ambiguity, efficiency for cognitive processes, or being more pleasant in oral use, many people, especially youths and children, are gradually losing interest in their native language, thus giving preference to English. This can be seen in how many schools are offering ILs as the subject of education and how many institutions are using ILs as the language of instruction. This study focuses on how ILs in Nigeria could be deployed as language of instruction in journalism training. Findings from the study revealed that if Hausa, Yoruba, and Igbo languages can be used to report in newspapers and radio, they can also be used for journalism education in tertiary institutions. Notwithstanding the identified challenges that may contend with using Yoruba as the language of instruction in the training of journalists during this 4IR, they are not insurmountable if there is appropriate LPLP and the government in conjunction with other stakeholders is determined to implement them.

REFERENCES

Ajepe, I. and Ademowo, A. J. (2016). English Language Dominance and the Fate of indigenous languages in Nigeria. *International Journal of History and International Studies,* 2(4):10–17. https://www.arcjournals.org/pdfs/ijhcs/v2-i4/2.pdf.

Akinfeleye, R. A. (2010). *Essentials of journalism an introductory text.* Lagos: Malthouse.

Akinkurolere, S. O., Akinfenwa, M. O. and Oluwapelumi, O. (2018). A Study on the extinction of indigenous languages in Nigeria: Causes and possible solution. *Annal of Language and Literature,* 2(1): 22–26.

Ayedun-Aluma, V. and Tijani-Adenle, G. (2014). Being "International": A Critique of Contemporary, Philosophies and Practices of Yoruba Language Journalism in Nigeria. In L. Oso, Olatunji, R. and Owen-Ibie, N. (eds.) *Journalism and Media in Nigeria: Context, Issues and Practice.* Ontario: University of Canada Press, p. 84–100.

Cann, R., Kempson, R., Marten, L. (2014). The Dynamics of Language. https://www.researchgate.net/publication/298544659_Dynamics_of_Language_An _Introduction.

Coker, I. (1968). *Landmarks of the Nigerian press: an outline of the origins and development of the newspaper press in Nigeria, 1859–1965.* Lagos: Nigerian National Press.

Dataphyte. (2022). International Literacy Day: Achieving SDG 4 still a long way off for Nigeria. https://www.dataphyte.com/latest-reports/international-literacy-day-achieving-sdg-4-still-a-long-way-off-for-Nigeria/#:~:text=An%20Illiteracy%20rate%20of%2031%25%20is%20equivalent%20to,21%20years%20to%20achieve%2094%25%20youth%20literacy%20rates.

David, R. (2010). Language Matters. http://www.randydavid.com/2010/08/language-matters/.

Egele, A. F. (2023). Language Death in Akoko-Edo: A Study of Some Students' Attitude to Native Dialects in Akoko-Edo LGA of Edo-State. https://www.researchgate.net/publication/363484743_Language_Death_in_Akoko_Edo_A_Study_of_Some_Students'_Attitude_to_Native_Dialects_in_Akoko-Edo_LGA_of_Edo-State Accessed June 02, 2023).

Ikoba, N. A., & Jolayemi, E. T. (2020). Investigation of Factors Contributing to Indigenous Language Decline in Nigeria. *The Philippine Statistician* 69(2). https://www.researchgate.net/publication/350131253_Investigation_of_Factors_Contributing_to_Indigenous_Language_Decline_in_Nigeria.

Iyinolakan, O. (2022). Digitizing Local Languages for the Fourth Industrial Revolution in *Business Day* https://businessday.ng/bd-weekender/article/digitizing-local-languages-for-the-fourth-industrial-revolution/.

Jung, D. (2019). Tackling Language Problems via Language Planning and Language Policy? Viability and Challenges Using the Example of Catalonia Term Paper in Advanced Seminar. https://www.grin.com/document/509681.

Kembo, J. (2000). Language in education and language learning in Africa. In V. Webb and K. Sure (eds.), *African Voices* (pp. 286–311). Oxford, UK: Oxford University Press.

Lavopa, A. and Delera, M. (2021) What Is the Fourth Industrial Revolution? https://iap.unido.org/articles/what-fourth-industrial-revolution.

National Board of Technical Education. (2024). NBTE unbundles Mass Communication program, shifting focus from generalists to specialists. https://edugist.org/nbte-unbundles-mass-communication-program-shifting-focus-from-generalists-to-specialists/.

National University Commission. (2020). NUC unbundles Mass Communication. https://www.nuc.edu.ng/nuc-unbundles-mass-communication/.

Nnabuihe, C., & Ikwubuzo, J. (2006). A peep into news publications and reading culture in Igbo language of Nigeria. In A. Salawu (ed.), *Indigenous language media in Africa*. Lagos: Centre for Black and African Arts and Civilization.

Odu, O. (2015). Social media and the Nigerian Youths. *Nigerian Monitor* https//.www.nigerianmonitor.com/social-media-and-the-nigerian-youths.

Ojebode, A. (2017). The role of community broadcast media in national development. In E. Soola (ed.), *Communicating for development purposes*. Ibadan: Kraft Books Limited.

Ojomo, O. W. (2015). Journalism and Mass Communication Training in Nigeria: Some Critical Thoughts DOI: 10.20287/ec.n20.a05. https://www.researchgate.net/publication/289495990_Journalism_and_Mass_Communication_Training_in_Nigeria_Some_Critical_Thoughts.

Oloruntola, S., Yusuff, A., Iretomiwa, S. G., Obia, V. A., & Ejiwunmi, S. (2018). Use of indigenous language for social media communication: The Nigerian experience. In A. Salau (ed.), *African language digital media and communication*. New York: Routledge.

Owiny, S. A., Mehta, K., Maretzki, A. N. (2014). The use of social media technologies to Create, Preserve and Disseminate Indigenous Knowledge and Skills to Communities in East Africa. *International Journal of Communication* vol. 8, p. 234–247.

Owolabi, T. O. S. (2014). Media Coverage of SMEs in Nigeria: Imperative for national development. Being a thesis submitted in partial fulfillment of the requirements for the degree of Doctor of Philosophy School of Humanities and Social Sciences, University of Strathclyde, Glasgow.

Owolabi, T. O. S. (2019). New Technology, Indigenous Language Media Practice and Management for Development in Nigeria. In A. Salawu (ed.), *African Language Digital Media and Communication,* London: Rutledge p.189–208.

Owolabi, T. O. S. (2021). The Political Economy of Indigenous Language Media in Nigeria and the Challenge of Survival in the Digital Age. In A. Salawu (ed.), *African Language Media, Development, Economics and Management.* New York: Routledge p. 15–34.

Salawu, A. (2011). Essentials of indigenous languages to journalism education in Nigeria. doi: 10.5789/2-1-31 https://www.researchgate.net/publication/307746948.

Salawu, A. (2019a). Not to be left behind by African languages, media, and the digital sphere. In A. Salawu (ed.) *African Language Digital media and Communication.* New York: Routledge, p. 1–7.

Salawu, A. (2019b). Alaroye, Isolezwe and the Adoption of Digital Technologies. In A. Salawu (ed.), *African Language Digital media and Communication.* New York: Routledge, p. 33–45.

Siebert, F. S., Peterson, T. B., & Schramm, W. (1956). Four theory of the press. Urbana: University of Illinois Press.

Sure, K., and Webb, V. (2010). Languages in competition. In V. Webb and K. Sure (eds.), *African Voices* (pp. 109–132). Oxford, UK: Oxford University Press.

Unaegbu, G. L, Obiamalu, G., Orji, D. A. (2023). Language Attitudes of Igbo Speakers: A Comparative Study of Igbo People at Homeland (Awka) and in Diaspora (Lagos). *Nigerian Journal of African Studies* (NJAS) 5(2). https://www.nigerianjournalsonline.com/index.php/NJAS/article/view/3373.

UNESCO Institute of Statistic (2014). Literacy rate. https://www.bing.com/search?q=UNESCO+Institute+of+Statistic+(2012).+Literacy+Rate.&cvid=79e09d862d9b4938be968bb575389cd1&gs_lcrp=EgZjaHJvbWUyBggAEEUYOdIBCDI0ODdqMGo5qAIEsAIB&FORM=ANAB01&PC=HCTS.

United Nations Department of Economic and Social Affairs UNDESA. (2016). Protecting languages, preserving cultures. https://www.un.org/development/desa/en/news/social/preserving-indigenous-languages.html.

Vos, T. (2018). Journalism. In T. Vos (ed.), *Journalism* (pp. 1–18). Berlin, Boston: De Gruyter Mouton. https://doi.org/10.1515/9781501500084-001.

Wittgenstein, L. (1926). Quotes on Language. https://www.azquotes.com/quote/319126.

Woods, N. (2016). *Describing Discourse: A Practical Guide to Discourse Analysis.* London: Hodder Education.

Chapter 10

Indigenous Language Preservation, Challenges, and Opportunities in the Social Media Age

Mawethu Glemar Mapulane, Amukelani Collen Mangaka, Edgar Julius Malatji, Nhlayisi Cedrick Baloyi, and Rudzanimbilu Muthambi

There has been a significant paradigm shift in recent years regarding the relationship between technology and language extinction, particularly indigenous languages (Abraham, 2020; Jany, 2017). Notwithstanding that previously technology was rejected due to its presumed threat toward the promotion and preservation of the previously marginalized indigenous languages. This presumption has challenged the proponents and speakers of the indigenous languages to rethink their attitudes toward technology. Thus, these proponents and speakers had to perceive social media as an alternative platform to the advancement of their native languages. It is worth noting that colonialism and apartheid had attempted to exterminate the indigenous languages as well as African cultures. The systematic dismantling of the Africans and their key attributes was perpetuated through mass media. According to Jany, "digital media and social networks have changed the status quo and are now viewed as vital tools in language preservation and revitalization endeavours" (2017, p. 44). Thus, this chapter explores the use of indigenous languages on social media in South Africa. This investigation analyses how speakers of Sepedi and Xitsonga use social media to preserve and promote these indigenous languages for posterity. As far as social media platforms are concerned, this chapter focuses on Instagram and Facebook.

Undoubtedly, new media, particularly social media platforms, transformed how media users generate, store, process, and share information in the public sphere. According to Owiny, Mheta, and Moretzki (2014), speakers of previously marginalized languages have an opportunity to elevate their status through social media. Historically, indigenous languages were sporadically used in the mainstream media. Social media platforms such as Facebook, Twitter, Instagram, TikTok, and WhatsApp have disrupted the injustices of censorship. Through social media, people have the space and freedom to generate content and disseminate it to a large audience (Malatji, 2019). According to Ligidima and Makananise (2020), the use of social media is imperative to advance the identity, culture, beliefs as well and languages of the previously stifled communities. In addition, Warren (1991) posits that indigenous languages should be preserved for posterity, so that the next generation of speakers of these languages should find their repository on social media.

Eyong (2007) and Gachanga (2005) argue that indigenous languages should not be perceived as archaic aspects of African culture. Furthermore, Malatji (2019) explains that the status and value of indigenous languages are undermined in the public sphere. As such, in the South African context, the use of these indigenous languages in the public sphere is uncommon as they are overshadowed by English (Thobejane, 2017). Owiny et al. (2014) make the additional claim that social media act as the creative minds' wings for those whose futures will be increasingly controlled by new technologies. Therefore, it is crucial to prevent children from being intentionally or unintentionally deprived of the indigenous knowledge that is their birthright by the quickly developing information society. Thobejane (2017) alludes to the possibility of using social media platforms as a tool for the advancement and promotion of African languages. Therefore, to ensure that these African languages are promoted and preserved, linguists and scholars who work on language analysis and research must pay attention to how languages are used on social media. Additionally, language revitalization is an effort by language activists to apply or develop techniques meant to sustain the language and stop it from perishing in collaboration with the community in which the language is spoken.

LITERATURE REVIEW

This section focuses on the reviewed literature on the brief description of social media, the use of social media in the promotion of South African indigenous languages, and the revitalization of indigenous languages through social media.

Brief Description of Social Media

The concept of "social media" refers to internet-based websites or applications which permit users to take part in establishing content (Fourie, 2017). These applications also allow users to connect in explicit ways which permits them to interconnect and interrelate directly with each other. This concept can also be explained as a cluster of internet applications that build on the ideological and technological grounds of Web 2.0 and ultimately permit users to construct and exchange user-generated content. These internet-based applications are typically called social networking sites (SNSs). Munyadziwa and Mncwango (2021) describe social networks as a universal term for different kinds of internet sites which are mostly used to connect users with similar attributes, interests, and backgrounds. Users normally create profiles comprising of their pictures and digital audio files (Thobejane, 2017). Social networking is communication between groups of people mediated through internet technologies. This mediation takes place through social networking sites which should be accessed through technological gadgets including smartphones, computers, and tablets. Eventually, these types of communication need one to have access to social media profiles, technological gadgets, and the internet (Outakoski, Cocq & Steggo, 2018). Some of the popular social networking include Facebook, Twitter (X), Instagram, YouTube, Myspace, TikTok, and LinkedIn.

This concept is mostly related to a social structure comprised of various factors, or collaboration using the internet. Clark, Algoe, and Green (2018) postulate that some of the attributes of social networks comprise involvement, communication, connectedness, community, and openness amongst others. Social networking sites allow users to create, communicate, share, and distribute information among themselves. These platforms also allow users to inculcate and perpetuate activism using hashtags. Social media has become an essential part of human life, and their usage has significantly improved in recent times (Malatji & Lesame, 2019). Moreover, Uysal (2015) postulates that social media has grown to become a vital part of mass communication among people.

Communication amongst social media mostly takes place using the English language, taking into consideration several factors including the popularity and the dominance of the language in the world, the popular culture and virtual communities created by people from diverse backgrounds and cultures, and the obliviousness of African indigenous languages by the internet in general, and the social media platforms (Ligidima & Makananise, 2020).

Social Media and its Role in the Promotion of South African Indigenous Languages

Despite the protection of all official languages by sections 6 and 30 of the South African Constitution Act 108 of 1996, and the commitment to advance multilingualism, establish environments for the development and use of all South African official languages, endorse respect and acknowledgment, particularly for the historically marginalized languages by the Pan South African Language Board (PanSALB), few strides have been made to promote the use South African indigenous languages on social media. According to Ligidima and Makananise (2020), Six Degree.com was the first social media platform to be launched in South Africa, followed by Mixt in 1997. These platforms permit users to establish profiles, connect with their virtual friends and relatives and collaborate in sharing information. Recently, Facebook has been the most prevalent social networking site to be used in South Africa (Piennar, 2018; Statista, 2023). More than 30 million users had a profile account on the platform. Furthermore, WhatsApp, Twitter (X), TikTok, Messenger, LinkedIn, and Instagram are also some of the popular social media networks used in South Africa. Malatji (2019) postulates that some minority South African languages, including Sepedi, Tshivenda, and Xitsonga, are silent on social media. Speakers of these languages and all South African indigenous languages in general hardly use their languages when communicating through social media platforms (Makananise, Malatji & Madima, 2023). The use of these languages in social media would preserve, develop, and make them popular among language speakers. Social media platforms permit the development and promulgation of user-generated content, in which users have an opportunity to establish their content in their languages. Li and Liu (2017) postulate that globally, English and other European languages make it simple for people around the world to access ICT resources. Social networking sites have English as a dominant language, with 80 percent of users who do not speak English as their first language. This picture also echoes the same situation in the South African context, with most of the population being non-whites. However, the dominance of indigenous South African languages in social media remains a conundrum (Malatji, Makananise & Madima, 2023; Aiseng, 2022). The nature of social media and the internet in general also makes it difficult for native speakers to use their indigenous languages due to the error detections whenever they are writing in their languages rather than English. This nature ultimately discourages users from using their indigenous languages on social media.

Opportunities for the Revitalization of Indigenous Languages through Social Media

Social media platforms provide an opportunity for indigenous language revitalization activists to develop and expand beyond geographical and cultural boundaries. These platforms permit indigenous language speakers the liberty to determine how to use their languages and bring their languages into milieus which make sense to themselves. For example, hashtag (#), which is an essential element of social media platforms, enables language users to disseminate their identities and position themselves with cultural and linguistic communities (Laucuka, 2018). The nature of social media surpasses geographical differences, implying that the use of indigenous language on these platforms is not constrained to a specific language's traditional territory.

Sepedi and Xitsonga languages are mostly spoken in the Limpopo province of South Africa. These are some of the historically disadvantaged languages in South Africa. However, the advent of social media permitted the popularization of these languages beyond the South African demarcations. Cru (2018) postulates that social media connects disconnected indigenous communities whose traditional territories are separated by national borders. This also allows the non-speakers to learn these languages through constant engagements via social media platforms. Language reactivation activists from diverse indigenous groupings in the world can simply mobilize and look to each other's activities on social media for encouragement (Dlaske, 2017). Furthermore, Jenkins (2016) highlights that one of the strong attributes of social media is participatory culture, where users participate in establishing and disseminating content. The nature of these platforms affords users space to experiment and adapt the use of languages to their understanding. Lillehaugen (2016) argues that the use of a language does not necessarily require an institutionalized orthography for an active writing culture; rather, standardized orthographies sometimes emerge from active writing cultures and not the other way around. Facebook posts, pictures on Instagram, videos on YouTube, and tweets in indigenous languages sometimes prompt comments which eventually enhance the establishment of an active writing culture in the language (Cru, 2018).

Most of the indigenous language content on social platforms echoes the prevalent exercise of code-mixing, where both popular and marginalized languages may be used in a single writing (Barman, 2018). Normalizing code-mixing is viewed to reduce perceived barricades to participation in indigenous language use in social media. Users can slowly begin to use their indigenous languages, one word at a time, and intermingle with the popular language in their posts and comments. Srinivasan (2006) postulates that communication through social media is at liberty from the traditional editorial processes, and this freedom makes these platforms a democratizing force where people are free to express themselves. Social media platforms expedite the natural production of indigenous literacies, unobstructed in their production by any ongoing issues about standardization.

THEORETICAL FRAMEWORK

The uses and gratification theory is perceived as the alternative theory against short-term effects theories (Fourie, 2010). It is used in scholarship to magnify the multifaceted nature of mass media theories. This theory illuminates the structural issues of media operations (Malatji, 2019). For centuries, theories about audience behavior patterns ignored the role of media users particularly how they use media for various purposes. The uses and gratification theory captures various aspects but is not limited to how media is used to satisfy the needs of the audience. Accordingly, the audience, in this regard dictates the way media are used. As far as this study is concerned this theory is key because social media create alternative platforms or the public sphere for social discourses. Thus, now the audience and media users have editorial and gatekeeping powers to generate content. One thing that is noteworthy, audience and users are not limited to these critical roles as it enables them to command their response to the same content. Social media is also known as user-generated content platforms which underscores the importance of the user. In other words, the audience has shifted from passive observers to active participants in both content creation and consumption. In this study, social media users dictate how they use their profiles and which language is apt for their posts. Accordingly, this theory is adopted to synthesize and analyze how indigenous languages are used on social media. The pillars of this theory particularly how the users use media (social media) to meet their personal goals anchor the golden thread in this chapter.

METHODOLOGY

The chapter adopted the exploratory research design and online observation to achieve the objectives of the phenomenon. According to Creswell, "Exploratory research typically seeks to create hypotheses rather than test them. Data from exploratory studies tend to be qualitative. Examples include brainstorming sessions, interviews with experts, and posting a short survey to a social networking website" (2014, p. 13). The research team made use of exploratory research design through desktop research and online observation because they were timely, practical, and applicable to the study. In addition, the study employed several methods to explore the main goal of the investigation, including a literature review, articles, and a scan of social media posts. Based on our experience as indigenous language media researchers and enthusiasts, we have chosen to focus on two social media networking sites: namely, Instagram and Facebook. These networking sites allow users to create and share user-generated content. The team has realized that such content is appropriate to be representative illustrations of indigenous languages, groups, and communities on social media. As a result, social media such as Instagram and Facebook can play a significant role in indigenous language preservation endeavors.

Sampling

The researchers used a purposive sampling technique within the non-probability sampling method. Thomas states that "Purposeful sampling is being used in various ways, based on study design, as according to research papers" (2022, p. 1). Every study has a tried-and-true method for collecting and analyzing data from a specific sample. The study used purposive sampling to document indigenous language content and posts on Instagram and Facebook accounts. This approach was used to identify accounts that generate content on indigenous languages. Additionally, it aided the selection of accounts, content creators, activists and organizations that use South African indigenous languages, particularly Sepedi and Xitsonga.

For this research, 110 social media posts were sampled from both Facebook and Instagram. Qualitative data were collated from the selected social media posts through online observations. Qualitative data were analyzed using critical discourse analysis. According to Campbell, "critical discourse analysis is concerned with the investigation of languages and one can reasonably expect linguistics to use this method" (2018, p. 44). In this chapter, this form of analysis was used to dissect the selected social media posts from both Instagram and Facebook.

Data Collection

The researchers documented social media posts related to indigenous languages. We limited our search to public posts from March to mid-June 2023 on Instagram and Facebook. The networking sites were purposively chosen to determine how indigenous languages are used on various platforms. These social media platforms were considered appropriate even though there were other social media sites such as Twitter, MySpace, TikTok, WhatsApp, and so forth. In addition, Instagram and Facebook were used because of their public nature, which offers a unique manner of inquiry into indigenous language use. The platforms were found to be more relevant, especially in the 4IR era. It is common knowledge that Facebook is the most popular social media platform, while Instagram has become resourceful to individuals and companies. Lastly, social media networks such as Instagram and Facebook posts are easily accessible since privacy settings are rarely used by users (Keegan et al., 2015). In addition, the study focused on social media accounts based in South Africa, which included posts from individuals, communities, activists, campaigns, and organizations.

Data collection and preliminary analysis of social media posts occurred simultaneously. The research team developed a spreadsheet and organized collected data into columns that enabled us to categorize posts around emerging themes. These themes included (1) Indigenous language promotion, (2) Using indigenous languages on posts, (3) Commenting in an indigenous language, (4) Challenges of using indigenous language, and (5) Frequency of using indigenous language. We also created a column for posts that did not fit into these categories or that we were unsure about at first. As we gathered posts, we arranged them within columns and titled them according to the themes. The approach helped us to identify the emerging themes.

Synopsis of Instagram

Instagram is mainly a photo-sharing social media platform and has become a useful networking site to instantly connect to individuals and companies (Mpofu & Salawu, 2020). User-generated content and posts were collected from Instagram. To identify accounts, the team followed hashtags related to indigenous languages, particularly South African minority languages; namely, Sepedi and Xitsonga. Hashtags such as #Xitsonga, #Sepedi, #speak-indigeneouslanguage, #indigeneouslangauge, and #indigenous were also followed to gather rich data. Hashtags are phrases used in social media to categorize topics, combine ideas, and create a flow of information around a particular topic (Malatji, 2019). Therefore, following these hashtags made it easier for the team to identify and organize data. Researchers began by sourcing public posts from accounts they already followed. This approach was appropriate because researchers, as indigenous language scholars and practitioners, already had a strong sense of what was happening in the communities where they lived and with whom they worked. The researchers ascertained the validity and reliability of the data by considering content and posts from verified and public accounts.

Synopsis of Facebook

According to Thobejane (2017), Facebook is one of the popular social networking sites in South Africa. A plethora of users on this platform use it to engage with friends and some of them view it as an advertising platform. In recent times, the same platform has been used to broadcast live events such as concerts, soccer matches, and political conferences.

RESULTS

This study collected data from social media platforms. Public accounts on Instagram and Facebook were used to collect data. The sample was made of Facebook and Instagram posts and texts. The results are presented as follows:

Instagram Users

The accounts used were purposively selected to explore the use of Sepedi and Xitsonga. The results were as follows:

@ntombiyamutsonga

In her profile, she describes her account as Arts and Entertainment. The profile has a South African flag to reflect her citizenship. The account has 54.7K followers. She describes herself as a #SONA2020 praise poet, multi-award-winning praise poet, and a published author. The account had a total of 592 posts at the time of data collection. Starting with her recent post, she posted on 20 June 2023. At the time of data collection, the post had 16 comments and 2,129 likes. The caption read: XEWANI from me and Moms. Only two comments were written in Xitsonga *"HeveenewXivambu" and "Nwa~Hlambela" (Nwa-Hlambela = Hlambela's daughter)*. On 09 June she posted a picture with the caption: *"LAHA HI HUMAKA KONA HI MFUWO NA NDHAWIUKO HI SWONA SWI TIYISAKA MUBYA WA LAHA HI YAKA KONA TANI HI RIXAKA."* XEWANI *(Knowing our Arts and Culture help us not to lose sight of where we're going as a nation) (Xewani = Good morning)*. In the comment section, 5 comments were in English, 8 with emoji, and 6 in Xitsonga.

On 3 April she posted several pictures: The first post had the caption as follows: *"THIS PAST WEEKEND- WAS MAGICAL." "We witnessed greatness. Felt good to do what I love most."* Only four people commented with one comment written in English and three with emojis. The post had 742 likes at the time of observation. In the second post, the caption reads: *"My greatest gift from God is my gift. It has allowed me to meet people who have become my family. I will always be thankful for your love and support Maxaka. "* The post had 2, 292 likes. Out of 15 comments, one commented with an emoji, nine in English and four In Xitsonga.

On 8 April she posted her graduation pictures. The caption was written in English. The post had 8,029 likes and 307 comments. Most comments were written in English, with few in Xitsonga. Lunje_77 commented:

"XaNkokaNgopfu a mi rivalangaXikwembu. Hambi switika a mi helangama-timba!!! Ha mi hoyozelaSesi!!!. " Another comment from mamananku- *"Haku tlangela. "*

Tsunduhatlani also commented *"HoyohoyoHahani"* (*XaNkokaNgopfu a mi rivalangaXikwembu. Hambi switika a mi helangamatimba!!! Ha mi hoyozelaSesi!!! = The most important thing is that you never forget God, even when things are difficult you never give up!!! Congratulations my sister!!!*)

(Haku tlangela = *we celebrate* you)

(HoyohoyoHahani = *Congratulations my aun*t).

On April 21 she posted a photo with the caption: *"DYONDZO I XITLHANGU XA VUTOMI. "* There were eight comments and 2,249 likes. Out of eight comments, four comments were in Xitsonga and others with emojis. One follower commented *"Halala ngwananga halala"* (*DYONDZO I XITLHANGU XA VUTOMI = Education is the key to a good life). (Halala nwananga halala = well done my child*).

@matalane_mokgatla

On his profile, he described himself as an award-winning praise poet, published author, heritage and cultural activist, social cohesion advocate, and Sepedi consultant. The account had 17.1K followers and 7,822 posts at the time of observations and data collection. Matalane posted a photo on May 11, 2023, with the caption *"Taking the Bapedi culture to the world #rebapedi. "* The post had 380 likes and seven comments at the time of observation. On 16 May 2023 post with the caption *"Embracing cultural diversity. Bapedi + Amazulu. " "#weareone #weareafrica #happyafricamonth. "* The post had 217 likes and nine comments. We observed that in the comment section, comments were written in Sepedi and English, whereas one was replied to with an emoji. He posted a photo on 9 April 2023. The caption was written in Sepedi which reads: *"Go bohlokwa go itshidulla" (It is important to exercise).* Only people commented on the post. Both the comments were written in English. The post had 134 likes.

@Sepedi_bapedi

The account falls under the category of community which posts mainly Sepedi traditional attires. The account had 138K followers with 1632 posts at the time of observation and data collection. A photo posted on 16 June 2023 with a caption that read *"Se motseresenatla"* *(The famous phrase for chanting that the groom has taken bride during traditional weddings)* had over two thousand likes and nine comments. We have observed that the followers used two languages in one sentence. The users were code-switching between English and Sepedi. Some of the comments are as follows:

"She is pretty, the doek e dutse perfect. Kempopi" *(She is pretty, the* head-wrap suits her perfectly. She is a doll!)

"Gorgeous bride. Keramakoti ka dukuyagagwe. O waswanelwa."
(Gorgeous bride. The bride with a headwrap. She is beautiful).

Facebook Users

The accounts used were purposively selected to explore the use of Sepedi and Xitsonga. The results were as follows:

Dj Brian Rikhozo

In his profile, he describes himself as a radio DJ, YouTuber, content creator, photographer, and voice-over artist. His account had over five hundred followers at the time of data collection.

On 28 June 2023, DJ Brian posted a video with the caption: *"Eka vhikileri hi rhambe Isaac Hlatshwayo kutwa to tala hi gondzo ra vona ra ntlangu wa swibakele"* *(This week we invited Issac Hlatshwayo to hear about his journey on boxing)* the post has 95 likes, 881 views, and 16 comments. Only five comments were written in Xitsonga, four were in English, and seven commented with emojis.

On 22 June 2023, he posted a picture with the caption *"Ndzawini! Kuna mani?"* *(Greetings, who is there?).* The post nearly more than 4,000 likes, and more than a thousand comments. Some of the comments were written in Xitsonga, some in English while some used code-switching combining Xitsonga and English. On 18 June 2023, DJ Brian posted two pictures with the caption *"Ëka mina u wankoka (For me you are special) BHARULE!!!!."* The post had around 3,000 likes, with nearly 300 comments. Like most of the posts, some of the followers would comment in Xitsonga, some in English, while some are code-switching. Some of the followers would comment with emojis.

DISCUSSION

The use of indigenous languages on social media is deliberate. According to the findings, the speakers of Sepedi and Xitsonga are using their languages to preserve and promote them. This is evident in how they presented their profiles. The Xitsonga poet stated in one of the posts that her activism about her culture and indigenous language is intentional. This suggests that her social media activities are meant to promote and preserve Xitsonga. Similarly, the Sepedi poet explicitly stated that the use of his mother tongue is instrumental toward preserving it for posterity. Thus, some of his posts are meant to move the previously marginalized languages from the periphery to the center of the public sphere. The use of indigenous languages on social media is linguistic and cultural activism (Ligidima & Makananise, 2020; Malatji & Lesame, 2019; Thobejane, 2017). Despite these identified issues, social media has the potential to preserve and promote African languages for posterity (Mpofu & Salawu, 2020). The activities on Instagram and Facebook underscore the importance of multilingualism. This aspect is pivoted using different languages on social media. As such, multilingualism can be a panacea for the preservation and promotion of previously marginalized languages (Barman, 2018).

It is integral to point out the significance of multilingualism against this phenomenon (Srinivasan, 2018). Moreover, this is crucially important because it disrupts the legacy of apartheid and colonialism. The literature exposed that the bilingual policy of apartheid eroded the value and currency of the indigenous languages in South Africa (Malatji, Makananise, & Madima, 2023). Therefore, alternative platforms such as Facebook and Instagram have created an opportunity to dismantle the injustices of apartheid and colonialism. The argument is that the indigenous languages were unfairly treated as inferior compared to ex-colonial languages. In addition, media was used to perpetuate the oppression of indigenous languages and cultures in South Africa (Mpofu & Salawu, 2020). Accordingly, studies of this nature attempt to magnify the previous disparities and cultivate a new way of disrupting the status quo.

According to the findings, the speakers of Sepedi and Xitsonga are using their languages to preserve and promote them. The use of indigenous languages on social media is linguistic and cultural activism. Also, the activities on Instagram and Facebook underscore the importance of multilingualism. This aspect is pivoted using different languages on social media. As such, multilingualism can be a panacea for the preservation and promotion of previously marginalized languages. It is integral to point out the significance of multilingualism within this phenomenon. Moreover, this is crucially important because it disrupts the legacy of apartheid and colonialism (Thobejane, 2017). The literature exposed that the bilingual policy of apartheid eroded the value and currency of the indigenous languages in Africa (Malatji, Makananise & Madima, 2023). Therefore, alternative platforms such as Facebook and Instagram have created an opportunity to dismantle the injustices of apartheid and colonialism. The argument is that the indigenous languages were unfairly treated as inferior compared to ex-colonial languages. And media was used to perpetuate the oppression of indigenous languages and cultures in South Africa. Accordingly, studies of this nature attempt to magnify the previous disparities and cultivate a new way of disrupting the status quo.

CONCLUSION AND RECOMMENDATIONS

This study exposed unique aspects as far as the use of indigenous languages on social media is concerned. Several conspicuous factors emerged from this study. First, the use of social media to preserve indigenous languages is a welcome move toward preserving African culture. The languages in the African context need to be preserved for posterity. Also, this is important to disrupt and dismantle the legacy of apartheid and colonialism. Second, the native speakers of the indigenous languages are the mainstay of their preservation. Additionally, some of the speakers perceive the use of their languages as activism against the apartheid legacy and remnants of colonialism. The speakers of these languages continue to post and comment in their mother tongues on social media. It is worth noting that some individuals subconsciously use indigenous languages on social media. Third, linguistical aspects such as code-switching, translanguaging, and multilingualism are presenting new opportunities and challenges. Code-switching can adversely affect the use of indigenous languages since English is mostly used in this exercise. Unfortunately, code-switching among indigenous languages is rare, which is detrimental for these languages. Translanguaging has some elements of eroding the key attributes of these indigenous. On the other hand, multilingualism presents an alternative way of promoting indigenous languages. This is because most languages are given fair opportunities through multilingualism. Also, it does not stifle minorities or previously marginalized languages.

In terms of recommendations, future research could focus on some of the emerging issues such as multilingualism in the public sphere to promote indigenous languages. Such studies could also investigate social media in balancing soft power based on languages. The importance of indigenous languages and their relationship with social media cannot be oversimplified. Thus, this chapter recommends that the speakers of indigenous languages should establish a strong network on social media to deal with their

236 *Mapulane, Mangaka, Malatji, Baloyi, and Muthambi*

preservation, identity, and culture. The same constituency should create multiple pages on Facebook for each indigenous language. Lastly, the speakers of these languages, particularly in the rural areas, need infrastructural support as well as digital literacy from both the public and private sectors. The digital divide which largely affects accessibility and connectivity issues remains a challenge in some areas in South Africa. These conundrums disrupt social media participation which adversely affects the use of social media to promote and preserve indigenous languages.

REFERENCES

Abraham, A. (2020). Impact of Digital Media on Society, *International Journal of Creative Thoughts*, 8(5):2742–2748.

Aiseng, K. (2022). Linguistic Dominance and Translanguaging: Language Issues in Generations: The Legacy. *Frontiers in Communication*, 7:880452. https://www.researchgate.net/publication/361767150_Linguistic_Dominance_and_Transl.anguaging_Language_Issues_in_Generations_The_Legacy/link/62c44adaa81be51e4090762d/download

Barman, U. (2018). Automatic Processing of Code-mixed Social Media Content. Doctoral thesis, Dublin City University. https://doras.dcu.ie/22919/1/UtsabBarmanThesis.pdf.

Campbell, M. (2018). Postmodernism and Educational Research, *Open Journal of Social Sciences*, 6(7): 34–44.

Clark, J. L., Algoe, S. B., and Green, M. C. (2018). Social Network Sites and Well-Being: The Role of Social Connection. *Current Directions in Psychological Science*, 27(1), 32–37.

Cru, J. (2018). Micro-level language planning and YouTube comments: Destigmatising indigenous languages through rap music. *Current Issues in Language Planning*, 19(4): 434–452.

Creswell, J. W. (2014). *Research Design: Qualitative, Quantitative and Mixed Methods Approaches,* fourth edition. London: Sage.

Dlaske, K. (2017). Music video covers, minoritized languages, and effective investments in the space of YouTube. *Language in Society*, 46(4): 451–475.

Eyong, C. T. (2007). Indigenous knowledge and sustainable development in Africa: A case study on Central Africa. in E.K. Boon and L. Hens (eds.), *Indigenous knowledge systems and development: Relevance for Africa*, 121–139. New Delhi: Kamla-Raj Enterprises.

Fourie, P. J. (ed.). (2010). 'New' paradigms, 'new' theory and four priorities for South African mass communication and media research. *Critical Arts*, 24(2):173–191.

Fourie, P. J. (ed.). (2017). *Media Studies: Social (New) Media and Mediated Communication Today*. Vol. 4. Cape Town: Juta and Company (Pty) Ltd.

Gachanga, T. (2007). *Education for peace in Kenya: Indigenous peace traditions and the Millennium Development goals.* At Issue Ezine, no.1 (February–June), available at www.africafiles.org/ atissueezine. asp?issue=issue1. Accessed 29 June 2023.

Jany, C. (2017). The role of new media technology and social media in reserving language loss. *Speech, Language and Hearing,* 21 (2): 73–76. http://dx.doi.org/10 .1080/2050571X.2017.1368971. Accessed 29 June 2023.

Keegan, T. T., Mato, P., & Ruru, S. (2015). Using Twitter in an indigenous Language: An analysis of te reo Maori tweets. *An International Journal of Indigenous Peoples,* (11)1: 59–75.

Laucuka, A. (2018). Communicative functions of hashtags. *Economics and Culture,* 15(1): 56–62.

Li, C., and Liu, J. (2017). Effects of using social networking sites in a different language: Does Spanish or English make a difference? *Computers in Human Behaviour,* 74: 257–24.

Ligidima, M. and Makananise, F. O. (2020). Social media as a communicative platform to promote indigenous African languages by young students at a rural-based university, in South Africa. *Gender and Behaviour,* 18(2): 15824–15832.

Lillehaugen, B. D. (2016). Why write in a language (almost) no one can read? *Language Documentation and Conservation,* 10(1): 356–393. http://hdl.handle.net /10125/24702.

Makananise, F. O., Malatji, E. J., and Madima, S. E. (2023). Indigenous Languages, Digital Media, and the COVID-19 Pandemic in the Global South: A South African Discourse. In *Indigenous Language for Social Change Communication in the Global South,* edited Salawu, A., Molale, T. B., Uribe-Jongbloed, E. and Ulla, M. S. London: Lexington Books.

Malatji, E. J., Makananise, F. O., and Madima, S. E. (2023). Critical Language Matters: The Fate of Indigenous Languages amid Covid-19 Pandemic in South Africa, In *Indigenous Language for Development Communication in the Global South,* edited by Salawu, A., Molale, T. B., Uribe-Jongbloed, E., and Ulla, M. S. London: Lexington Books.

Malatji, E. and Lesame, C. (2019). The use of South African languages by youth on social media: The case of Limpopo Province. Communicare: *Journal for Communication Studies in Africa,* 38(1): 76–95. https://journals.co.za/doi/epdf/10 .10520/EJC-173da01d4c.

Malatji, E. J. (2019). The impact of social media in conserving African languages amongst youth in Limpopo province. Doctoral thesis, University of Limpopo. ULSpace.http://ulspace.ul.ac.za/bitstream/handle/10386/2921/malatji_ej_2019.pdf ?sequence=3&isAllowed=y.

Mpofu, P., and Salawu, A. (2020). African language use in the digital public sphere: Functionality of the localised Google webpage in Zimbabwe, *South African Journal of African Languages,* 40(1): 78–84.

Muyadziwa, M. A. and Mncwango, E. M. (2021). Promoting the Use of Indigenous Languages on social media. *International Journal of Research and Innovation in Social Science (IJRISS),* 5(5): 310–314.

Outakoski, H., Cocq, C., and Steggo, P. (2018). Strengthening indigenous languages in the digital age: Social media-supported learning in Sápmi.

Owiny, S. A., Mehta, K., and Maretzki, A. N. (2014). The Use of Social Media Technologies to Create, Preserve, and Disseminate Indigenous Knowledge and Skills to Communities in East Africa. *International Journal of Communication*, 8: 234–247.

Pienaar, J. (2018). Profiling the social media users in South Africa. *The language used in Twitter for posts* is 18(1):1–2.

RSA (1996). *Constitution of the Republic of South Africa.* Cape Town: Government Printers.

Srinivasan, R. (2006). Indigenous, ethnic and cultural articulations of new media. *International Journal of Cultural Studies, 9*(4): 497–518.

Statista. (2023). Number of social media users in South Africa as of May 2023, by platform. https://www.statista.com/statistics/1312488/social-media-users-by -platform-in-south-africa.

Thobejane, L. N. (2017). The impact of social media on the development and promotion of indigenous African languages: A case study of the rural university. Unpublished Master of Arts Dissertation. University of Venda.

Thomas, B. (2022). The Role of Purposive Sampling Technique as a Tool for Informal Choices in a Social Sciences in Research Methods, *Just Agriculture,* 2(5): 1–8.

Uysal, R. (2015). The predictive role of social safeness and flourishing on problematic Facebook use. *South African Journal of Psychology,* 45(2): 182–193. https://doi.org/10.1177/0081246314560010

Warren, D. M. (1991). *Using indigenous knowledge in agricultural development,* World Bank discussion paper no. 127, Washington, DC: World Bank.

PART IV

Orality on Social Media, Indigenous Epistemic Cultures, and Minority Languages in Digital Media

Chapter 11

Promotion of Indigenous Languages and Culture through Social Media

Kganathi Shaku

The emergence of social networking (SN) has resulted in various digital communication platforms that enable the instant exchange of information. Such platforms include Facebook, X, Instagram, TikTok, and WhatsApp. These platforms became popular internationally and have easily dominated the digital space since many people have access to electronic gadgets. Statista (2023) reports that worldwide, many people have access to the internet, with Facebook having 2,989 million users, WhatsApp 2,000 million users, Instagram 2,000 million users, TikTok 1,081 million users, and X 564 million users. In Africa, Statista (2023) reports that social media users favor Facebook, WhatsApp, YouTube, X, TikTok, and Instagram. Africa alone has 384 million social media users. North and southern Africa dominate the social media space, with 56 percent of the population in northern Africa and 45 percent in southern Africa using social media.

Al-Tarawneh (2014:1) observes that "social media is the fastest growing web application in the 21st century. The nature of applications like Wikis, video streaming and application, and social networks makes it the phenomenon of the century." With the growth of social networks worldwide, Datareportal (2023) shows the active participation of youth, wherein they spend a minimum of three hours a day on social media. Shaku (2021) also reports that messaging (texting) is one of the main reasons why youth visit social media platforms. This means that most of the time, social media users exchange communication rather than scrolling or using such platforms for passive entertainment purposes.

Furthermore, when engagements take place on social media, language becomes central as a channel through which messages travel. According to Chapelle (2019) and Fromkin, Rodman, and Hyams (2011), language is a channel through which intangible knowledge, such as cultural heritage, is disseminated. Chapelle (2019) further notes that language is a carrier of an imperceptible cultural heritage that holds the representation, expressions, and knowledge that the communities regard as their cultural treasure. Furthermore, UNESCO (2020) regards language as a tool used to develop and resuscitate cultural values and an enabler for the delivery of information and knowledge coded in different sociocultural, political, and economic contexts (UNESCO, 2020). Likewise, Bella (2021) notes that culture and language are inextricably linked; that is, one cannot understand a culture without understanding the language. Additionally, a specific language is usually associated with a particular group of people. When you interact with a speech community, by default, you also interact with their culture.

For instance, more often, social media users dedicate discussions to cultural issues such as lobola or wedding and funeral procedures and the cultural life of the people. In such discussions, language becomes central as a communication tool. Moreover, when language matters such as the teaching of idioms and proverbs, language development, and language anthropologies are discussed, issues of culture are also embedded. This makes language and culture inseparable. Thus, we cannot talk about language without touching on the issues of culture and vice versa.

Moreover, in social media platforms where communication takes place, the use of language is also a factor since people use language for communication. Simultaneously, the sharing of cultural information also develops. Therefore, social media enables exposure to both language and culture. Shaku (2021) observed that in South Africa, communication takes place in both official and unofficial languages. These include eleven of the twelve official languages of the country (Sepedi, Setswana, Sesotho, isiNdebele, isiXhosa, isiZulu, SiSwati, Xitsonga, Tshivenda, Afrikaans, and English) and their dialects. As social media platforms have no language policy, users can choose any language for communication. Consequently, users have created various communication spaces where interactions solely take place in specific languages. For instance, on social media platforms, you would find *#BapediTwitterSpace, #SepediSeReng, Diema tša Sepedi*, and *Sešego Pukuntšutlhaloši ya Sepedi* (Basket: Sepedi monolingual dictionary) as platforms created by the Sepedi-speaking community to engage in issues relating to culture and language. Such platforms keep the Bapedi people connected regardless of their location, age, and educational level. These platforms empower Bapedi people linguistically and culturally, as they constantly engage in various topics concerning language and culture.

Promotion of Indigenous Languages and Culture through Social Media   243

This chapter uses Facebook, TikTok, and X because of their popularity worldwide and in South Africa. Table 11.1 demonstrates the Statista (2023) and Datareportal (2023) social media statistics of Facebook, Instagram, TikTok, and X worldwide and in South Africa.

Table 11.1 shows that Facebook is a leading social media platform (2,989 million users worldwide and 22.2 million locally), followed by Instagram (2,000 million worldwide and 5.7 million locally), TikTok (1,081 million worldwide and 5.4 million locally), and finally X (564 million worldwide and 3.6 million locally). Table 11.1 justifies the use of Facebook, TikTok, and X as social media platforms of focus. These social media platforms show the dominance of social media internationally and locally and their potential impact as channels for information distributors.

This chapter explores the use of social media platforms to promote language and culture. It looks at the Sepedi language and its cultures and how the Sepedi speech community, on social media, embraces their linguistic and cultural values. The role of social media in the promotion of indigenous languages and cultures has not been appreciated; hence, this chapter closes that gap.

FACILITATION OF LANGUAGE AND CULTURE THROUGH SOCIAL MEDIA: A BACKGROUND

Social media has become a platform of communication, enabling effective communication between its users. The nature of communication is effective because users can either have synchronous or asynchronous interactions. Synchronous communication allows them to have live chats, audio, and voice conferencing. In contrast, asynchronous interactions allow users to leave messages, and targeted people can respond when ready to do so. This means that people are allowed to engage without communication barriers, such as time and location. This creates compatibility between people's mode of communication and the concepts carried by the communication—language and culture in the context of this chapter. Language and culture are constant

Table 11.1. Social media distribution worldwide and in South Africa. Data from Statista (2023) and Datareportal (2023).

Social media platform	Worldwide statistics per billion/ million	South African statistics per million
Facebook	2,989 million	22.2 million
Instagram	2,000 million	5.7 million
TikTok	1,081 million	11.8 million
X	564 million	3.6 million

social pillars that require nurturing. Therefore, social media could facilitate and resuscitate cultural and linguistic awareness within a group of people. For instance, Sepedi language speakers on social media constantly promote language and culture through social media features such as the following:

- Status posting;
- Hashtagging;
- Video conferencing;
- Audio conferencing; and
- Gamification.

More often, social media users share information by posting statuses, using hashtags (#) to open a trail of discussions, using video and/or audio conferencing to facilitate engagements, and using gamification to test language and culture knowledge. The mentioned social media features allow users to have continuous engagement regardless of their various remote locations. The synchronous and asynchronous nature of these channels makes social interactions more effective.

On Facebook, there is a page such as *Sešego: Pukuntšutlhaloši ya Sepedi* (Basket: Sepedi monolingual dictionary), which is created to promote the Sepedi language through the teaching of proverbs and explanation of unfamiliar vocabulary. On this page, users post terms to understand their meaning or post a proverb to test others' knowledge of Sepedi proverbs. Ultimately, group pages such as these become educational and have much potential for developing the Sepedi language (Ngoepe, Shaku, & Letsoalo, 2022).

On X, a hashtag such as *#BapediTwitterSpace* is a synchronous space initiated by Sepedi speakers to discuss language issues, culture (teaching of lobola procedure), and issues concerning the Bapedi youth. In addition, on X, there is a handle such as *@Sepedi Bapedi*, created for the promotion of Sepedi cultural attire and music and for the teaching of the taboos within Bapedi society. On TikTok, language and culture are also promoted. The nature of TikTok allows users to engage in various components of language and culture. These include cultural music, language tutoring, cultural practices relating to marriage, the naming of children, and wedding and funeral procedures. This shows that the new media and social media platforms are potent tools for the promotion of cultural values and that through them, the cultural system will resist extinction (Asemah, Ekhareafo, & Olaniran, 2013).

This chapter also falls within anthropological linguistics—a branch of linguistics and anthropology that focuses on language from the cultural and social points of view and the role it plays in cultural practices and societal structures. In the context of this chapter, anthropological linguistics facilitates the relationship between language and culture and shows the importance of language and culture promotion. Sepedi social media users are a social media community that relates to common experiences and interests; Douma (2007) categorizes them under a community of interest. Daily, the community engages in interesting and ongoing topics relating to language and culture. The following figure is an example.

Figure 11.1 demonstrates Douma's (2007) point about social media's ability to create communities of interest. In the group "*Learning Sepedi 'twii' [Are boleleng]*" (Learning the correct Sepedi [Let us speak]), the concerned community is interested in preserving the Sepedi language and culture by creating an inter- and intra-cultural and linguistic transfer environment. The other group, "*MAREMA KA DIKA: DIKA LE DIEMA TSA SEPEDI. . . . LE DITHAI*" (Idioms: idioms, proverbs, and riddles of the Sepedi language), is concerned with the teaching of Sepedi idioms, proverbs, and riddles.

THEORETICAL PERSPECTIVES

Sociocultural Theory and Constructivism

The learning of language and culture through social media can be positioned within sociocultural and constructivism perspectives and uses and gratification perspectives. This section positions social media platforms within sociocultural and uses and gratification theories. According to Osuna (2000:3), "Vygotsky's socio-cultural theory posits that learning is grounded in social contexts." Furthermore, Vygotsky's sociocultural theory, as a learning theory, suits well with the learning of a language, as Magnan (2008) regards the social environment of an individual to be very fundamental for the development of

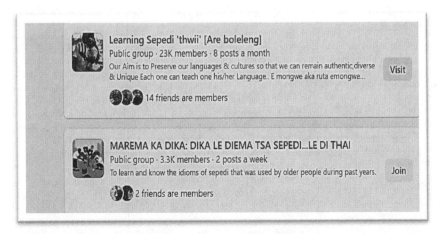

Figure 11.1. Sepedi Facebook Groups for Language Promotion

language. Therefore, social media, as an environment where communication about language and culture continually takes place, should be acknowledged, and explored fully. This will help with the understanding of how learning takes place on social media.

Panhwar, Ansari, and Ansari (2016) argue that the sociocultural approach can be intertwined with constructivism if it focuses on teaching and learning. Panhwar, Ansari, and Ansari (2016:522) emphasize that "constructivism is the philosophy, or belief, that learners create their own knowledge based on interactions with their environment including their interactions with other people." In the context of social media as a teaching and learning environment, social media users can understand the Sepedi language and culture through their engagement with knowledgeable Sepedi speakers. Therefore, the Bapedi content creators on social media ultimately contribute to the linguistic and cultural empowerment of others.

Uses and Gratification Theory (UGT)

Whiting and Williams (2013:363) opine that uses and gratifications theory is relevant to social media because of its origins in communications literature. Social media is a communication mechanism that allows users to communicate with thousands, and perhaps billions, of individuals all over the world. The basic premise of uses and gratifications theory is that individuals will seek out media among competitors that fulfils their needs and leads to ultimate gratifications.

This means that social media users compare different social media platforms and choose relevant platforms that meet their needs. With the widespread use of social media platforms internationally and locally, social media users are spoiled for choice. However, Facebook, X, and TikTok appear to be some of the highly favored social media platforms; hence, they are used as environments for learning. The content put on these platforms gratifies the needs of the users.

Furthermore, Eginli and Tas (2018:88) observe that:

> Most users of social network sites regard social media not only as an alternative communication medium but also as an expressional environment in which they can express their ideas and take ideas. However, another important reason why social network sites provide satisfaction for individuals is that information can be acquired immediately, and this can be done at the global level.

Uses and gratification theory posits that individuals actively seek out certain media content to satisfy specific needs. Individuals may have different needs that drive them to seek out types of media content. As Douma (2007) posits that social media creates communities of interest and different users use social media to satisfy different needs. Therefore, the uses and gratification of the social media users who consume Sepedi content on social media is twofold. There are those who access the content to gratify their eagerness to learn the Sepedi culture and other groups that consume the Sepedi content for them to learn the language.

SOCIAL MEDIA AS AN EDUCATIONAL ENVIRONMENT FOR CULTURE AND LANGUAGE

This section looks at the promotion of language and culture on social media. Although language and culture are discussed separately in this section, they should not be treated or regarded as two separate or unrelated concepts. Mohiuddin (2016:181) captures the relationship between language and culture by stating the following:

> Every language has a culture, and every culture bears a language. Every culture nourishes a language, and every language accomplishes a culture. Hence a language is a "Barometer" and a "Thermometer" of the culture as well. A minor motion, or vibration or under current at the level of culture may be well depicted through the language and its literature. The language and literature acts like a seismograph of the relative culture. In short language and culture are the paradigms to the social maturity.

Thus, language is an important aspect of culture, as is culture to language. The following subsection discusses the promotion of the Sepedi language and culture through social media.

Social Media and Language Promotion

The promotion of language on social media contributes to language development and maintenance. Therefore, when social media users share information and knowledge through their languages, particularly indigenous languages such as Sepedi, such languages gain strength, increasing their chances of sustainability. UNESCO (2020) opines that it is within the people's rights to preserve, revitalize, and promote their languages. Therefore, this implies that no one besides the speakers of the Sepedi language can develop the Sepedi language. Social media has become a convenient platform for the promotion of the Sepedi language. This is confirmed by Outakoski, Cocq, and Steggo (2018) who see social media as one of the digital spaces that open doors for the promotion and strengthening of languages.

This discussion explores the promotion of the Sepedi language on the following social media platforms: Facebook, TikTok, and X. The presented excerpts are extracted from these social media platforms to demonstrate how Sepedi speakers promote the Sepedi language on social media.

Promotion of Sepedi on Facebook

The Facebook platform creates a conducive environment for the promotion of the Sepedi language by enabling the operation of groups such as "*SEPEDI SE RE MOPEDI OMANG?*" (Sepedi says Mopedi who are you?) and "*Sešego: Pukuntšutlhaloši ya Sepedi*" (Basket: Sepedi monolingual dictionary). See figure 11.2 for reference.

The Facebook groups displayed in figure 11.2 show social media users' commitment to the promotion of the Sepedi language. The first group, "*SEPEDI SERE MOPEDI OMANG?*" (Sepedi says Mopedi who are?) focuses on the use of the Sepedi language to communicate issues relating to kingship, customs, music, attire, and history. Therefore, groups such as these are dynamic, as they simultaneously promote language and culture. The "*Sešego: Pukuntšutlhaloši ya Sepedi*" (Basket: Sepedi monolingual dictionary) also deals with the promotion of the Sepedi language through the discussion of less-known vocabulary. This group is a platform for Sepedi users on Facebook to inquire about the unfamiliar vocabulary of the Sepedi language or to understand anything related to the Sepedi language. For instance, figure 11.3 is an excerpt showing a member of "*Sešego: Pukuntšutlhaloši ya Sepedi*" asking about the Sepedi word for technology.

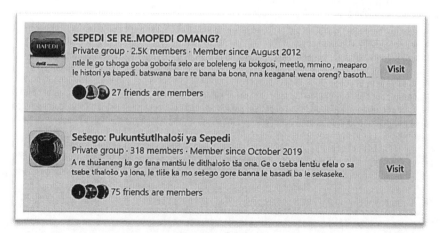

Figure 11.2. Sepedi Facebook Groups for Language Promotion

Promotion of Indigenous Languages and Culture through Social Media 249

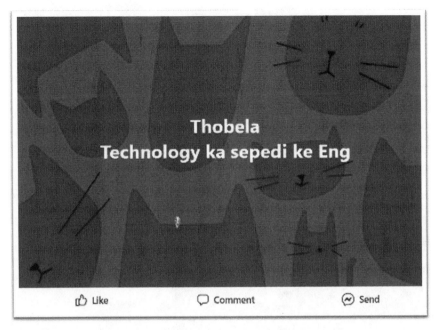

Figure 11.3. Sepedi Facebook Post for Language Consultations

In addition to consultation purposes, social media is used as a space for the learning of proverbs, idioms, and riddles. Sepedi speakers also use social media for the teaching of proverbs (Figure 11.4).
It is inevitable that groups such as *"Diema le dika tsa Sepedi"* (Proverbs and Idiom of the Sepedi language) exist because learning of a language involves the understanding of both its literal and figurative aspects. This speaks to the understanding of how language is used on a daily basis and the messages hidden in its figurative expressions, such as proverbs and idioms. The Facebook group displayed in figure 11.4 focuses on the teaching and continual use of Sepedi proverbs and idioms. The group has 431.2 thousand followers, which implies that many Bapedi users and those interested in learning the language on Facebook take pride in the learning of proverbs and idioms as figurative entities of a language.

Promotion of Sepedi on TikTok

The TikTok platform also enables the promotion of the Sepedi language. Its video mode of communication adds value, as TikTokers can have live interactions for the purposes of language learning. Some of the TikTok posts are illustrated in figure 11.5 and table 11.2.

Figure 11.4. Sepedi Facebook Group About the Teaching of Proverbs and Idioms

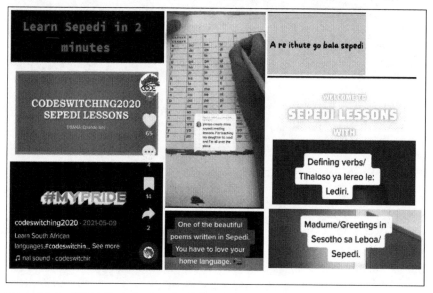

Figure 11.5. TikTok Posts for Language Promotion

Table 11.2 Translation (Excerpts are translated sequentially.)

A re ithuteng go bala Sepedi (English translation: Let us learn to read Sepedi)
Tlhalošo ya lereo le "Lediri" (English translation: Definition of the word "verb")

The TikTok posts shown in figure 11.5 display different TikTok handles created for the teaching and learning of the Sepedi language. Ultimately, the Sepedi language is promoted, as TikTokers share information about the Sepedi language. The TikTok handle "Learn Sepedi in 2 minutes" uses a

Promotion of Indigenous Languages and Culture through Social Media 251

code-switching teaching strategy to teach the Sepedi language. The content creator switches between English and Sepedi language to make language learning easier and more fascinating. There is also the presence of TikTokers who voluntarily teach basic Sepedi grammar aspects such as phonology and morphology. For instance, the middle post in figure 11.5 shows a TikToker teaching Sepedi phonetics. Following the teaching post on Sepedi phonetics, someone provided a comment illustrated in figure 11.6 below.

Moreover, from figure 11.5, we also see other TikTokers who dedicate their time to the promotion of the Sepedi language by providing Sepedi lessons. In essence, this also contributes to the availability of language learning resources of the Sepedi language, as Outakoski, Cocq, and Steggo (2018, p. 21) state that "social media has become an arena where resources are created and shared, enabling communities of speakers to support each other and promote their languages." For previously marginalized languages such as the Sepedi language, which lacks digital resources, social media is significant because it contributes greatly to the growth of the language. Outakoski, Cocq, and Steggo (2018) emphasize that the availability of digital tools and social media platforms plays a significant role in the promotion of languages.

Compared to Facebook, TikTok appears to be more dynamic and more effective in the promotion of the Sepedi language. This is because the "TikTok news feed is essentially based on a system called 'Discovery Engine.' This tool combines a complex algorithm that customizes the content displayed to each user based on their previous interests and positive interactions" (Bastien, 2023). Thus, if you are a fan of the Sepedi language on TikTok, you will

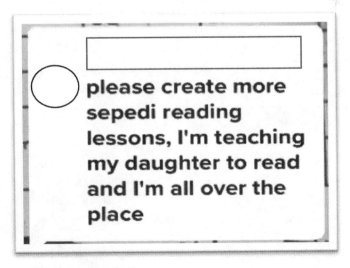

Figure 11.6. TikTok Appreciative Post

always be fed with content relating to the Sepedi language. This complex algorithm makes it easy to get your favorite content updates.

Promotion of Sepedi on X

The X platform also opens a space for the promotion of a language. Tweeps (people who use X) can use their X handles or create hashtags (#) for content related to the promotion of the Sepedi language. Language could be promoted through the teaching of proverbs or other linguistic subcategories. The cases in point are the X posts about the promotion of the Sepedi language, displayed in figure 11.7 and table 11.3 below.

Figure 11.7 displays a promotion of the Sepedi language on X. The selected posters focus on the teaching of months and proverbs of the Sepedi language. The poster under *"Bolelang Sepedi"* (Speak Sepedi) shows a detailed teaching of proverbs because the author of this tweet provided a proverb and its meaning. Notably, the middle poster shows a gamification approach to the teaching of Sepedi proverbs. This is done through the combination of emojis and having people guess the combination.

The use of the Sepedi language on social media is advantageous for the promotion, development, and sustainability of language, as Outakoski, Cocq, and Steggo (2018) mention that for language to develop, it should be used in as many domains as possible. Consequently, the Sepedi language as a previously marginalized language (previously confined to being used at home or between mutual speakers) gets exposure and room for sustainability. Therefore, it is worth appreciating the role played by social media in the promotion of languages and, more importantly, the previously marginalized.

Figure 11.7. X Posts for the Promotion of the Sepedi language

Table 11.3 Translation (Excerpts are translated sequentially)

Months in Sepedi	I am a teacher here on Twitter. This is the assignment for the long weekend. The Sepedi proverbs. What do they mean?	As we conclude the month of August, and go into September, we will share the Sepedi proverbs, every day, until the end of September
		--------------------
		Proverb
		You cannot sever two masters.
		Explanation:
		If someone tries to do two duties simultaneously, both those duties might fail. If someone loves two people, he will end up being committed to only one and making the other one a fool.

Nonetheless, social media is not confined to the promotion of just a language, but also culture (Aydin, 2012). Aydin (2012:1098) states that "culture and language are intimately related, the uses and meanings of language are shaped and dictated by culture, while conversely, to some extent, culture is determined by language." Hence, the following section discusses social media and the promotion of the Sepedi culture.

Social Media and Culture Promotion

According to Aydin (2012), social media platforms have recently become environments for the teaching and learning of culture. This is the case, as people traditionally meet physically to share knowledge about culture. These platforms also provide exciting possibilities for cultural transfer, as they are constituted by heterogeneous users. The promotion of culture on social media more often comes in the form of social media groups, the posting of messages, video conferencing, and hashtags (#). Social media communication platforms are shaped to be intercultural (happening between people of different cultures) and intracultural (happening between people of the same culture). Therefore, learning of culture may occur between Bapedi users or between Bapedi and other tribes with an interest in learning about Bapedi culture. A case in point is the Facebook group *"Learning Sepedi 'twii' [Are boleleng]*," displayed in figure 11.8. Its description states that the aim of the group is to preserve language and culture and to facilitate inter- and intracultural transfer.

The promotion of Bapedi culture on social media is deemed significant. Asemah, Ekhareafo, and Olaniran (2014) report that social media can

Figure 11.8. Facebook Public Group on the Promotion of Bapedi Culture

redefine and promote culture's core values. Thus, when cultural transfer, learning, and teaching take place, promotion prevails. One of the key points realized by Asemah, Ekhareafo, and Olaniran (2014) is social media's ability to promote the core values of a culture. Essien (2020) states that cultural values are the core principles and ideals upon which an entire community exists and protects and relies upon for existence and harmonious relationships. The concept is made up of several parts: customs, which involve traditions and rituals; values, which are beliefs; and culture, which is a group's guiding values. The core cultural values of the Bapedi include traditionalism relating to funeral procedures, marriage procedures, traditional medicines, healing procedures, and the naming of children. In this section, we look at how social media promotes Bapedi cultural norms relating to the marriage procedure and naming of children. Extracts from different social media platforms are used for clarification.

CORE CULTURAL VALUES OF BAPEDI

Marriage Procedure

Teaching and learning about the marriage procedure of the Bapedi people can also be found on social media platforms. X, Facebook, and TikTok are used to provide evidence.

Figure 11.9 shows an announcement about the topic of an X Space known as "*Sepedi Leleme la Gae*" (Sepedi Home Language). This announcement informed the Bapedi speech community on X that the topic of discussion for the night would be the explanation of the wedding procedure for the Bapedi people in detail.

In addition to conversations over X spaces, Sepedi users also share information about wedding procedures through X posts. This can be seen in figure 11.10 and table 11.4.

"Rutang bana ditaola, seke laya le tšona Badimong"

Leina **la** space ke "**Sepedi**, Leleme **la** Gae"

Nako: 21h00

Hlogo taba;
Tlabe re rutana tshepidišo ka botlalo ya **lenyalo** gore ditaba tša gona ka **Sepedi** di sepetšwa bjang.
Go tloga kago thiba sefero go fihla ka mohlobolo sekotlelong.

♡ 9   ↻ 26   ♥ 82

Figure 11.9. Bapedi X Space Announcement for the Wedding Procedure from X

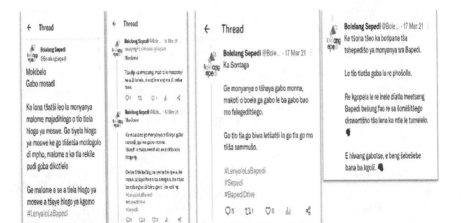

Figure 11.10.   X Thread for the Bapedi Wedding Procedure

Table 11.4 Translations Excerpts are translated sequentially)

Saturday	Saturday	Sunday	That is a brief procedure of the Bapedi wedding.
Bridal home	I will leave out the	After the wedding cer-	
On the day of the	issues of put-	emony, the bride	You will add or cor-
wedding, the	ting a sound	will return with her	rect us.
uncle of the bride	system on the	companion.	We apologise for
will bring gifts to	walls, the bridal	Later, they will put a date	using some of your
the bride. He can	dress, bridal and	to officially bring her	pictures without
come with a goat	groom's mates,	to the groom's place.	your permission.
or bowls.	everyone knows		Have a good day.
If not bringing the	about that.		We wish you all
gifts, he will take	Saturday		the best.
a cow's head.	After the wedding		
	ceremony has		
	been completed		
	at the bridal		
	home, the same		
	night people will		
	go to the groom's		
	home. The bride		
	will carry the		
	mohlobolo bowl.		
	When they arrive at		
	the groom home's		
	gate they sing and		
	get welcomed.		
	When they are		
	still at the gate		
	a bride would		
	be given a mari-		
	tal name.		

An X handle *@BolelangSepedi* explains the activities that are supposed to take place during the Bapedi wedding. Since Bapedi wedding ceremonies often occur on Saturday and Sunday, this X thread explains activities to take at the bridal home on Saturday and what is to happen at the groom's home on Sunday. Since culture is a complex social element whereby Bapedi have slightly different but related practices (depending on the geographic areas), the author of the above thread concludes by putting a disclaimer that what is communicated can be added or corrected.

X enables mass communication and has a greater reach than other social media platforms, as De Villiers (2020:27–28) states that "X can be seen as a synchronous microblogging service that allows users to share short thoughts and ideas in the form of Tweets to a timeline wherein users can read and access anyone's messages, even though they do not follow that specific person." This means that information about Bapedi culture could be reached by anyone regardless of being a member of a particular group or a follower of someone. Once you type in any keyword, such as *Bapedi culture, Sepedi wedding, Setšo sa Bapedi* (culture of Bapedi), *Lenyalo la Bapedi* (wedding of Bapedi), etc., a list of available information will be provided.

Naming of Children

The Bapedi people have a unique way of naming their children, known as "*theo ya maina* or *go rea maina*." This forms part of the cultural and traditional practices of the Bapedi people. In some Bapedi speech communities, children are named after their family members from the paternal and maternal family sides. However, there is a procedure to follow when names are given. Bapedi social media users take advantage of social media and use it to share information about the naming of children. On social media platforms such as Facebook and TikTok, some users dedicate their time to sharing information regarding the naming of children. For example, figure 11.11 and table 11.5 show an example of what one Facebook user wrote about naming children.

Figure 11.11 and Table 11.5 show a Facebooker who needed guidance about the procedure of naming children in the Bapedi speech community and to confirm the repercussions of giving a child a wrong name. The user posted this on social media with the knowledge that the Bapedi speech community on Facebook would provide helpful information.

Consequently, many Bapedi followers of the person who inquired about the correct procedure of naming children replied. One of the respondents wrote what is illustrated in figure 11.12 and table 11.6.

The response provided in figure 11.12 and table 11.6 emphasize the convenience of social media as a source of information. Thus, the effectiveness of social media should also be acknowledged since users make the sharing of information easy by being active and responsive to queries posted.

Moreover, TikTok plays a role in the promotion of Bapedi culture. The teaching of naming procedures for Bapedi people also takes place on TikTok. For instance, after one of the Bapedi TiKTokers who leads the conversation about culture and language shared similar information about the naming procedure, the following was said, as illustrated in figure 11.13 and table 11.7.

June 16, 2022

Ke no fela ke ekwa Bapedi ba re ngwana o tshwenywa ke leina. Taba e le gore batswadi ba mo fele leina (leina la go theelwa ka yo mongwe wa leloko) leo le sego la mo lebana. Ge eba taba ye ke nnete, ke kgopela go tseba gore tsela ya maleba ya go theela maina ka segagabolena ke efe.

Figure 11.11. Facebook Post About the Naming of Children

258   Kganathi Shaku

Table 11.5 Translation

Post translation

I often hear Bapedi saying a child suffers because of a name. The reason being that their parents gave the child a wrong name (family name given to a child). If this is true, I would like to know the correct procedure of giving name to children.

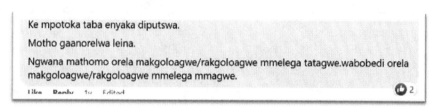

Figure 11.12. Facebook Responses for Naming of Children

Table 11.6 Translation

That issue is difficult it needs elders.
You do not just give a person a name.
The first-born is named after her paternal grandmother or his paternal grandfather, the second-born is named after her maternal grandmother or his maternal grandfather.

Figure 11.13. TikTok Conversation on the Naming of Children

The chain of conversation depicted in figure 11.13 and table 11.7 followed a TikTok video created about the naming procedure of the Bapedi people. The responses appreciate the content of the video, as it helped them to resolve challenges they had in naming their children. More importantly, they regard the sharing of such content as a provision of great wisdom.

Promotion of Indigenous Languages and Culture through Social Media 259

Table 11.7 Translation (Excerpts are translated sequentially)

My child would cry day and night.	Therefore, what happens if we are many at home, maybe you are an 8th born among the 10 children and the older ones have already allocated names to their children. How do you do?
--	
I needed this information. I thank you. Tag me on part 2.	
	--
	You should name your children after your brother, if is a boy and after your sister if is a girl.

Social media plays an important role in the promotion of culture. The promotion of Bapedi culture on Facebook, X, and TikTok is a case in point, as Bapedi speech communities on social media take advantage of its effectiveness as an information-sharing channel. Therefore, although social media cannot replace physical interaction between people, it enables them to engage more often (Mas, Arilla, and Gómez, 2021). This means that even though the Bapedi speech community is still able to have face-to-face interaction for the teaching, learning, and transmission of cultural knowledge, social media provide an effective and convenient mode of communication.

For instance, the Facebook page Sepedi Bapedi, presented in figure 11.14, is one of the groups that aims to promote Sepedi culture.

Figure 11.14 shows that social media sites such as Facebook serve as platforms for the promotion of Bapedi culture. Figure 11.14 depicts a Facebook page, Sepedi Bapedi, which was created for the promotion of Bapedi culture. Its description reads: "We are proud of our identity. This group is a space for Bapedi and those who love culture. Its main purpose is to promote our culture and share information." As Ahmed et al. (2022:195) state, "mass media play a significant role in modern society by providing content that shapes values, positively impacts shared identity and fosters a sense of belonging," which shows that people see value and positivity in mass media platforms such as Facebook. Sepedi Bapedi's membership of 106.2 thousand people implies that users have enthusiasm to learn about Sepedi culture. Consequently, when the Sepedi culture is communicated on social media, it becomes sustainable, as Baran (2002) holds that culture is socially constructed and maintained through communication.

CONCLUSION

This chapter explored the use of social media in promoting Sepedi language and culture. It demonstrated different initiatives taken by the Bapedi speech community on Facebook, X, and TikTok regarding the promotion of their

Figure 11.14. Facebook Group for Culture Promotion

language and culture. Through social media, Bapedi social media users are given the chance to understand and know their surroundings. Additionally, it is noted that they use social media for various purposes and to gratify different needs. Therefore, social media must be appreciated for playing an important role in enabling the promotion of language and culture. As UNESCO strives to promote all indigenous languages, in its Decade of Indigenous Languages, social media should be considered an effective digital platform for the promotion and preservation of language and culture. This is because more often, African researchers focus on the negative effects of social media on languages and overlook or report less about the positive side. The research on how language is used on social media should also be expanded to unveil some of the positives of social media.

REFERENCES

Ahmed, I. S. Y., Miladi, N., Messaoud, M. B., Labidi, F., Ashour, A., Almohannadi, H., & Alorfe, A. (2022). Social media networks as platforms for culture and identity interplay among Qatari youth. *Journal of Arab and Muslim Media Research, 15*(2), 179–203.

Al-Tarawneh, H. A. (2014). The influence of social networks on students' performance. *Journal of Emerging Trends in Computing and Information Sciences, 5*(3), 200–205.

Asemah, E. S., Ekhareafo, D. O., & Olaniran, S. (2013). Nigeria's core values and the use of social media to promote cultural values. *International Journal of Information and Communication Technology Education, 9*(4), 58–59.

Aydin, S. (2012). A review of research on Facebook as an educational environment. *Educational Technology Research and Development, 60*, 1093–1106.

Baran, S. (2002). *Introduction to mass communication, media literacy and culture*, second ed. New York: McGraw Hill Higher Education.

Bastien. (2023). TikTok vs Facebook: The duel of social networks. Debugbar. Accessed June 2023, https://www.debugbar.com/tiktok-vs-facebook.

Bella. (2021). Language and culture relationship – A detailed guide. Accessed June 2023, https://thelanguagedoctors.org/blog/what-is-the-language-and-culture-relationship/.

Chapelle, C. A. (2019). *The Concise Encyclopedia of Applied Linguistics*. John Wiley and Sons: New York.

Cru, J. (2015). Language revitalisation from the ground up: promoting Yucatec Maya on Facebook. *Journal of Multilingual and Multicultural Development, 36*(3), 284–296.

Datareportal, Digital (2023), *Global Digital Overview*. Accessed April 2023, https://datareportal.com/.

De Villiers, J. M. (2020). Introduction to social media for Research. In Du Plessis, C. and Satar, A. A. (eds). *Introduction to social media research: Theory and application*. Cape Town: Juta.

Douma, C. (2007). The 3 Types of Social Media Communities. Accessed May 2023, https://www.socialmediatoday.com/content/3-types-social-media-communities.

Draper, R. J. (2002). School mathematics reform, constructivism, and literacy: A case for literacy instruction in the reform-oriented math classroom. *Journal of Adolescent and Adult Literacy, 45*(6), 520–529.

Eginli, A. T., & Tas, N. O. (2018). Interpersonal communication in social networking sites: An investigation in the framework of uses and gratification theory. *Online Journal of Communication and Media Technologies, 8*(2), 81–104.

Essien, E. (2020). Exploring Culture and Entrepreneurship Nexus in Peacebuilding: Beyond Fragility of Institutions as Source of Conflict. In Essein (ed.), *Handbook of Research on the Impact of Culture in Conflict Prevention and Peacebuilding* (pp. 347–371). IGI Global.

Fromkin, V., Rodman, R., & Hyams, N. (2011). *An introduction to language* (Int. ed.). Boston, MA: Wadsworth.

Magnan, S. S. (2008). The unfulfilled promise of teaching for communicative competence: Insights from sociocultural theory. *Sociocultural theory and the teaching of second languages*, 349–379.

Mas, J. M., Arilla, R., & Gómez, A. (2021). Facebook as a promotional tool for Spanish museums 2016–2020 and COVID influence. *Journal of promotion management, 27*(6), 812–831.

Mohiuddin, S. (2016). Crossing the borders: Language, literature and social media a case study of Urdu. *Language in India, 16*(7) 179–188.

Ngoepe, M., Shaku, K., & Letsoalo, N. (2022). Development of an indigenous language through crowd-sourcing on social media. *Bulletin of the National Library of South Africa,* 76 (1), 63 – 78

Asemah, E. S., Ekhareafo, D. O., & Olaniran, S. (2014). Nigeria's core values and the use of social media to promote cultural values. In *Digital Arts and Entertainment: Concepts, Methodologies, Tools, and Applications* (924–935). IGI Global.

Osuna, M. (2000). Promoting foreign culture acquisition via the Internet in a sociocultural context. *Journal of educational computing Research, 22*(3), 323–345.

Outakoski, H., Cocq, C., & Steggo, P. (2018). Strengthening Indigenous languages in the digital age: social media–supported learning in Sápmi. *Media International Australia, 169*(1), 21–31.

Panhwar, A. H., Ansari, S., & Ansari, K. (2016). Sociocultural theory and its role in the development of language pedagogy. *Advances in language and literary studies, 7*(6), 183–188.

Shaku, K. J. (2021). The impact of social media on the writing of Sepedi in secondary schools. Doctoral dissertation. University of South Africa.

Social Media Today. (2007). *The Three Types of Social Media Communities*. Accessed June 2023, https://www.socialmediatoday.com/content/3-types-social -media-communities.

Statista. (2023). *Distribution of languages spoken by individuals inside and outside of households in South Africa 2018*. Accessed June 2023, https://www.statista.com/.

The Language Doctors. (2021), *Language and Culture Relationship—A detailed Guide*. Accessed May 2023, https://thelanguagedoctors.org/what-is-the-language -and-culture-relationship/.

UNESCO. (2020). *Indigenous Languages Decade (2022–2032)*. Accessed May 2023, https://www.unesco.org/en/decades/indigenous-languages.

Whiting, A., & Williams, D. (2013). Why people use social media: A uses and gratifications approach. *Qualitative Market Research: An International Journal, 16*(4), 362–369.

Chapter 12

Orality On Social Media Language

Linguistic Texts and Images Portraying Elements of Isizulu Folklore

Beryl Babsy Boniwe MaMchunu Xaba

The storyteller's role in early human culture was like that of the historian in modern times: to preserve the past by recounting its events. In ballads and epic poems, which recounted what men believe to have happened many centuries ago, medieval men presented their experiences in poetry while singing them in banquet halls. However, as society advanced, these storytellers became aware of the significance of their experiences for society as a whole and shifted to prose storytelling in the form of stories, myths, and tales. Over time, the bardic verse stories that were mostly spoken at the inns, crossroads, and palaces of the nobility evolved into utilitarian prose, which was the style used by professional compilers to create what is now known as folklore tale (Campa, 1965). Everything is folklore in a completely oral culture. The dominance of the passed down over the learned element in modern society's folklore, as well as the prominence that the popular imagination derives from and accords to custom and tradition, are what set it apart from the rest of civilization. While freezing or solidifying its form, the transfer of oral tradition to writing and print serves to keep it alive and spread it among those to whom it is not native or fundamental, rather than negating its validity as folklore (Leach, 1959).

Orature is made up of indigenous knowledge and conventions vary from tribe to tribe in the form of customs, traditions, and beliefs. Social media channels are used by tribes like the AmaZulu to spread texts and cultural materials that contain ancient wisdom. An information of a blended style that contains both oral and written characteristics together with numerous sets of symbols and scripts, as well as prosodic attributes, has arisen as a result of new trends in how people write in digital environments (Cutler et al., 2022:13). Eventually, the above outline defines the concept of folklore: generally tracing it back to ancient times. This lays a knowledge background for this chapter where modern presentation of folklore is via digital spaces on social media platforms like Facebook.

Among the few scholars who researched isiZulu folklore, Masuku (2005) examines folktales, proverbs, and praises to ascertain how society wants women and girls to behave in order to be recognized as members of society. She examines how women were portrayed in folktales, how women responded to society, and how women felt about marriage with a focus on the stereotypes associated with women.

There is a shift in oral tradition, passed on from one generation to the other through word of mouth, to the literacy era where folklore literary works were introduced. Social media has recently taken over as applications are introduced daily on cellphones and computers to improve communication. According to Griffith and Liyenage (2008), the impact of technology on social interaction influences how people engage and build relationships across geographic boundaries. Nowadays, people from various countries use social networks to connect and share information and opinions even when they have never met. Various apps and programs are used to distribute and transmit messages on computers and mobile devices. These smartphones and laptops, the backbone of social media, are instructive, amusing, and educational. It should be noted that these elements serve the same functional purposes as folklore.

Internet access is required on computers and mobile devices to access social media communication. The extent to which people and organizations can freely participate in discourse across extensive time-space is drastically changing due to the internet. Internet access creates new avenues for discussion and discourse, gives individuals more control over their lives, and allows new kinds of cooperation and solidarity. Slevin (2000:47) articulates that the internet serves as a platform for personal development, group sharing, and community discussion on significant topics affecting their daily existence. As reported by Slevin (2000) above, the internet enables unfettered debate between those with similar opinions and those with opposing viewpoints. This is all accomplished through linguistic repertoires, which this research aims to investigate, among other things.

In addition, societies use social media to share linguistic repertoires because oral tradition and storytelling seem to be falling away. For instance, words are given new meanings and written in brevity on social media, impacting verbal communication.

What further captures the researcher's attention is that oral communication was/is permitted like social media users do to express their feelings, ideas, and daily experiences. Similarly, traditional prose and poetry were invented in the same way that oral language was, through everyday occurrences. The same is true for social media posts formed by daily events and experiences. In this chapter, the researcher's main contention is that folklore-inspired aesthetic expressions can also be found in social media posts, which are illustrated, analyzed, and discussed using extracted posts from Facebook and other social media platforms.

The objectives of this chapter are:

- To examine how idioms, proverbs, and themes from folktales, such as witchcraft, extraterrestrial prowess, magical knowledge, evil, terror, misfortune, beliefs, and spiritual possession, are presented on social media platforms.
- To identify moral lessons in textual and truncated images posted as messages on social media platforms.
- To explore the impact these roles, have on the teaching and maintenance of the isiZulu language.

The intended outcomes of this study are to find out if orality has a place in digital world and to discover if social media platforms, like Facebook in this case, has a role in teaching and learning of orality. As a result, this research analyses fictionalized orality taken from social media posts. Furthermore, it elaborates on the effect of social media posts on the educational and cultural archiving process. This either presents the idea that oral tradition (by word of mouth) has progressed or the point that it has collapsed with the advent of the 4IR. The study's objective is, what if oral tradition has deteriorated to the extent that social media has raised it as a presentation tool? Ferris (2022) suggests that social media platforms be viewed as an alternative teaching and learning model, particularly for traditional orature, which is no longer passed down from generation to generation through word of mouth. In the same way, this chapter explores how idioms and proverbs are shared and examined through social media platforms using messages and images. It is an educational opportunity for both isiZulu language speakers and non-speakers who access these uploaded messages to learn and understand the linguistic terms of isiZulu.

This study is motivated by the realization that social media sites like Facebook offer isiZulu speakers a means of disseminating indigenous knowledge, instructing the general public, and conserving knowledge for future generations. Against this backdrop, this research highlights the significance of social media posts' effects on the understanding and distribution of orality.

266   *Chapter 12*

THEORETICAL FRAMEWORK

The discourse analysis theory frames this study. According to Paltridge (2021), the purpose of discourse analysis is to:

- Investigate language trends across texts and consider the connection between language and the social and cultural environment in which it is utilized.
- Consider the many ways language is used to convey various worldviews and understandings.
- Examine how participant interactions affect language usage and how language use affects social identities and relationships.
- Consider how language is used to form identities and worldviews.

The definitions above support the notion that discourse analysis is a suitable theory to base this study on. This study focuses on how isiZulu literature is distributed via social media. One would also agree that the introduction of social media has positively affected modernizing traditional literature, which was archaic and outdated in terms of vocabulary. Discourse analysis was created to focus on language in studying society and people as social beings, particularly in sociology and social psychology. Researchers studying discourse examine both public and private language use to gain access to a society's standard, if not cohesive, "world view." Some of these elements include how individuals and their actions are identified, valued, and situated in hierarchical relationships. One action or practice that people engage in as part of their ongoing social lives and connections is language use. The researcher thus creates a picture of society and how it operates through the investigation of language and language use (Taylor, 2013:2). This study's focus is defined by social media users' behavior toward the isiZulu language on a public platform, as their point of view is mirrored in their actions and practices of a language at that specific moment in time (Taylor, 2013). The current chapter concerns itself with idiomatic and proverbial phrases; thus, discourse analysis underpins this research.

In addition to the above, Mhlambi (2012:3) alluded that thematic art form repertoires reflect life's common experiences and effects. These repertoires firmly anchor the literature inside popular discourses by focusing on African cultural demands, features of religiosity and modernity, and African nationalism. As this chapter argues, folktale elements and themes like witchcraft, extraterrestrial prowess, magical knowledge, evil, terror, misfortune, beliefs, and spiritual possession, are also topics presented on social media platforms in the form of truncated images and illustrations, and these ideas are a part of the Zulu society's cultural beliefs; hence this chapter employs discourse analysis as its framework for argumentation background based on the aforementioned supporting notions. Since this study is based on the analysis of spoken, written, or sign language use and any significant semiotic event, it can be conducted through discourse analysis, also known as discourse studies.

LITERATURE REVIEW

The research on how isiZulu orality is conveyed on social media is scarce, if not nonexistent. Only related subjects are quoted and discussed concerning this topic. The scholars reviewed in this chapter generally investigated orality after the invention of technology, not isiZulu orature per se. Fitrahayunitisna and Zulvarina (2017) hypothesize that oral literature has a specific function to educate people, such that it has particular ideals about ethics and local wisdom. Those values will not be effectively transmitted to the next generation without a current and compelling formula. The authors are certain that transferring the importance of oral literature using digital technology will be successful since the new digital generation cannot be separated from technology. Examining this new method of passing down oral literature from one generation to the next is crucial as society accepts technology as a substitute media for oral literary content. Following a brief overview of the debate over the connections between oral literature, the written word, and technology, Kaschula and Mostert (2011) propose that the term technauriture might provide a useful all-encompassing paradigm for further discussion of the oral word and its useful application in contemporary society. In Kaschula's definition of a recently invented term for orality in technology, "techno" stands for technology, "aura" for "auriture," and "ture" for literature. Since primary orality, literacy, and technology interact triangularly, technauriture is defined as "an attempt to capture the modalities associated with the three-way dialectic between primary orality, literacy, and technology" (Kaschula, 2017). Ekesa et al. (2022) define technauriture as any type of literature distributed through print or oral medium employing technology. Thus, spoken word poetry shared on social media platforms may be categorized as technological. Social media mimic the oral tradition. Using the share button, information spreads quickly from one person to the next, giving social media an excellent platform for disseminating oral literature to an audience.

On the other hand, Ekesa et al. (2022) articulate that the emergence of social media technologies has changed how spoken word poetry is performed in Kenya. As a result, virtual spaces are now used in these performances instead of actual spaces. These digital environments simulate existing spaces. They enable interaction between audience members and between the poet and the audience. On social media platforms, spoken word poetry is displayed as written texts, video poems, live recordings, and virtual live performances. Orality is present in all these spoken word poetry genres. Ekesa et al. (2022) investigated the virtual live performances to see how much they demonstrate the three main oral literature's performance, audience, and setting features. Mnenuka (2019) interrogates the consistency of the notion of literature based solely on its verbal/oral and written forms of transmission. Literary compositions and their presentations are no longer limited to spoken and written forms in modern contexts. New, creative forms of communication have emerged and are heavily involved in presenting and disseminating literary compositions. Both written and oral communication are included in these advances in communication. Therefore, Mnenuka (2019) states that literary compositions are no longer only available in verbal (oral literature) or written (written literature) formats, but also in ingenious communication formats made possible by special computer-mediated programs that take the place of verbal and written modes of delivery. Against this backdrop, this study investigates the orality of truncated images posted on social media platforms like Facebook. This chapter explores how the shift to the digital era has implicated the isiZulu language orality. The prevalence of social media has shaped all elements of language influences, whether modern or classic literature.

Rajunayak (2021) concludes that it is essential to first comprehend how oral literature varies from written literature to grasp it. A study of "orality" in contrast to "literacy" reveals the importance of oral literature. The struggle of oral literature is defined by the distinction between the oral and written forms and by the written forms' dominance over the former. For a long time, accessibility to the written word has been kept on the periphery and associated with privilege. Previously, someone's tongue was severed if they attempted to read. Reading is a skill that can be developed over time. The historical context of South African education presented difficulties in terms of reading. Correlations between words, understanding, and fluency are a part of reading. Other skills must be used in order to improve reading. Folklore was formerly removed from the basic education curriculum in South African schools, but it has recently been reinstated in the language curriculum for grade 12 students. The issue of how the students would learn in their higher phases without exposure in foundation phase still needs to be addressed. This study is attempting to close that gap in some way. It was a misconception that people could be represented or have a voice in print media, which is still the case today. We must acknowledge that while Turin (2013) contends that the archiving of audio and video recordings of oral literature through online platforms is a form of cultural documentation and preservation welcomed by many indigenous communities worldwide, there is little consensus on how such collections should be appropriately managed, archived, and curated

Orality On Social Media Language

for the future. Rajunayak (2021) concludes that oral traditions are reflexive forms of expression, unlike the conventional documentary reporting mode. By accumulating experiences and sentimental connections, they produce an experienced type of history since oral traditions highlight the creative worth of human perception.

RESEARCH METHODOLOGY

This study employs a qualitative, inductive research methodology where the researcher typically looks at insights and meanings in a particular setting, according to Mohajan (2017). Qualitative research is a powerful paradigm that occurs in a natural setting. The researcher is able to produce a level of depth because of their intense involvement in the genuine scenarios (Creswell, 2009). In other words, it is a collection of interpretive techniques that let us see the outside world. For instance, in our setting of investigating orality on Facebook, applying linguistic insights as part of a qualitative research approach to make the meaning of proverbs idioms and truncated images is evident. This task is to reveal meanings that have been carefully specified by the posted linguistic text and images portraying orality. It has a multi-method approach with an interpretive, naturalistic perspective on its subject (Denzin & Lincoln, 2005).

Data Collection

Identification of Data

Data was collected from the researcher's Facebook page and feed between August 2019 and June 2020. At this point, the topic's proverbs, idioms, and shortened imagery, truncated images were identified. According to the data collection listed below, they were extracted on various dates. Research design refers to the early planning of the approaches to be taken for gathering the pertinent data and the approaches to be utilized for their analysis, keeping in mind the goal of the research and the amount of staff time and money that is available (Pandey & Pandey, 2021). Supporting this statement, it is crucial to remember that internet connection is necessary in order to access social media platforms and that is expensive. Logging in, extracting data, and logging out were thus limited to the days of data gathering.

270   *Chapter 12*

Classification of Data

Following the collection of data from the researcher's Facebook page, each piece of the data is broken down into sections corresponding to an oral tradition researched.

Data processing

Each section's explanation and analysis are provided using these attributes of data analysis:

- Description content analysis approach—defining the meanings of proverbs and idioms together with how they are used on these Facebook posts. Results are presented together with morale of the posts.
- Interpretation—using historical perspective approach- analyzing witchcraft, cultural representations, and African ways of sustaining families is provided with results and morale of the posts.

Allowing the meaning of the text to depend on an act of interpretation is another method to open the door for a more contextual interpretation of it (Ifversen, 2003). This chapter contains textual representations of images and abbreviated illustrations.

TEXTUAL REPRESENTATION OF ORALITY EXTRACTED FROM FACEBOOK

Textual presentation of idioms, proverbs, and truncated images that incorporate elements or themes from folktales, such as witchcraft, extraterrestrial prowess, magical knowledge, evil, terror, misfortune, beliefs, and spiritual possession, are presented and analyzed below. A projective system views proverbs in this way and has frequently described them as the condensed wisdom of the previous generation (Ogundokun, 2015).

Proverbs and Idioms Representations on Facebook

Language is a tool for communication employed daily. Without a language, people cannot communicate in a meaningful way. Humans use language to communicate with one another and exchange information. When engaging with others, language is used to send messages, express concepts, and accomplish goals (Fadilla & Sari, 2022). Supporting these ideas is this chapter that hypothesizes that orality has been elevated to a different platform with different audiences, but with the same characteristics and aims; that platform happens to be social media.

Fadilla and Sari (2022) indicate that idioms can take many different forms and are often used in written and spoken communication in both informal and formal contexts. Thus, to communicate and transmit meaning more easily, native speakers employ idioms in everyday discussions. Depending on the situation, idiomatic terms might be used, for example, in formal or informal settings; hence this chapter represents the informal way of using idioms and proverbs in social media language.

The structure and meaning of the following proverbs, which feature on Facebook, are explained in figure 12.1.

While this written comment is amusing, it also illustrates the significantly high unemployment rate in South Africa. Due to the high unemployment rate in the country, this Facebook post encourages unemployed people to act and start their businesses rather than waiting for someone to hire them; entrepreneurial skills are humorously highlighted. Like other linguistic items, the sayings were formed and verbally transmitted from one isiZulu user to another through word of mouth. Thus, social media users have started using and disseminating these sayings more recently.

Proverbs Results and Characteristics of Folklore Portrayed Above

Entertainment is a component of folklore; it discreetly teaches about social obligations and proper conduct in society. Publicly mentioning that one has the skills to beat others and get paid for it is inappropriate. Additionally, it unintentionally teaches one to respect community members and live in harmony with them instead of hiring someone who will mistreat them on your behalf. According to Marsellaa and Putri (2020), folklore is believed to exist to give kids an enjoyable bedtime story. Many clear and organized meanings

Ngawushiya phansi umsebenzi, ngiyazisebenza manje nginezinyanga ezintathu ngiqale *ibusiness* lami lokubhonya abantu.

UMA UFUNA NGISHAYE UMNAKWENU R500

UMA UFUNA NGISHAYE UMAKHELWANE WAKHO ONGAZWANI NAYE R300

UMA UFUNA NGISHAYE INDODA YAKHO EKUHLUKUMEZAYO R1000

Angishayi nginomuntu phansi, ngikubuyela namazinyo 1che lowo muntu uwabone cos ngiwakhipha ngesibhakela. PLZ inbox me uma ufuna ngikubhonyele umuntu.

Figure 12.1. www.facebook.com izisho nezaga nencazelo. *Ukubhonya* is a proverb meaning to assault someone physically. *Nginomuntu phansi* is a proverb meaning one is skillful in what they do.

272   *Chapter 12*

in folklore are present throughout reality. Folklore frequently depicts the creativity of traditional cultures by sustaining tradition as an art form that exists
and is passed down from one generation to the next.

Pictorial Presentations with Truncated Proverbs

> Umfazi oqotho akavele avuke nje GULUKUDU! Uyabuza; "Ubaba
> ubesazongisebenzisa yini noma sengingavuka?"
> www.facebook.com izisho nezaga nencazelo accessed on
> 17/10/2022.
> *Usazongisebenzisa yini*? Is a proverb that asks whether the husband
> will use the wife for sexual enjoyment?

Although the scenario is modern since respect is one of the primary characteristics expected of a woman in a cultural context, it appears as exhibited
in the scene. One of the most crucial cultural principles is respect and subor-
dination, which this Facebook post teaches. The proverb has humor because
folklore occasionally has humorous components (the woman is quietly asking for something). According to Ogundokun (2015), proverbs are regularly
used to solve problems, establish organizations, and strengthen interpersonal
relationships. They create strong mental images in people's heads that can
motivate them. The message of a proverb is never disputed because it is a
proven conclusion; consequently, no one is bold enough to do so.

Proverbs results and features of folklore portrayed above

In African culture, wives have obligations, chores, and anticipated behavior.
In addition to their duties, husbands must provide for their families.

> Cultural representation (dating game content)
> Weqa lo layini "uyangithanda"
> Wadlula eceleni "uyangifuna"
> Waphinda emuva "sofa silahlane"
> www.facebook.com amasiko nokuziphatha accessed on 26/10/2022.

When a boy asks a girl out, it is a cultural game. A common occurrence is
a game during which a man draws a line in front of the woman and gives her
three options:

1. If the drawn line is crossed, the request for courtship is granted.
2. Doing so indicates that the girl is giving herself over to the guy.
3. Returning signifies that the girl is the boy's forever.

He wants her to decide, but when she considers the options, no one would be advantageous if she declined. Folklore offers amusement and fun; playing this mind game as a proposer is fascinating and entertaining.

Sofa silahlane is a linguistic item (proverb), meaning, we will spend our lives together.

Dating Game Results and Features of Folklore Portrayed Above

Zulu love proposals were based on a young man's verbal skills. Both linguistic and dramatic tools for persuading a lady to fall in love are included in the post. These techniques persuaded a woman that being in a relationship was her only viable alternative. These are features and attributes of orature because language and sketches are drawn.

AN AFRICAN WAY OF LIVING POSTED ON FACEBOOK

Posting such activities on social media teaches youth and upcoming generations about life's "good olden days." The modern way of life has changed how Africans sustain their families. Ploughing fields, milking cows, and slaughtering farm animals to feed families is a myth in some modern generations.

> Ukusenga inkomazi kusetshenziswa ibhakede nezandla.
> www.facebook.com amasiko nendlela yokuphila accessed on 05/07/2022.

Proverbs and idioms form part of orature. The above picture depicts the traditional way of milking a cow; thus, proverbs and idioms have been coined from milking cows.

> IsiZulu proverb/idiom (surface structure)   Semantic representation (deep structure)
> Selidumela emasumpeni   Problems are about to be solved
> Kochitheka gula linamasi   Hell will break loose
> Kwankomo isengwa ilele
> Good life

> Ukulima ngamageja ezandla endaweni yasemaphandleni.
> www.facebook.com amasiko nendlela yokuphila accessed on 11/08/2021.

274   *Chapter 12*

Ploughing fields and cultivating vegetables using a span of oxen by the whole family.

> IsiZulu proverb/idiom (surface structure)   Semantic representation (deep structure)
> Umvunisi ubuya nengqobe
> Assisting each other has great rewards

Idioms

Images Replacing Words 1

Using the definition of folklore provided, it is described as art. A language speaker must be familiar with the linguistic item being presented and be able to see and understand art to identify an idiom when words are represented by imagery. These pictures were shared on Facebook, with the user requesting comments with a linguistic interpretation of the idiom.

Sithini lesi saga?

Isithombe semvubu esinophawu lokuphika, isithombe semfologo nommese okumele 'ukudla,' isithombe sengwenya, isithombe samanzi acwebile, isithombe sesiziba

www.facebook.com izisho nezaga nencazelo accessed on 30/04.2021.

Incazelo yezithombe eyisaga: *Akukho zinyane lemvubu ladliwa ingwenya maqede kwacweba isiziba.*

Idiom Semantics

People whom you have harmed should prepare for retaliation. Although it might not happen immediately, waiting does not imply it will be forgotten. In certain circumstances, great-grandchildren exact revenge, adding a new linguistic element referred to as *icala aliboli.*

Moral Lesson and Results

People should be respected and be respectful; any harm you cause them will return to haunt you. It discourages cruel conduct. Although it is addressed to humans, it uses characters from nature (the river) and animals, which supports the idea that oral language has a more profound significance.

Images Replacing Words 2

The title's orthographic shortcomings reflect the era in which it was written. Since language is typically utilized in social media posts without regard to linguistic or grammatical conventions, Facebook language use destroys the isiZulu language or is an invention of a brand-new slang language and grammatical rules. This can be viewed as language death or a new language invention.

Sithini lesi saga?

Isithombe sesisu, isithombe somuntu ohambayo, isithombe sophawu lwezibalo (=), isithombe senso, isithombe senyoni

www.facebook.com izisho nezaga nencazelo accessed on 20/11/2021.

Incazelo yezithombe eziyisaga: *Isisu* somhambi asingakanani singangenso yenyoni

Meaning: This phrase suggests that strangers will accept whatever they are given, regardless of how little food they receive. Hence, the notion "beggars are not choosers." The definition of oral tradition includes the artistic use of items to convey idioms. This idiom promotes acts of Ubuntu by emphasizing giving to those in need.

Moral Lesson and Results
The idioms mentioned above promote cooperation, kindness, and humane conduct among members of families, communities, countries, and ethnic groups. Unyawo alunampumulo, which means that "one day one could improbably be somewhere far away from home and crave for assistance of strangers around," is the phrase that it most closely relates to.

IMAGE AND THEMES OF FOLKLORE AND ANALYSIS

Folklore's major goal is to impart knowledge and create new concepts for various kinds of knowledge. Using social media as a forum, we can end the debate on cultural teachings from ancestors and how we could participate in language development and use.

According to Yaseen (2014:13), witchcraft beliefs, accusations, and the violent behaviors that frequently accompany them affect how people view women and are reflected at several levels of society. According to Briggs (2002), witchcraft is the practice of witches forming cults and imparting their magical knowledge to their offspring. On the other hand, Swartz (2002) believes that people's relationships with others are translated into their belief in supernatural beings through religious or cultural texts and unwritten legends, which gives one a model of health, illness, and bad luck.

Owl and Black Cat Facebook Post
Numerous folktales, myths, legends, and proverbs feature supernatural entities with strong personalities and sway who act like humans (Ogundokun, 2015).

276 *Chapter 12*

Isithombe sekati elimnyama nesikhova esinombhalo othi: ZULUS WORSE NIGHTMARE

www.facebook.com ubuthakathi accessed on 09/02/2021.

Folktale Narration

A long time ago, in a remote village, lived two witches who were fierce rivals; one lived in a cabin on the left bank of the river and the other on the right. They got into a heated argument over clients who recently preferred the witch on the right side of the river to the one on the left. The witch from the right side of the river used an owl as her mode of transportation, whereas the one from the left used a black cat.

They used bewitching to evaluate the potency of their plant as a result of the competition. The plants belonging to the witch on the right side were set on fire by a cat dispatched by the other witch. The cat could not cross the river to its owner since a storm had developed on its way back. It was compelled to return to the home of its adversary. The witch on the right side was pleased to see the cat return. The witch tricked the cat, and the situation with the burned plants changed. Later that afternoon, the rain ceased, allowing the cat to cross.

Through bewitching one another, they were able to evaluate the potency of their herbs due to the competition. The witch on the left instructed the cat to destroy all the herbs on the right side. While returning, a storm began, the river was full, and the cat could not cross to its owner. It was compelled to return to its adversary's home. The cat returning impressed the witch on the right side. The witch successfully tricked the cat into reversing the burnt herb predicament. That afternoon, after it stopped pouring, the cat could cross.

Due to its loyalty to its owner, the cat told him what had transpired. She wished to discipline the witch on the right side. He was unaware that the owl was listening to their conversation atop their hut. When the owl returned to its owner, it told them what had been spoken. The owl flew away when the black cat discovered it on the roof while hunting in the garden.

With the cat's assistance, the witch on the right side charmed the owl's former perch on their hut's roof. The owl arrived the following morning, and as soon as it landed on the roof, all its feathers separated from its body.

The moral of the story is that if you believe you are superior to others, you will eventually experience something that will make you inferior. The witch who owned an owl thought she was superior because her agent could fly, but she was unaware of other methods to harness its power.

To support the possession of magical abilities, Swartz (2002) states that people's relationships with others are translated into their belief in

Orality On Social Media Language

supernatural beings through religious or cultural texts and unwritten legends, which gives one a model of health, illness, and bad luck.

Wicked spirits and physical entities spread witchcraft. These two creatures are regarded as witchcraft agents; as such, they employ sounds to carry out their tasks as required. Upon reaching their destination (where they are instructed to bewitch), they speak, which has the following intentions or implications:

> "Thatha ezakho, awumbiwa ndawonye" is used as a means of delivery because neither of these animals has hands, so they use their mouths to carry whatever they need. I have arrived (to report to the sender [witch doctor]), and I am reporting to the bewitched that it is here to work.

People emerge from their homes to chase these animals away when they make noises because they represent witchcraft and bad luck.

Thunder and Lightning

Isithombe semibani edweba isibhakabhaka esikhombisa ukuduma kwezulu esinalo mbhalo:

> My neighbor: Msah uqeda nini ukufunda?
> Mina: Hopefullly this year, ebese ngiyasebenza.
> www.facebook.com ubuthakathi accessed on 09/02/2021.

This picture and the previous conversation evoke the memory of a folktale about a girl attending a university whose mother used to advise her not to discuss her academic achievement with others. One day, her neighbor inquired about when she would complete her studies. The girl informed her that she was in her final year of school and that her first job interview would be right after. The girl was killed by a lightning strike the same night when there was thunder and lightning.

The Moral of the Story and Results

Respect the privacy of others; people are jealous; thus, one must be cautious about whom they share their goals and future dreams with. Oral storytelling supports and validates spiritual realities and experiences (Ogundokun, 2015).

> *Customs and traditions*
> *Witchcraft*
> *Spiritual possession*   *Beliefs*
> *Magical power*

278 *Chapter 12*

Isithombe seziko, kubasiwe kwabekwa ibhodwe elivaliwe laze labe-
kwa netshe phezulu.
www.facebook.com ulwazi nobuhlakani assessed on 10/02/2021.

Elderly Wisdom

The Folktale Narration

There was once a single mother raising twin boys. She ran away from her
family members who wanted to practice the *ukwendisa iwele* custom. Her
love for her children did not allow her to offer them as a ritual or sacrifice.
Living in a cave with her children, she would hunt for food for them every day
so they would not go to bed hungry. One day she came home empty-handed;
thinking about how disappointed her children would be, she devised a plan.
Her children came out of the cave happy to see their mother carrying a heavy
sack; they helped her carry it inside the house. She then placed a large stone
on the lid to prevent the children from messing with what was cooking. She
made a fire, put something inside a pot, poured water, and started to cook; she
put a big stone on top of the lid so that her children would not tamper with
what was cooking. As the kids were tired from the games they had played
during the day, they fell asleep before their mother finished cooking.

The Moral of the Story and Results

Do not expose all your failures as a parent, especially those involving failure to provide for your children. As their provider, you lose their trust. The
elderly know how to maintain dignity and trust.

DISCUSSION

In this instance, Facebook provides isiZulu speakers with definitions of idioms and proverbs. Although the cost of an internet connection is high, this is
the fastest way to receive information. There is no guarantee that the proverbs
and idioms uploaded represent the actual linguistic repertoires contained in
dictionaries. Because anyone can publish anything on social media, even
slang within the primary isiZulu can be wrongly interpreted as the original
language. These data sets were gathered and analyzed on themes that are
rarely studied in the area of religion, such as witchcraft, alien ability, magical
knowledge, evil, horror, bad luck, and spiritual possession. They are considered to be immoral, which attracted the researcher's attention and interest
and made him feel the necessity for such a study. When data images were
processed, the most crucial part was figuring out how a discourse transforms

something into an object that can be categorized, explained, used as a basis for action, institutionalized, etc. (Ifversen, 2003).

Comparatively, the advantages and the disadvantages of social media folklore representation and word of mouth are that social media usage is costly while word of mouth is cheap. Secondly, orality is coined daily via word of mouth, social media only present already invented orature. Both social media and word-of-mouth orality are not published.

Summing up the discussion on collected data there are components, old and new concepts that are coined and discovered by different scholars that are in one way or another related to this study like the word "technauriture" alludes to this study's use of social media platforms as a tool for redefining, rethinking, and archiving traditional literature for use by present-day readers as well as future generations. Additionally, Facebook-posted orature has a teaching and belonging—instilling a sense of belonging and a reminder about our roots, particularly for the current age for whom folklore seems useless and a primitive way of life. Technauriture is the way of reaching the unreachable, thinking the unthinkable, and also an exploration of traditional literature through modern platforms.

Consequently, orality on social media, notably Facebook, teaches about linguistic repertoires that isiZulu language speakers hardly ever use since they are not exposed to or lack meaning and understanding. Additionally, it has a sense of folklore narratology and imaginative resonance with speakers of the isiZulu language, which are both results of this study. This is the easiest way to get information. The sociopolitical climate of our nation requires that African art be preserved; any opportunity to do so must be grasped with both hands and seized. The fact that African indigenous languages have been disadvantaged in South Africa, for preservation and teaching, the researcher felt the necessity to do this.

FINDINGS, LIMITATIONS, AND RECOMMENDATIONS

Orality can be used to restore the essence of socio-cultural order, that is, object manipulation (lightning and thunder) that can harm people and the use of social media as an educational tool. Traditionally grounded activities are posted for learners to explore social and cultural knowledge. Competitions to create orature should be sponsored to renew interest and cultural advancement.

Even the dominating systems that exploited their position of authority to restrict the distribution of written and oral literature are falling behind in the teaching and acknowledgment of orality. Additionally, language users consider orality to be an outmoded field that only researchers and linguists find interesting.

280 *Chapter 12*

Images of the African way of life (cow milking and field plowing) demonstrate how traditional traditions have mostly been updated and adjusted to fit the modern world. It is a component of the theater in that it exhibits customs that are based on the history and culture of the amaZulu tribe. African science is underrated and undermined in the sense that muthi influences nature (clouds and thunder) to strike at any given time when accused. That is wisdom beyond comprehension on its own. People who practice witchcraft, unlike doctors and other professionals, have no proper training, but they execute such acts; that is orality.

The creative process of converting words into images to communicate idioms is a higher form of art. Social media creativity is to be praised since it provides internet users the chance to explore their artistic abilities and showcase their skills for others to view, learn from, understand, and get new linguistic repertoires that have never been produced before. While some linguists could contend that this dilutes language, others might uphold the idea that language evolves.

The limitation of content analysis means that interpretation and comprehension of idioms, proverbs, and other presentations depend on knowledge of the isiZulu language. Facebook is used to share information and expertise, and it serves as a helpful archive that can be accessed by users of all languages from anywhere at any time. Therefore, Africans should use technology to advance our native culture and traditions as it is a product of the West. Social media platforms have been found to impact how people think and perceive social concerns, how languages are taught, and how society's unavoidable realities are reflected.

Additionally, communities with high levels of poverty still struggle with internet access. Due to a lack of gadgets, internet connection, and technical knowledge, especially among older generations, not everyone can access Facebook and other social media sites. Youth and middle-aged people utilize social media the most. These are a few of the restrictions. The government is attempting to give citizens access to the Internet by putting in cables and offering free bandwidth in public locations like malls and airports.

This study suggests further research into other social media sites like YouTube and TikTok. For example, for elementary education, there are films on how to study and subject material videos, questions, and answers. These platforms include a great amount of content with knowledge and information for all age groups. There are videos on how to cook, bake, etc., for adults and entrepreneurial purposes. On these networks and others, even college and tech students are catered for. Social media platforms also educate users about the emotional, spiritual, physical, and social well-being of netizens (citizens of the network).

Since these myths were handed down orally and spread by professional storytellers, later generations could only go by them, seeing the number of current principalities as the justified and correct quantity (Goody, 1977). Although there are limitations stated above, the aim should be to stop mourning the ways of the past and remain optimistic by grabbing this opportunity of accessible publishing in social media and embracing change as the way to go.

FUTURE RESEARCH

African indigenous languages contain a wealth of linguistic knowledge that must be compiled and published, and it is the responsibility of all linguists to embark on this effort to create archives for future generations. Another issue facing African languages is exploring modified and Westernized traditional knowledge.

CONCLUSION

Oral traditions construct an experienced kind of history by gathering events and emotional connections because they highlight the creative value of human perception. Speaking orally involves preserving knowledge, memories, and history. Traditional spirituality is oral in the sense that it entails education, intellectual growth, and the cultivation of one's fictitious universe (witchcraft). Both contemporary and conventional scientific knowledge systems have roots in Africanism. Facebook, a platform used to disseminate posts, adds monotony, yet the information placed there is valuable historical information that should be preserved. It's interesting to see how these many cultures have come together to celebrate the digital age.

Social media is a platform for oral tradition; thus, it should be used to give children a sense of belonging through oral tradition. This study demonstrated how technology is currently used, and its potential to educate about languages, disseminate knowledge, and preserve cultural heritage. Old linguistic information is presented in new ways (social media platforms) for preservation and accessibility to generations of the Fourth Industrial Revolution and beyond. This study suggests that to enhance the preservation and archiving of this traditional knowledge that language users and non-language speakers around the world share through oral tradition, apps and compilations of social media sites should be established.

REFERENCES

Adegbola, T. 2021. Orality and information communication technology. In A. Akinyemi & T. Falola (eds.). *The Palgrave Handbook of African Oral Traditions and Folklore*. Palgrave Macmillan, Cham. https://doi.org/10.1007/978 -3-030-55517-7_41.

Briggs, R. 2002. *Witches and neighbours: The social and cultural context of European witchcraft*. USA: Blackwell Publishers.

Campa, A. L. 1965. Folklore and History. *Western Folklore, 24*(1), pp.1–5.

Creswell, J. W. 2009. *Research Design: Qualitative, Quantitative and Mixed Method Approaches (3rd Ed.)*. Los Angeles: SAGE Publications.

Cutler, C., Ahmar, M., & Bahri, S. eds., 2022. *Digital orality: Vernacular writing in online spaces*. Springer Nature.

Denzin, N. K., & Lincoln, Y. S. 2005. Introduction: The Discipline and Practice of Qualitative Research. In N. K. Denzin & Y. S. Lincoln (eds.). *The SAGE Handbook of Qualitative Research (3rd Ed.)* (pp. 1–32). Thousand Oaks, CA: SAGE.

Ekesa, B., Rinkanya, A., & Wabende, K. 2022. Spoken word poetry in Kenya: An emerging genre of oral literature in social media spaces—Beatrice Ekesa. *The Nairobi Journal of Literature, 10*(1).

www.facebook.com accessed in 2021 and 2022.

Fadillah, I., & Sari, P. (2022). The idiomatic expression found in the movie script of Beauty and the Beast: A Semantics Study. *Ethical Lingua: Journal of Language Teaching and Literature, 9*(2), 645–651. https://doi.org/10.30605/25409190.477.

Fairclough, N. 1995. *Media discourse*. Arnold: A member of the Headline Group: London.

Ferris, S. P. 2022. The affordance of secondary orality. *Solutions for Distance Learning in Higher Education,* 108.

Fitrahayunitisna, F., & Zulvarina, P. 2017. The efforts to strengthen national identity through ethical values and local wisdom in oral literature. *ISLLAC: Journal of Intensive Studies on Language, Literature, Art, and Culture, 1*(2), 19–23.

Goody, J. 1977. *The domestication of the savage mind*. Cambridge University Press: Cambridge.

Griffith, S., & Liyanage. 2008. An introduction to the potential of social network- ing sites in education In I. Olney, G. Lefoe, J. Mantei, & J. Herrington (eds.). Proceedings of the second emerging technologies conference (pp. 76–81). University of Wollongong: Wollongong.

Ifversen, J., 2003. Text, discourse, concept: Approaches to textual analysis. *Kontur– Tidsskrift for Kulturstudier, 7*, pp.61–69.

Kaschula, R. H. 2004. *Myth and reality in the new South Africa: Contemporary oral literature*. Alizés: Revue angliciste de La Réunion, Founding Myths of the New South Africa / Les mythes fondateurs de la nouvelle Afrique du Sud.

Kaschula, R. H. 2017. Technauriture as a platform to create an inclusive environment for the sharing of research. *Searching for Sharing: Heritage and Multimedia in Africa, 7*, 2.

Kaschula, R., & Mostert, A. 2011. From oral literature to technauriture. Unpublished MS. dissertation, Rhodes University, South Africa.

Lankshear, C., Gee J. P., Knobel, M., & Searle, C. 1997. *Changing literacies.* Open University Press.

Leach, M. 1959. *Definition of Folklore: Mythology and Legend.* Indiana University Press Stable URL: https://www.jstor.org/stable/3814683.

Marsellaa, E., & Putri, D. M. 2020. Folklore as ethnic embodiment bias: Value analysis on Karo folklore. *Budapest International Research and Critics Institute-Journal (BIRCI-Journal), 3*(4), 2619–2628.

Masuku, N. (2005). Perceived Oppression of Woman in Zulu Folklore: A Feminist Critique. Doctoral thesis, University of South Africa, Pretoria.

Mhlambi, I. J. 2012. *African language literature: Perspective of isiZulu fiction and popular black television series.* Wits University Press: Johannesburg.

Mnenuka, A. 2019. Online performance of Swahili orature: The need for a new category? *Eastern African Literary and Cultural Studies, 5*(3–4), 274–297. DOI: 10.1080/23277408.2019.1685752.

Mohajan, H. K. 2017. Two Criteria for Good Measurements in Research: Validity and Reliability. *Annals of Spiru Haret University Economic Series*, 17(3), 58–82.

Ogundokun, S. 2015. The role of orature in African soci-cultural space. *Journal of English Language and Literature*, 6(10), 179–185.

Paltridge, B. 2021. *Discourse analysis: An introduction.* Bloomsbury Publishing.

Pandey, P., & Pandey, M. M., 2021. *Research methodology tools and techniques.* Bridge Center.

Rajunayak, V. 2021. Oral traditions and literature: A discourse on the need to democratize literature. *Turkish Online Journal of Qualitative Inquiry, 12*(9).

Slevin, J. 2000. *The Internet and Society*: Polity Press: Cambridge: UK.

Swartz, L. 2002. *Culture and mental health: A Southern African view.* Cape Town: Oxford University Press.

Taylor, S. 2013. *What is discourse analysis?* Bloomsbury Publishing PLC: London

Thetela, P. 2001. Critique discourses and ideology in newspaper reports: A discourse analysis of the South African press reports on the 1998 SADC's military intervention in Lesotho. *Discourse and Society, 12*(3), 347–370.

Turin, M. 2013. Orality and technology, or the bit and the byte: The work of the world oral literature project. *Oral Tradition, 28*(2).

Yaseen, A. 2014. *Witchcraft accusations in South Africa: A feminist psychological exploration.* UNISA: Pretoria.

Index

African languages, promotion of, 226
Afrocentricity approach, 30
artificial intelligence (AI), 82, 85, 127

clan organization, 163
collaborative strategies, 51–52, 55
colonial era, 80; colonial languages, 42; colonial legacy, 79–80; colonial systems, 1; coloniality, 25, 33
computational linguistics, 104, 106–8, 118
computer-generated communication, 100
core cultural values, 254–59
Creative Commons license, 36
cultural domination, 82
cultural heritage, 56

digital media, 6, 8, 37; digital documentation, 120; digital emancipation, 31; digital ethnography, 101–2; digital management, 33; digital media technology, 50, 51, 202; digital preservation, 3, 21, 58–60, 113–14, 124, 126; digital revolution, 3; digital technologies, challenges of, 129–30; digital tools, 61, 142
dominant languages, 3

economic development, 34–35
emojis, indigenous meaning of, 97–100, 103–7
endangered indigenous languages, 54
endangered language revitalization, 12
epistemic knowledge, 1, 8, 23
epistemic strategies, 36
ethical considerations, 63–65
ethnicity, 107
extinction, risk of indigenous languages, 10, 50, 54, 203

folklore, 264
Fourth Industrial Revolution (4IR), 4, 6, 11, 49, 89, 137–38, 204, 214; impact of, 139
functional linguistics, 116

global initiatives, 113, 118
global languages, 176
government policies, 65–66
gratification theory, 246

hegemonic languages, 1

indigenous epistemologies, 3; indigenous African languages, 77, 79, 85, 90, 135, 143; indigenous knowledge systems, 40; indigenous

285

286   *Index*

language media, 205–6, 215; indigenous language preservation, importance of, 51; indigenous languages, 2, 9, 11, 26, 41, 115,178–80, 212, 224; indigenous languages, attitudes toward, 147; indigenous languages and journalism, 214–15; indigenous media organizations, 218; indigenous names, 156
intercultural, 253
intracultural, 253

journalism education, 210–11

labeling languages, 144
language and culture, 242, 247
language development, strategies for, 145, 218, 247
language policy, 78
language preservation, 85–87, 91, 103–4, 140–41, 145; challenges of, 56–58
language resources, digitalization of, 148
language revitalization, 120
language survival strategy, 208
linguistic and cultural activism, 234
linguistic diversity, 88, 115–17, 124
local languages, 177

marginalized languages, 2, 8, 251–52
mass media, 223
mobile television, 177
modernization, 81

modernization theory, 28–30
multilingual, 80, 86–87

native languages, 42
native speakers, 77

onomastics, 160
oral communication, 26, 265
oral tradition, 30, 264
orality, 13–14
orature, 263

participatory epistemic knowledge, 22–23, 25, 27, 31, 33
preventing language extinction, 55

regulatory policies, 39

social communication, 81, 83–84
social media: description of, 225; features, 244; platforms, 226–27, 229, 231, 243, 265; social networking, 241

teaching journalism in indigenous languages, challenges of, 216–17
technologies, AI, 4
toponymic heritage, 159
toponyms, 153–56
traditional literature, 266
TV landscape, 178, 181, 183, 194

universal language, 101

About the Editors and Contributors

Fulufhelo Oscar Makananise is associate professor in the Department of Communication Science at the University of South Africa. He holds a doctoral degree in media studies from the University of Limpopo. Prof. Makananise obtained a PG (dip)HE from Rhodes University and his master's degree in media studies from the University of Limpopo. He also serves as an external examiner in other South African universities and acts as a reviewer in both international and national scholarly journals. Prof. Makananise has authored and published academic articles in peer-reviewed and DHET-accredited journals. In addition, Prof. Makananise has presented papers both at national and international conferences. His research interest is in new media technology, digital media, indigenous language media and social media, political communication, digital diplomacy, and news media consumption.

Shumani Eric Madima is linguistics senior lecturer at the University of Venda in the Department of English, Media Studies and Linguistics, Faculty of Humanities, Social Sciences and Education. He teaches linguistics to undergraduate and postgraduate students. He completed his BA degree at the University of South Africa (Unisa), BA (Hons) in applied linguistics at the University of Pretoria, MA (Cum Laude) in linguistics, and doctor of philosophy (PhD) in linguistics at the University of Venda. He has been a teacher and a lecturer at South African Teacher Education (SACTE). His fields of specialization are sociolinguistics, language planning, psycholinguistics, language and gender, linguistics in educational context, and media studies. He has written several articles on various themes such as linguistics and media studies, published in different international journals.

* * *

Yusuf Ayodeji Ajani is a postgraduate student at the Department of Library and Information Science, University of Ilorin, Nigeria. He has published over

288 *About the Editors and Contributors*

forty articles in local and international journal outlets in the field of librarianship. In 2023, he won the Emerald Literati Award.

Nhlayisi Cedrick Baloyi is senior lecturer in the Department of Communication, Media, and Information Studies at the University of Limpopo (UL) where he teaches courses in radio broadcasting, journalism, and mass media research. He obtained his PhD in media studies from UL in the year 2021. Dr. Baloyi joined academia after gaining extensive hands-on experience as a journalist and current affairs news producer at the South African Broadcasting Corporation's (SABC) Munghana Lonene FM between 2014–2022. As part of his academic contribution, Dr. Baloyi has supervised master's students in the field of media studies and published several papers in the form of journal articles and conference proceedings. His research interests include broadcasting, new media, media, and education. Dr. Baloyi is a beneficiary of the South African Humanities Deans Association (SAHUDA) scholarship in collaboration with the National Institute for the Humanities and Social Sciences (NIHSS).

Jennings Joy Chibike is lecturer in media and communication in the Department of Languages at Lupane State University. He holds a master of science and an honours degree in journalism and media studies from the National University of Science and Technology in Zimbabwe. His research interests are in indigenous language media, political communication, identity politics, memory studies, digital media, and human rights and democracy.

Nhlavu Petros Dlamini is senior lecturer in the Department of Information Studies, at the University of Zululand. My area of interest is indigenous knowledge, knowledge management, ICTs for development, cataloging and classification, research methods, and marketing of information products and services in libraries. I have published several papers in accredited journals and book chapters. I have also presented several papers at national and international conferences.

Zelda Elisifa hails from the small village of Kinyamvuo, situated within Kilimanjaro, Tanzania. She is a devoted wife and mother to Lazarus and Mary respectively. Currently, she resides in the Ubungo district in Tanzania. At the esteemed Open University of Tanzania, Zelda holds a distinguished senior lecturer position at the Department of Linguistics and Literary Studies under the Faculty of Arts and Social Sciences. Her areas of expertise comprise second language acquisition/ learning, language assessment, and semantics. Zelda reads and gardens in her free time, watches movies, and exercises for fitness.

About the Editors and Contributors   289

Remah Joyce Lubambo is a Siswati lecturer at the University of South Africa who teaches literature, grammar, and research to level 1 to postgraduate students. African Languages Department. Dr. Lubambo believes that teaching an indigenous language is critical because it restores our African people's identity and pride, which were misdirected during colonization. She believes that native speakers of a language should be knowledgeable about the science of the language. Furthermore, she believes that African languages should be recognized as a language of teaching and learning as well as a language of research, as this can help to decolonize our African people's minds and eliminate attitudes toward our indigenous languages. Dr. Lubambo is senior lecturer and the head of the Siswati Section in the Department of African Languages. Dr. Lubambo has a teaching diploma from Elijah Mango College of Higher Education, a BA degree with education and Siswati as a major subject, a BA honours degree in Siswati, and a PhD in languages, linguistics, and literature from the University of South Africa. She also has a BA honors degree in education management law and policy from Northwest University. Dr. Lubambo's research interests include literature, linguistics, and discourse analysis.

Memory Mabika is lecturer in the media studies section of the Department of English, Media Studies, and Linguistics at the University of Venda's Faculty of Humanities, Social Sciences, and Education. She has over twenty-four years of experience in the media industry. Dr. Mabika earned her tertiary degrees in Zimbabwe and South Africa, respectively. She has a PhD in social science in communication from the University of Fort Hare and a postgraduate diploma in teaching and learning attained from Stellenbosch University. Her secondary field of study is communication, journalism, and media studies. Dr. Mabika's research interests include media and society and indigenous language media.

Amukelani Collen Mangaka holds a master of arts (media studies), a bachelor of arts honours (media studies), and a bachelor of arts in media studies in 2014 from the University of Limpopo. Currently, he is media studies lecturer at the University of Limpopo. Apart from being a lecturer at the university, he is also pursuing a doctoral degree in communication science at the University of South Africa (Unisa). In 2018, he obtained a post-graduate diploma in education from Unisa. Moreover, he published several scholarly contributions including three book chapters, journal articles as well as full conference papers. His research interests are in new media, new media and education, corporate and organization communication, and health and political communication.

Edgar Julius Malatji is senior lecturer and program coordinator in media studies at the University of Limpopo. He holds a PhD in media studies, and his thesis is titled "The Impact of Social Media in Conserving African Languages amongst Youth in Limpopo Province." The findings of his doctoral study were presented at the International Conference (2019) in Russia-themed Preservation of Languages and Development of Linguistics in Cyberspace: Context, Policies and Practices. In addition, he recently acquired a post-graduate diploma in higher education from the Durban University of Technology. Also, Dr. Malatji is part of the UNESCO team and Information for All Programme (IFAP) that advocates for the preservation and revitalization of the endangered indigenous languages in the world. Moreover, he published several scholarly contributions including three book chapters, journal articles as well as full conference papers. His research work focuses on broadcasting studies, media and society, new media, languages, culture, and identity. Dr. Malatji is a beneficiary of the South African Humanities Deans Association (SAHUDA) scholarship under the auspices of the National Institute for the Humanities and Social Sciences (NIHSS).

Mawethu Glemar Mapulane is lecturer in media studies at the Department of Communication, Media, and Information Studies (University of Limpopo). She holds a master of arts in media studies (University of Limpopo), and a post-graduate diploma in teaching and learning in higher education (University of Fort Hare). She has lectured in diverse courses in media and society, media law, media theory, radio production, and gender in media. She also supervises postgraduate students at the honor's and master's levels. Her research interests are media audience, advertising, broadcast and social media, media and society, and gender studies. Mawethu has played a mentorship role for both undergraduate and postgraduate students at UL through the Centre of Academic Excellence (CAE) from 2010 to date. She is currently serving on the Executive Kindi (senior mentor) Committee as the deputy secretary from 2022 to date. She has also played leadership roles as the chairperson of the University of Limpopo Women Academics and Student Association (ULWASA) in 2017–2018. Mawethu is also involved in community engagement serving as the Chairperson of the Board of Directors at Radio Turf from 2022 to date. She is currently in the process of pursuing a PhD.

Rudzanimbilu Muthambi is a PhD candidate in communication science at the University of Free State, South Africa, where her thesis is on the black experience in contemporary South African film: a study of ten filmmakers. She is lecturer at the University of Limpopo, where she has been teaching for over twelve years. Moreover, she is responsible for the development of film students from around South Africa and the Southern African Development

Communities (SADC). A senior adjunct lecturer at UNISA School of Business Leadership where she is responsible for developing courses in Digital Innovation, she is also a founder of a project called iBioscope yeCommunity—Cinema for People's Development where she exhibits films to the marginalized communities through her company Rudzani Muthambi Properties (RMP). Through experience gathered over the years, the power of storytelling and narrative-setting in shaping society's perspectives and informing culture has become clearer to her.

Joseph M. Ngoaketsi is doctoral researcher at the University of Witwatersrand and lecturer at the University of South Africa (UNISA). His teaching focus and interests are research, digital archives and records management modules development, and ICT applications in Archives and Records management. Ngoaketsi has written journal articles and book chapters on open access, memory and commemoration, library science, and media. He is involved in community engagement projects relating to memory studies.

Toyosi Olugbenga Samson Owolabi, associate professor, holds a PhD in journalism and development from Strathclyde University, United Kingdom. Before this, he obtained a bachelor's degree in language and linguistics from the University of Ilorin, an MA (linguistics), and an MA (language and communication arts) from the University of Ibadan in addition to a postgraduate diploma (journalism) from the Nigerian Institute of Journalism. He teaches journalism, media, and development communication at Lagos State University. Also, he at different times taught mass communication at Igbinedion University and Benson Idahosa University, respectively. He had been the Group Political Editor and Member of the Editorial Board of Concord Group of Newspapers. He was also the Editor of Credit Market Magazines, all in Lagos. He is widely published locally and internationally. His research interests in journalism, indigenous language media, communication, and development have been published in reputable journals and books.

Kganathi Shaku is senior lecturer and researcher in the Department of Linguistics and Modern Languages, at the University of South Africa (UNISA). He has a PhD in languages, linguistics, and literature. His areas of research interest include applied linguistics, internet linguistics, paremiology, and general linguistics. His current focus is on social media and language. He is involved in multiple projects which aim at the development of African languages and the promotion of multilingualism.

Adeyinka Tella is associate professor at the Department of Library and Information Science at the University of Ilorin in Nigeria and is currently a visiting researcher in the Department of Information Science at the University of South Africa in Pretoria, South Africa. Before this time, Tella had been a research fellow in this same department. Tella was a Commonwealth scholar who finished his PhD at the University of Botswana in September 2009. Tella is a three-time winner of the Dr. TM Salishu Most Published Librarian Award by the Nigerian Library Association (2015, 2017, and 2018), and a 2007 winner of the CODESRIA small grant for thesis writing for the PhD students' category. He has authored many articles in high-impact Web of Science/Scopus-rated journals.

Beryl Babsy Boniwe MaMchunu Xaba was born in Nyanyadu, a rural region between Dundee and Newcastle. She is the third child to be born to Smangele and Mlungisi Mchunu. She attended Mdutshulwa and Rutland for her elementary schooling, she matriculated at Malambule High School. Her undergraduate studies were completed at the University of Zululand, her honors degree at the University of South Africa, and her master's and doctoral degrees at the University of KwaZulu Natal. She served more than twenty years under the basic department of education. From 2018 to current she is the IsiZulu Section Head and senior lecturer in the Department of African Languages at the Unisa.